True Myth

True Myth

C. S. Lewis and Joseph Campbell
on the Veracity of Christianity

JAMES W. MENZIES

PICKWICK *Publications* · Eugene, Oregon

TRUE MYTH
C. S. Lewis and Joseph Campbell on the Veracity of Christianity

Pickwick Publications
An Imprint of Wipf and Stock Publishers
199 W. 8th Ave., Suite 3
Eugene, OR 97401

www.wipfandstock.com

ISBN 13: 978–1-62564-443-5

Cataloging-in-Publication data:

Menzies, James W.

    True myth : C. S. Lewis and Joseph Campbell on the veracity of Christianity / James W. Menzies.

    xii + 258 p. ; 23 cm. —Includes bibliographical references.

    ISBN 13: 978–1-62564-443-5

    1. Lewis, C. S. (Clive Staples), 1898–1963. 2. Campbell, Joseph, 1904–1987. 3. Mythology. I. Title.

BL304 M35 2014

Manufactured in the U.S.A.

12/23/14

For Jay and Alina
Soli Deo gloria

Contents

Preface

THIS BOOK EXAMINES THE meaning and significance of myth as understood by Joseph Campbell and C. S. Lewis and its place in the Christian faith in a technological society. My thesis is that, despite the many similarities in their life experiences, the high regard each man had for myth, and their shared belief that myth has an important place in Christianity, they differed considerably on myth's role concerning faith.

Joseph Campbell understood Christianity as comprised of mythical themes similar to those in other myths, religious and secular. Admitting that certain portions of the biblical record are historical, he taught the theological and miraculous aspects as symbolic, as stories in which the reader can find life-lessons for today. Campbell believed that these life-lessons are the heart of Christianity and that taking the theological or miraculous elements literally not only undermines Christianity's credibility, but results in sectarianism and a misunderstanding of the universal themes held in common by all humanity.

C. S. Lewis defined Christianity as a relationship between the personal Creator and his creation mediated through faith in His son, Jesus Christ. As such, Lewis was a supernaturalist who took the theological and miraculous literally. Although Lewis understood how one could see symbolism and life-lessons in miraculous events, he believed miraculous events took place in human history.

Joseph Campbell understood critical doctrines of Christianity as myth and maintained that understanding myth was a key to making sense of key doctrines of Christianity in any society, including a highly-technological one. C. S. Lewis understood myth as one means among many used by God to point people to His Son, Jesus Christ.

Acknowledgments

THIS BOOK OWES ITS existence to many people who encouraged and supported me throughout the writing process. Originally a doctoral dissertation delivered in pursuit of a PhD in Humanities at Salve Regina University, I first want to thank the members of my class—Jennifer Fallas, Suzanne Baldaia, Mea Simanski, Jeff Shaw, and Washington Irving—for their encouragement and friendship over the course of study in the program. I would like to especially thank my friend and mentor, Timothy Demy, without whose encouragement, patience, and guidance this project would never have been completed. Also on my committee were Dan Cowdin and Craig Condella, both of whom challenged my thinking and provided additional guidance. My thanks goes out to them and to everyone at Salve Regina University.

Others who deserve thanks are Carol Zurcher who took on the herculean task of editing and Craig Noll and George Anderson who offered me their expertise and encouragement. I would also like to thank Christian Amondson and Chris Spinks of Pickwick Publications for help and oversight of this project.

Most important, thanks to my wife Jay and daughter Alina who got used to looking for me in my study. It is therefore dedicated to them with deepest gratitude and affection. "He who finds a wife finds a good thing and obtains favor from the LORD" (Prov 18:22); "O noble daughter" (Song 7:1).

1

Introduction

NEED

THIS BOOK SEEKS TO answer the question "What was the meaning and significance of myth as understood by Joseph Campbell and C. S. Lewis and how did each man apply his understanding of myth to the Christian faith?" In the process of answering this question the Christian faith is represented by certain historical doctrines held by the church since its inception as recorded in the Bible; the central record of the early Christian experience and faith upon which Christian doctrines, traditions, and experiences were subsequently built and therefore central in the interpretations of Campbell and Lewis. Attention is also given to the role of myth in a highly technological society as understood by each author.

A question asked by each generation is "What does it mean to be human in an age of advanced technology?" This book will address the question by exploring not only the thinking of Joseph Campbell and C. S. Lewis regarding myth and religion, but by investigating the influence and presence of myth in philosophy, media, ethics, history, literature, art, music, and religion in a contemporary context. A comparison, analysis, and critique of the perspectives of these two men will enable individuals working in these disciplines to integrate the thoughts of Campbell and Lewis in further reflection upon the relationship between humans and technology in the twenty-first century. For both men, myth held significance, even in a technological society.

BACKGROUND

Throughout history humanity has pondered matters beyond sensory perceptions. These include hopes, dreams, hunches, intuition, life after death, a realm of "spirituality" and spiritual beings, and even the thought process itself. But because humans often limit certainty to sensory perceptions, assurance about such things remains elusive. And at those rare moments when someone thinks he or she is closest to certainty, where reasoning is able to make sense of existence, such confidence can collapse by a simple change in circumstances. For instance, at the moment a village is convinced how best to please the gods by thinking, "If we offer up our children as a sacrifice the gods will repulse the enemy," tragedy can strike as an enemy breaks down the walls, invades, and conquers, leaving the people to wonder why the gods remain angry. Individually one may be convinced that his or her act of lust or anger certainly must enrage the "unknown other" but then rewards come. So the question remains: How can I make sense of my existence?

One response to this existential question found throughout primitive and technologically advanced cultures is understanding the role of myth. Throughout human history, myth has served as a source to explain questions of creation and human origins, making sense of tragedy, finding meaning for one's existence, and to help prepare for life after death. And whether one examines indigenous cultures steeped in religion or highly technological cultures espousing many (or no) religions, there is frequently an evidence of myth handed down through generations resulting in ideas and beliefs that intentionally and unintentionally become part of such cultures and societies.

But as universal as *myth* is, few words are used with more definitions, or with as many meanings as there are authors to offer them. Following the first entry, from the *Westminster Review* in 1830, the *Oxford English Dictionary* has the following definition:

> A traditional story, typically involving supernatural beings or forces, which embodies and provides an explanation, aetiology, or justification for something such as the early history of a society, a religious belief or ritual, or a natural phenomenon. *Myth* is strictly distinguished from *allegory* and *legend* by some scholars, but in general use it is often used interchangeably with these terms.[1]

---

1. *Oxford English Dictionary*, s.v. "myth."

But as traditional and succinct as this definition is, myth appears to be as old as humanity and as profound as the most challenging philosophy.

Further confusing the study are the numerous scholarly writings that each offer their own variation on the term. One dictionary provides the definition,

> In popular usage the term . . . connotes something untrue, imaginative, or unbelievable; or, in older parlance, "a purely fictitious narrative usually involving supernatural persons, actions, or events";[2]

Professor of philosophy Tom Snyder comments,

> . . . some myths are grounded in pure fantasy while others convey a strong sense of realism. In the past many scholars identified different kinds of myths, such as creation myths, initiation myths, captivity myths, and trickster myths. Each of these different kinds of myth does different things;[3]

While professor of religion Ian Barbour remarks,

> . . . in popular usage, a myth refers to fictional and untrue tale, so I have come to prefer the term *story*, since the status of a story is clearly left open[4]

And literary theorist and philosopher Roland Barthes writes,

> Myth is not defined by the object of its message, but by the way in which it utters this message: there are formal limits to myth, there are no 'substantial' ones. Everything, then, can be a myth? Yes, I believe this, for the universe is fertile in suggestions.[5]

The scope of usage of myth is so vast that it causes New Testament scholar Richard Soulen to admit, "There is, however, no agreed-upon definition, whether in terms of its form (that is, its relationship to fairy tales, sagas, legends, tales, epics, etc.), or in terms of its content and function."[6] Professor of Philosophy Richard Purtill observes "So much has been written about myth, from all kinds of standpoints, with all kinds of purposes, that the boundaries of the concept of myth have been considerably stretched."[7] And

2. Soulen, *Handbook of Biblical Criticism*, 124.

3. Snyder, *Myth Conceptions*, 20.

4. Barbour, *Religion and Science*, 114; italics in original.

5. Barthes, *Mythologies*, 109.

6. Soulen, *Handbook of Biblical Criticism*, 125.

7. Purtill, *J. R. R. Tolkien*, 1.

in the opinion of Old Testament research professor John Oswalt, the thorniest problem in the entire study is how to define myth.[8]

But as Oswalt goes on to point out, the question of definition faces two challenges: "We must first ask whether it is broad enough to include all the items that manifestly share the majority of the common characteristics of the class being defined. Then we must ask whether the definition is narrow enough to exclude those items that only exhibit one or two of the common characteristics. This is a major problem with the definitions of myth."[9] In exploring the question Oswalt presents two approaches: a historical-philosophical approach and a phenomenological or descriptive approach. He further discusses the semantics and history of the word and concept of myth by writing, "We may further subdivide the historical-philosophical definitions into three groups: the etymological, the sociological, and the literary."[10]

Purtill also categorizes myths into sections or groups. He points out that to some scholars myth is, first, related to *gospel*, "which includes but is not confined to the four New Testament accounts."[11] While Purtill is careful to point out that traditional Christian believers, such as J. R. R. Tolkien, regarded the gospels as historical accounts, others see a resemblance between the gospels and myth. For instance, gospels and myth are stories concerning acts of God or the people of God with moral or religious significance. A second category is *literary* myth, "which is the use of mythical characters and heroes for purely literary purposes."[12] In this case neither the audience nor author considers the story as true. His third grouping is *philosophical* myth, "the conveying of philosophical ideas by allegories or metaphors that have a greater or lesser resemblance to original myth."[13] Yale professor of divinity, Brevard Childs, adds this comment concerning myth and *true* myth:

> Not every story with a reference to a primeval event can be classified as a true myth. In order to be a myth, such a story must bear a 'truth,' that is, myth must relate to the basic structure of being within the world order. This 'truth' consists in a recognition of the life-determining reality which the mythical mind has apprehended in the powers of nature . . . Such stories concern themselves with the creative acts of power of the primeval age

8. Oswalt, *The Bible Among the Myths*, 32.

9. Ibid.

10. Ibid., 33.

11. Purtill, *J. R. R. Tolkien*, 3.

12. Ibid.

13. Ibid.

which establish the order of being, such as the discovery of the hunt and agriculture, or the origin of life and death.[14]

So just as science and religion scholar Ian Barbour defines technology as "the application of organized knowledge to practical tasks by ordered systems of people and machines,"[15] one can perhaps understand myth as the application of faith (or imagination) and reason (or experience) to the practical events of daily life and existence.

> The mythological world . . . provide[s] the individual with a model in order to understand the meaning of his or her existence. For this reason, any mythology must feature an ample range of characters, gods, enemies, places and circumstances to ensure the possibility of a personal relationship, for all the members of the community, to the primordial world.[16]

So myth is a story, potentially real or symbolic whose main figures are divine, human, or even animal in which the story accomplishes something significant for its adherents.[17] Myth brings significance and meaning to life as much as life brings meaning to myth.

In considering Christianity, the role of myth and history is essential because, as Purtill alludes to above, since its inception some of Christianity's adherents have maintained that myth is antithetical to the faith; that Christianity is a historically-based belief (e.g., Lewis in his later years), while others (e.g., Lewis in his early years and Campbell), have argued for origins based on ancient and universal myths. Orthodox Christianity maintains that Christian history is not legend or imagination, that the events of Christ's birth, life, miracles, death, resurrection, and ascension happened in a specific time and place in history, and that Jesus was, in fact, "a historical person crucified (it is all in order) *under Pontius Pilate.*"[18] So for the Christian evaluating myth with regard to the historicity of the biblical text upon which Christianity relies, the question is, in the words of anthropologist Claude Levi-Strauss, "Where does mythology end and where does history start?"[19]

---

14. Childs, *Myth and Reality in the Old Testament*, 20.

15. Barbour, *Ethics in an Age of Technology*, 3.

16. Simonson, *The Lord of the Rings*, 67.

17. Segal, *Myth*, 4–6.

18. Lewis, *God in the Dock*, 67; italics in original.

19. Levi-Strauss, *Myth and Meaning*, 38.

STATEMENT OF THESIS

The thesis of this book is that Joseph Campbell and C. S. Lewis started with a similar understanding of myth and its role in explaining basic tenets of the Christian faith. Events such as the incarnation and physical resurrection of Jesus Christ are doctrinal and *not* historical. But while Campbell maintained his perspective and beliefs throughout his life Lewis underwent a transformation causing him to rethink the nature of myth and the historicity of Christianity. This book will explore the beginnings and individual developments in the thought of each author.

This objective is accomplished through an exploration of the role and relevancy of myth in an age of advanced technology. Specifically, this book considers myth as understood and explained by Joseph John Campbell (1904–1987) and Clive Staples Lewis (1898–1963), two scholars who devoted much time and effort to the topic. Their major works, as well as nuances in their definition, understanding, and application of myth, are also considered. Additionally, this book gives attention to each thinker's understanding of historical Christianity; it considers the ways in which myth can serve as an aid in understanding basic Christian beliefs.

Rationale of Research Validity

Comparing these writers is important because of the influence both have in the study of myth as a genre and the role that religion plays as part of the worldview of individuals in a technological society. Lewis's influence is not only evident in his primary fields of medieval and renaissance literature and English literature of the sixteenth century, but also in his wide-ranging essays on culture, ethics, and religion. And with his twenty books on mythology and close to forty years of teaching about myth at Sarah Lawrence College, Joseph Campbell's influence can be anticipated whenever myth is studied. Anyone embarking on research of the nexus of myth and faith in contemporary society will do well to be familiar with the thinking and contributions of C. S. Lewis and Joseph Campbell.

C. S. Lewis

By the time Joseph Campbell began teaching at Sarah Lawrence College, NYC (1934), Clive Staples Lewis had been teaching English for ten years at Magdalen College, Oxford, UK. Just prior to Campbell's appointment, Lewis had professed faith in Christianity and published his first theological work, *The Pilgrim's Regress: An Allegorical Apology for Christianity, Reason, and Romanticism*,[20] where he shares in allegory his journey from atheism to belief. And later, in *Surprised by Joy*, he explains, "This book is written partly in answer to requests that I would tell how I passed from Atheism to Christianity."[21] So at the time Joseph Campbell is developing his understanding of myth at Sarah Lawrence, Lewis, in these works, is introducing the reading public to his later and revised understanding of myth.

During his youth Lewis showed little interest in religious matters. In speaking of his upbringing and the religious influence of his parents he states "I was taught the usual things and made to say my prayers and in due time taken to church. I naturally accepted what I was told but I cannot remember feeling much interest in it."[22] Of his mother's religion he could "say almost nothing," concluding, "My childhood, at all events, was not in the least other-worldly."[23] He considered his mother's death, when Lewis was only ten, to be his "first religious experience."[24]

Prior to his conversion, Lewis held a common "mythical" view of Christianity. Early in his life Lewis believed the virgin birth, miracles, death, resurrection, and ascension of Christ were fictional events that did not take place in history. As Armand Nicholi observes, "Many of these myths, as those of Balder, Adonis, Bacchus, contained stories similar to the one of the Bible—of a god coming to earth, dying to save his people, and rising again from the dead. Lewis had always considered the New Testament story simply another one of these myths."[25] White sums up Lewis's view of Christianity prior to his conversion:

> He considered all religions to be mythologies, stories created by simple, primitive people to explain the complexities and terrors of the world, and to him in 1914 Christianity was no different from sun worship or the pagan religions associated with the gods of Olympus.[26]

Lewis's faith in Jesus Christ resulted in his revisiting and revising his understanding of myth. At the age of sixty-three, Lewis devoted the fourth chapter of his work *An Experiment in Criticism* to explaining his approach:

20. Lewis, *The Pilgrim's Regress*.

21. Lewis, *Surprised by Joy*, vii.

22. Ibid., 7.

23. Ibid., 8.

24. Ibid., 20.

25. Nicholi, *The Question of God*, 86. See "Myth Became Fact" in Lewis, *God in the Dock*, 63–67.

26. White, *C. S. Lewis*, 36.

"I define myths by their effect on us."[27] For Lewis, at this point in his thinking, a myth was "a particular kind of story which has a value in itself—a value independent of its embodiment in any literary work."[28] Lewis admits he was not satisfied with the word "myth" and would have preferred another. He saw the challenge with myth as being two-fold: first, the Greek word *mythos* originally meant any sort of story and not just the kind Lewis considered mythical, and second, Lewis admitted that anthropologists understood myth differently from how he used the term. But he felt myth was the only word available. "It is difficult to give such stories any name except *myths,* but that word is in many ways unfortunate."[29] Here, Lewis admits the word can be confusing and his only options were *myth,* or to invent a new word, and myth seemed to him to be "the lesser evil."[30]

As Lewis further explains, "(S)ince I define myths by their effect on us, it is plain that for me the same story may be a myth to one man and not to another. This would be a fatal defect if my aim were to provide criteria by which we can classify stories as mythical or non-mythical. But that is not my aim. I am concerned with ways of reading . . ."[31] Further, he writes, "the degree to which any story is a myth depends very largely on the person who hears and reads it."[32] For Lewis, what one person considers mythical another reader considers historical, thus bringing history, theology, and personal faith into the study of myth.

One area to be studied and answered in relation to myth, therefore, is how did Lewis regard the biblical record? Did he consider it a collection of stories that reflected myths on God, creation, and redemption? Or did he understand it as a historical account of real people and events? This book will explore these questions. Initial research points to a conclusion that, in Lewis's thinking, the life of Jesus Christ was the literal incarnation of the perfect myth: Jesus Christ as God Incarnate in true humanity embodied everything myths seek to describe. As one of his chapter titles put it, in Christ "Myth Became Fact."[33]

Lewis had a complex understanding of myth. It was the means by which the abstractions of the mind and the spiritual (or what people consider the perfect or ideal existence) find concreteness in human experience,

---

27. Lewis, *An Experiment in Criticism*, 45.

28. Ibid., 42.

29. Ibid.; italics in original.

30. Ibid., 43.

31. Ibid., 45–46.

32. Ibid., 48.

33. Ibid., 63–67.

bringing together "the two hemispheres [of mind] in sharp contrast. On the one side, a many-islanded sea of poetry and myth; on the other, a glib and shallow 'rationalism.'"[34] As Lewis describes it,

> Now as myth transcends thought, Incarnation transcends myth. The heart of Christianity is a myth which is also a fact. The old myth of the dying God, *without ceasing to be myth,* comes down from the heaven of legend and imagination to the earth of history. It *happens*—at a particular day, in a particular place, followed by definable historical consequences. We pass from a Balder or an Osiris, dying nobody knows when or where, to a historical person crucified (it is all in order) *under Pontius Pilate.* By becoming fact it does not cease to be myth: that is the miracle . . . to be truly Christian we must both assent to the historical fact and also receive the myth (fact though it has become) with the same imaginative embrace which we accord to all myths. The one is hardly more necessary than the other.[35]

Yet, to Lewis, myth corresponds to the imagination much as history and fact corresponds to reason. It was possible for myth to be historical, that is, for myth to "happen."

Though Lewis studied the many categories or genres of the Bible—poetry, prophecy, epistles—of particular interest to him were the gospel accounts of Jesus' life. As a first-in-his-class recipient in Greek and Latin literature, Philosophy and Ancient History and English Literature, and a professor of medieval and renaissance literature, Lewis was also well versed in literary criticism. He refers to his expertise when he writes,

> I was by now too experienced in literary criticism to regard the Gospels as myths. They had not the mythical taste. And yet the very matter which they set down in their artless, historical fashion—those in narrow, unattractive Jews, too blind to the mythical wealth of the Pagan world around them—was precisely the matter of the great myths. If ever a myth had become fact, had become incarnate, it would be just like this. And nothing else in all literature was just like this. Myths were like it in one way. Histories were like it in another. But nothing was simply like it. And no person was like a person it depicted; as real, as recognizable, to all that depth of time, as Plato's Socrates or Boswell's Johnson

---

34. Lewis, *Surprised by Joy,* 170.
35. Lewis, *God in the Dock,* 66–67; italics in original.

... this is not 'a religion,' nor 'a philosophy.' It is the summing up in actuality of them all."[36]

And in a sentence that could serve as his own summary of things, Lewis concludes, "Now the story of Christ is simply a true myth: a myth working on us in the same way as the others, but with this tremendous difference that *it really happened*: and one must be content to accept it the same way."[37]

Initial research indicates that Lewis's conclusion of the Gospels is that they are not legends; indeed, everything about them convinced him they could *not* be legends.

> Now as a literary historian, I am perfectly convinced that whatever else the Gospels are they are not legends. I have read a great deal of legend and I am quite clear that they are not the same sort of thing. They are not artistic enough to be legends. From an imaginative point of view they are clumsy, they don't work ... Most of the life of Jesus is totally unknown to us ... and no people building up a legend would allow that to be so.[38]

The very fact that so little is known of Jesus' life convinced Lewis that what is known does not fit the pattern of legend, the story is not creative enough. As he said concerning the details in the account of Christ's encounter with the woman caught in adultery,[39] "Surely the only explanation of this passage is that the thing really happened? The author put it in simply because he had *seen* it."[40]

Joseph Campbell

Perhaps no individual in the twentieth century has a better claim on the title, *mythologist*, than Joseph Campbell. As the author of twenty books and professor at Sarah Lawrence College (Yonkers, NY) for thirty-eight years until his retirement in 1972, Campbell is perhaps best known through the six, one-hour interviews aired on PBS, *The Power of Myth with Bill Moyers*, first aired in 1988 (a year after Campbell's death), and later published into a bestselling book.[41] The towering influence of Campbell in the world of

36. Lewis, *Surprised by Joy*, 236.

37. Hooper, *The Collected Letters of C. S. Lewis*, 1:977; italics in original.

38. Lewis, *God in the Dock*, 158–59.

39. John 8:1–11.

40. Lewis, *God in the Dock*, 159; italics in original.

41. Campbell, interview by Moyers, Episode 1: "The Hero's Adventure," June 21, 1988; Episode 2: "The Message of the Myth," June 22, 1988; Episode 3: "The First

mythology is evident in the estimation of Campbell made by Sam Keen, the psychologist-theologian who, like Campbell, was the subject of a Bill Moyers television special and for many years served as contributing editor at *Psychology Today*. As someone who knew Campbell personally and interviewed him for an issue of *Psychology Today*, Keen pays this tribute to Campbell,

> I often say Joseph didn't know more than *any* of us, he knew more than *all* of us. I think he was the Encyclopedia—all by himself. None of us had as much data as he did. I don't think even Eliade rivaled him. . . . .You don't get light without a shadow. Joseph was a man who had a single enthusiasm for a lifetime. He paid certain things for it. We all do.[42]

Everyone who knew Campbell personally, as well as those who worked with him professionally, considered him one of the greatest students and teachers of myth.

Campbell's interest in religion and myth began at an early age. As he describes it in *The Power of Myth*:

> I was brought up in terms of the seasonal relationships to the cycle of Christ's coming into the world, teaching in the world, dying, resurrecting, and returning to heaven. The ceremonies all through the year keep you in mind of the eternal core of all that changes in time. Sin is simply getting out of touch with that harmony . . . It wasn't long before I found the same motifs in the American Indian stories that I was being taught by the nuns at school.
>
> In those days there was still American Indian lore in the air. Indians were still around. Even now, when I deal with myths from all parts of the world, I find the American Indian tales and narratives to be very rich, very well developed.
>
> And then my parents had a place out in the woods where the Delaware Indians had lived, and the Iroquois had come down and fought them. There was a big ledge where we could dig for Indian arrowheads and things like that. And the very animals that play the role in the Indian stories were there in the woods around me.
>
> It was a grand introduction to this material.[43]

Storytellers," June 23, 1988; Episode 4: "Sacrifice and Bliss," June 24, 1988; Episode 5: "Love and the Goddess," June 25, 1988; and Episode 6: "Masks of Eternity," June 26, 1988.

42. Larsen and Larsen, *Joseph Campbell*, 490–91.

43. Campbell, *The Power of Myth*, 10.

Evident in this personal narrative is Campbell's early attention to similarities and synchronicities of American Indian folklore to the miraculous elements of Christianity.

His childhood exposure to Roman Catholicism and early interest in Native American Indian beliefs combined to lead Campbell to the conclusion that both religious beliefs were mythical. His assumption that faith had basis neither in history or in the material world—other than both being rooted in nature—would launch Campbell on a trajectory culminating in the assumption that the Biblical testimony of many of the events of Christ's life were never intended to be taken literally.

Regarding Roman Catholicism, Campbell would formally abandon the Catholic Church before his mid-twenties; "he felt that the Church was teaching a literal and concrete faith that could not sustain an adult."[44] His feelings toward the church have been termed "bitter"[45] and even though he did see a pedagogical need to teach children "through concrete interpretations, rather than through metaphor they could not understand," he never returned to attending Mass.[46] But Campbell saw a religious function of myth, "the mystical function, which represents the discovery and recognition of the dimension of the mystery of being."[47]

Regarding myth and the Christian faith, understanding Campbell is challenging since he taught and wrote so much about myth and, as seen above, *myth* is open to an almost endless array of definitions. Further complicating the issues is how Campbell and his interpreters understand the Biblical narrative as it pertains to history and metaphor. For instance, in the editor's forward to *Thou Art That*, Eugene Kennedy writes, "To describe the [Old and New] testaments as myth is not, as Campbell points out, to debunk them . . . Joseph Campbell's purpose in exploring the biblical myths is not to dismiss them as unbelievable but to lay open once again their living and nourishing core."[48] And seven pages into the same book Campbell writes, "The problem, as we have noted many times, is that these metaphors, which concern that which cannot in any other way be told, are misread prosaically as referring to tangible facts and historical occurrences."[49] And in another place he remarks, "Jesus dies, is resurrected, and goes to Heaven.

---

44. Kennedy, *Thou Art That*, xvii.

45. Ibid.

46. Ibid.

47. Ibid., 3.

48. Ibid., xiv–xv.

49. Ibid., 7.

This metaphor expresses something religiously mysterious. Jesus could not literally have gone to Heaven because there is no geographical place to go."[50]

While some Christians understand the life-giving core of the gospel message as mediated by a faith in historical facts, facts that contain a power that transcends time and space, such as the physical resurrection and ascension of Jesus Christ, Joseph Campbell believed that though aspects of the Christian faith were historical, the message is mediated through metaphor. How one distinguishes the historical occurrences from the use of metaphor to lay open this nourishing core is paramount in the thinking of Joseph Campbell.

As will be seen, Campbell's approach to the *purposes* of myth is fourfold: myths (1) awaken the conscience to the universe, (2) give one an image of the order of the universe, (3) validate the moral order of the culture in which the myth arose, and (4) help an individual through personal crisis and various stages of life (i.e., youth, adolescence, middle age, death).[51] So myths might be understood as having therapeutic value since they offer a world-view, a way of looking at reality that notices similarities in all of humanity such as birth and death, and offering an explanation that sustains people in times of loss and crisis.

STRUCTURE OF THE STUDY

To properly analyze myth, myth and Christianity, and the views of Lewis and Campbell regarding myth, it is necessary to establish the need, purpose, and method of such a study. In a highly technological society one must ask if a need remains for research into myth and its role in Christianity. Does myth continue to have a place in the present postmodern age and, if it does, are the views of C. S. Lewis and Joseph Campbell relevant to establishing and understanding that place?

To answer such questions requires research into the meaning of myth. Therefore, the first chapter will explore myth's definition, genre, lexical history, usage, and application. This chapter will also study the role of myth in a technological culture by tracing its history from the primitive culture of hunters and gatherers to today's highly scientific and computerized Western society. Does the power of myth decrease as culture becomes more technological? Or does myth remain and simply adapt itself to the changes in culture? Does myth, in fact, become strengthened as a society moves away

50. Ibid., 48.
51. Ibid., 2–5.

from the humanities and science finds itself unable to answer the deeper questions of meaning and life?

This chapter will also explore the tension of history and belief regarding the Christian faith. Both Campbell and Lewis believed people and events in the Bible existed in history, but they differed on the historicity of the supernatural and miraculous. Did the human Jesus, who both men believed lived and died, ascend to heaven? Can the same text that has Jesus saying "Come forth" be believed when it records "And he that was dead came forth"?[52]

Finally, this chapter will introduce Joseph Campbell and C. S. Lewis by giving a summary of their upbringing, educational pursuits, achievements and writings, their religious heritage (and disagreements with that heritage), and their understanding of myth and Christianity and how this understanding changed over the years.

The second chapter will explore myth by reviewing attempts to define its meaning and role in society. Because myth defies any single, complete and satisfactory definition, it will be put in context by showing its place and role in the areas of religion and culture. Are religion and myth synonymous or antithetical? Does myth help one better understand religion or does it confuse and mislead? How much does culture influence myth and myth influence culture? Can ancient myths find a place in a technological culture?

Following this investigation, myth is considered as a literary genre by considering comparisons and contrasts of myth to other genres such as fantasy and allegory. The purpose of this chapter is not necessarily to arrive at a definition of myth, but to consider the character, attributes, and benefits of myth.

The third chapter will review the pertinent information with respect to the life and writing of C. S. Lewis. Although most of his education was grounded in philosophy and literature, Lewis devoted much time, thought, and writing to the subjects of myth, fantasy, and the role of myth in the Christian faith.

To understand Lewis's approach to myth one needs to be familiar with the literary, experiential, and religious sources that influenced Lewis. Literary influences include Scottish social anthropologist James Frazer (1854–1941), English writer G. K. Chesterton (1874–1936), Scottish author and poet George MacDonald (1824–1905), and the English writer and poet J. R. R. Tolkien (1892–1973). Experiential influences include his boyhood interest in fantasy and his witnessing the death of his (then forty-six year old) mother and the grief of his father when Lewis was only ten years old.

---

52. John 11:44.

This event had a tremendous impact upon the boy who prayed that his mother would not die.

Religion too had a great influence on Lewis's view of myth. He would refer to his conversion to the Christian faith time and again in his writings and, although he would make it clear that he was a layman and not a theologian and that he had many reservations and disagreements with organized religion, from this point on when Lewis spoke about myth he did so as one who believed in the historicity of the Gospel accounts of both the life and miracles of Jesus Christ.

The clearest and perhaps most comprehensive explanation for Lewis's view of myth is his attempt to pin down the meaning of myth in *An Experiment in Criticism*.[53] According to Lewis, six characteristics were required for a story to be myth: (1) independence in the form of the words used; (2) a minimal use of suspense or surprise; (3) minimal empathy with the characters of the story; (4) dealings with fantasy, the impossible, and preternatural; (5) no comic sense; even if the experience is joyful, it is also grave, and it must (6) contain a numinous or all-pervasive sense of the other.[54]

Early in life Lewis recognized a great chasm between myth and history and prior to his conversion he wrestled with how to bring these two concepts together. After his conversion he was able to see myth as a means by which the natural and supernatural could meet. In fact, it could be said that, to Lewis, the Christian view of myth is history plus miracle equals myth.

What makes Lewis's arguments stand out in his day as well as in ours was his countercultural insistence that not only was a supernatural view far from being passé, but it was necessary as a way for humans to think and make sense of their existence. In his own day Lewis wrestled with the widely influential views of scholars such as James Frazer and the University of Marburg New Testament theologian, Rudolf Bultmann (1884–1976). In studying magic and religion throughout the world, Fraser saw no need for asking whether religions were true or false and so Christianity, not being unique, was only one religion among many. Meanwhile, Bultmann, considered by many to be the most significant and influential New Testament scholar of the century, maintained that the gospel records were myths that helped explain events in a world comfortable with supernatural causes. But Bultmann believed that since the modern person could not accept the idea of supernatural causes, the gospels needed to be stripped of their myths in order to get to the core of what the early disciples believed about the person and work of Jesus Christ.

53. Lewis, *An Experiment in Criticism*.

54. Ibid., 43–44.

Lewis found both approaches inadequate and misleading. Regarding Frazer, Lewis believed the similarities between myth and Christianity could just as easily be used to argue in favor of the truth of Christianity as against it, and as a literary critic and lifelong reader of myth, Lewis felt Bultmann did not fully understand what myth actually was.

In spite of differing with these authors, Lewis nevertheless recognized that people have difficulties with the miraculous. But instead of dismissing the truthfulness of the gospel accounts or the veracity of the miraculous, Lewis sought to find a way forward that would allow the tension between myth and fact to blend together harmoniously and thus concluded that, in the birth of Christ, myth became fact although it still remains a myth.

The fourth chapter will examine the approach to myth of Joseph Campbell, considered by many as the leading mythographer of the modern era. Influenced early in his childhood by his Roman Catholic upbringing and an early interest in Native American spirituality, Campbell would later recall that as early as the age of six or seven he was captured by the beliefs of Native Americans. As he wrote later in a personal journal, "I early became fascinated, seized, obsessed by the figure of a naked American Indian with his ear to the ground, a bow and arrow in his hand, and a look of special knowledge in his eyes."[55]

But his parents' Catholicism would also leave an indelible impression upon Campbell. From serving as a young altar boy, through elementary school and into his college years, Campbell faithfully attended Catholic services. Even so, this loyalty was not without reservation, for Campbell is often found expressing dismay and criticism of the Church in his private writings until he finally decided to abandon his formal practice of attending Mass, finding more spiritual satisfaction in the natural world around him than in the incense and candles of the Catholic liturgy.

As Campbell matured and started to consider myth academically, two authors greatly influenced his thinking. They were the anthropologist James Frazer (who, in a different way, influenced Lewis) and the Swiss psychiatrist Carl Jung (1875–1961). While Lewis would find Frazer's observations on universal themes of myth running throughout all cultures and religions lacking, Campbell would find such explanations fascinating and persuasive.

Campbell explains his view of myth arguing that myths (1) awaken the conscience to the universe, (2) give one an image of the order of the universe, (3) validate the moral order of the culture in which the myth arose, and (4) help an individual through personal crisis and various stages of life

55. Larsen and Larsen, *Joseph Campbell*, 3.

(i.e., youth, adolescence, middle age, death).[56] In these four points it is easy to see how myth and religion coalesce in Campbell's thinking.

Before his introduction to Jung, Campbell was influenced by the writing of the Austrian neurologist and father of the psychoanalytic school of psychiatry, Sigmund Freud (1856–1939). And although Campbell would later find Jung's approach more appealing, he would admit that his classic work *The Hero with a Thousand Faces*[57] was the result of the "Freudian insight on the universality of the Oedipus myth."[58]

A final and critical issue to explore is Campbell's understanding of the relation of myth to Christianity. Unlike Lewis, who would come to look at all things from a Christian worldview, Campbell looked at the world and its religions from a mythological view. His travels around the world and his study of various religions and cultures allowed him to flatten out all religions so that whatever they had in common became prominent, thus enabling him to identify universal themes and conclude mythological underpinnings to all the world's great religions.

This fourth chapter will also explore the divergent views of Lewis and Campbell regarding myth and its place within Christian doctrine pointing out areas of agreement as well as evaluating their differences. The purpose of this exploration is to arrive at some conclusions about the place and role of myth within Christianity.

The fifth chapter will address Christianity as history, mystery, and myth. Since both Lewis and Campbell see history, mystery, and myth within the Christian faith, the question is how to identify each. Both men were comfortable using myth as a hermeneutical tool in reading the Bible, but differed on how it was used and the conclusions one might derive from applying myth to the biblical record.

Is an element of myth necessary to understand the true message of Christianity or does myth serve to undermine the truth claims of the faith? C. S. Lewis often spoke about the role of myth in Christianity, yet he believed in the historicity of the gospel accounts. How did he reconcile myth to history?

And Campbell, though raised in the Catholic faith, came to conclude that a historical reading of the Bible missed the true meaning of the narrative, confusing the literal and metaphorical interpretations of the religious stories. To Campbell, a literal reading of biblical passages clearly meant as

---

56. Campbell, *Thou Art That*, 2–5.

57. Campbell, *The Hero with a Thousand Faces*.

58. Larsen and Larsen, *Joseph Campbell*, 106.

myth serve only to further divide humanity along religious lines and do a disservice to religion by misunderstanding the original intention of the text.

For C. S. Lewis, Christianity is a true myth; that is, a myth which is also a fact. This blending together of two ideas often understood as diametrically opposed enabled Lewis to reconcile the seemingly irreconcilable: the universal allure of myth with the historical convictions he held concerning the gospels.

For Joseph Campbell it is the mystery of myth that gives Christianity its power; a historical reading of the gospels, especially of the miraculous elements, works against the message and purpose of the Christian faith. For Christianity and the Bible to accomplish their purpose and remain a viable faith with meaning in a technological and scientific age, it is necessary to understand their mythological nature.

The sixth chapter will summarize the role of myth in a technological society as understood by Campbell and Lewis. For each of these authors, myth is timeless and has a vital place in every culture as a means by which one can understand truth and find some meaning in the vicissitudes of life. And because religion is also an important component in culture as it too seeks to address many of the same issues of life, myth's role in religious belief will be addressed as well.

Because culture is comprised of individuals, this chapter will also discuss myth and the significance of the individual as well as myth and the significance of society and culture. How significant is the individual to myth and can the individual significantly influence myth? As individuals progress from birth to adolescence and from adulthood to death, how does myth help them face such changes in a world also undergoing change?

And how does myth influence culture? And when it does, does the influence differ from culture to culture or does each culture influence the meaning of myth? As cultures advance in fields such as science, education, and technology, what becomes of myth? Like religion, can myth exist and even thrive in a culture dominated by science and technology or does it become weakened or even extinct? If it does remain, what form must myth take to remain a vital part of human existence? Does myth, like religion, need to be organized with agreed upon doctrines and creed, or can it survive with no clear set of values simply by becoming a part of everyday life in thinking and conversation? And what is the significance of the abundance of words, titles, terms, logos, and trademarks in the West with mythical origins? In cultures where the stories are no longer told or believed, why do the names and figures have such lasting value? Is it just a matter of trademark recognition or is there some deeper meaning in myth that the human psyche does not recognize but cannot ignore?

In closing, the seventh and concluding chapter will review the salient points as they pertain to the topic, "Belief in an age of technology: C. S. Lewis and Joseph Campbell on myth and its application to the Christian faith in a technological society." Following the conclusion and a brief review, recommendations for further study will be made to students interested in exploring further the influence of C. S. Lewis and Joseph Campbell on myth and the influence of myth in religion and culture.

The topics of religion, spirituality, technology, and culture along with the range and limits of scientific method are common themes in classroom discussions. When one realizes that scholarship continues to investigate these issues and publish books addressing the tensions between religion, myth, and the influence of technology, the timelessness and relevancy of such a study is apparent.

Summary Review of the Literature

In preparing for this project a literature review was conducted and a bibliography of approximately 100 (and growing) books, journal articles, and internet selections was created. These selections fall into a number of categories. The first body of work seeks to put into context the life and thinking of Joseph Campbell. Specifically included are Campbell's own works including *Myths to Live By*; *The Hero with a Thousand Faces*; *The Inner Reaches of Outer Space: Metaphor as Myth and Religion*; *The Masks of God*; *Pathways to Bliss: Mythology and Personal Transformation*; *The Power of Myth* (with Bill Moyers*)*; *The Flight of the Gander: Explorations in the Mythological Dimensions of Fairy Tales*; *Legends, and Symbols*; and *Thou Art That: Transforming Religious Metaphor*.

Closely tied to the study of Joseph Campbell are the works of those who have investigated Campbell's life and work. Included in this field are: Stephen and Robin Larson's biography, *A Fire in the Mind: The Life of Joseph Campbell*; Joseph Felser's "Was Joseph Campbell a Postmodernist?"; Tom Collin's "Mythic Reflections: Thoughts on myth, spirit, and our times, an interview with Joseph Campbell, by Tom Collins"; Robert Segal's *Joseph Campbell: An Introduction*; and Jonathan Young's "Joseph Campbell's Mythic Journey."

The second body of work explores the life and thinking of C. S. Lewis and his understanding of myth as explained by Lewis and those who have studied him. Specifically these include collected works edited by Walter Hooper such as *Of Other Worlds: C. S. Lewis, Essays and Stories*; *The Collected Letters of C. S. Lewis: Family Letters 1905–1931. Vol.1*; *The Collected*

Letters of C. S. Lewis: Books, Broadcasts, and the War 1931–1949, *Vol. II*, and *The Collected Letters of C. S. Lewis: Narnia, Cambridge, and Joy* 1950–1963 *Vol. 3*. Works by Lewis, both fiction and non-fiction, include *An Experiment in Criticism; God in the Dock; Essays on Theology and Ethics; Mere Christianity; Out of the Silent Planet; Perelandra; Surprised by Joy; The Abolition of Man; That Hideous Strength; The Joyful Christian; Till We Have Faces: A Myth Retold.*

Closely tied to the above works are those that study Lewis's understanding of myth such as Louis Markos' "Lewis Agonistes: Wrestling with the Modern and Postmodern World" and "The Myth Made Fact"; William Gray's *Fantasy, Myth and the Measure of Truth: Tales of Pullman, Lewis, Tolkien, MacDonald and Hoffman;* David Downing's *Planets in Peril: A Critical Study of C. S. Lewis's Ransom Trilogy;* Bruce Edwards' *C. S. Lewis: Life, Works, and Legacy;* Don Elgin's "True and False Myth in C. S. Lewis's 'Till We Have Faces'"; Charles Moorman's "Space Ship and Grail: The Myths of C. S. Lewis," and Duncan Sprague's "The Unfundamental C. S. Lewis."

A third body of resources is composed of works that explore the meaning of myth in language and culture. These include Roland Barthes' *Mythologies;* Tom Collins' "Mythic Reflections: Thoughts on Myth, Spirit, and our Times"; Mircea Eliade's *Myths, Dreams and Mysteries: The Encounter between Contemporary Faiths and Archaic Realities;* G. A. Gaskell's *Dictionary of All Scriptures and Myths;* Michael Grant's *Myths of the Greeks and Romans,* and Claude Levi-Strauss' *Myth and Meaning.*

The fourth body of work will be resources that engage myth from the religious perspective with some focus on Christianity. These include Mortimer Adler's *Truth in Religion: The Plurality of Religions and the Unity of Truth;* J. J. Bachofen's *Myth, Religion, & Mother Right;* Ian Barbour's *Religion and Science: Historical and Contemporary Issues;* William Cobble's "C. S. Lewis's Understanding of God's Work in Paganism"; Tom Collins' "Mythic Reflections: Thoughts on Myth, Spirit, and our Times"; Winfried Corduan's *A Tapestry of Faiths: The Common Threads Between Christianity and World Religions;* Louis Markos' "Culture, Religion, Philosophy, and Myth: What Christianity is Not" and "From Homer to Christ: Why Christians Should Read the Pagan Classics"; John Oswalt's *The Bible Among the Myths;* Clark Pinnock's "Theology and Myth: An Evangelical Response to Demythologizing," and Thomas Snyder's *Myth Conceptions: Joseph Campbell and the New Age.*

Scholarly Contribution

To date there has been no comprehensive study comparing the similarities and differences of these two leading scholars concerning their respective understanding of myth and its role in the thinking of Western culture where both religion and technology remain persuasive aspects of daily life. Such a study is needed not only because it fills a gap in Campbell and Lewis studies, but also because an exploration of their views provides information and assistance for a greater understanding of the role of religion and literature in a technological age. Such a study of religion, myth, culture, and technology as discussed in the writings of C. S. Lewis and Joseph Campbell can serve as an invaluable contribution in exploring the question, "What does it mean to be human in an age of advanced technology?"

2

Myth, An Attempt to Define the Indefinable

MYTH, FANTASY, AND ALLEGORY are terms that identify a genre familiar to many in the reading public. More difficult to understand is how these terms have been defined. In what ways are they similar and in what ways are they unique? In the context of this study, it is necessary to ask what bearing, if any, these concepts have on religious faith.

To further understand these ideas and their relevance in a technological society, it is important to explore the meaning of myth and its influence upon religion. To accomplish this purpose the idea of myth as a religious phenomenon will be considered, then myth as a cultural phenomenon, and finally myth as a literary genre.

THE CHALLENGE OF A DEFINITION

In commenting on the challenges of defining and explaining myth, J. R. R. Tolkien astutely observes that "Mythology is not a disease at all, though it may like all human things become diseased."[1] This observation serves as a caution to anyone claiming to have the last word regarding a definition of myth. A review of the literature reveals that no single definition of myth satisfies those who study the topic, and yet how one defines myth determines what one reads or writes on it. Robert Segal, who has spent a lifetime teaching on myth, comments, "I have attended many a conference at which speakers fervently propound on 'the nature of myth' in novel X or play Y or

1. Tolkien, *Tolkien Reader*, 21.

film Z. Yet so much of the argument depends on the definition of : Segal follows this remark with his own succinct definition: "I will : define myth as simply a story about something significant . . . the stc., ... take place in the past . . . or in the present or the future."[3]

In a personal correspondence to his friend Owen Barfield, C. S. Lewis shared the state of affairs concerning the word among academics in the latter half of the 1920's:

> By the bye, we now need a new word for the 'science of the nature of the myths' since 'mythology' has been appropriated to the myths themselves. Would 'mythonomy' do? I am quite serious. If your views are not a complete error this subject will become more important and it's worth while trying to get a good word before they invent the beastly one. 'Mytho-logic' (noun) wouldn't be bad, but people wd [*sic*] read it as an adjective. I have also thought of 'mythopoeics' (cf. 'Metaphysics') but that leads to ' mythopoeician' wh. [*sic*] is frightful: whereas 'a mythonomer' (better still 'The Mythonomer Royal') is nice. Or should we just invent a new word—like 'gas.' (Nay Sir, I meant nothing.)[4]

There seems to have never been a time when myth, or the kind of story that qualifies as myth, was unanimously understood. As Peretti observers, "There is no single form of the myth, though some forms are more common than others."[5]

Part of the difficulty in understanding the nature of myth, especially concerning its role in religion, is the question of its veracity: Can a myth be true?[6] In contemporary usage, myth often conveys an idea of invention, falsehood, or something imaginary. For instance, a book claiming to be a *history* of the United States conveys a very different message from a book claiming to be a *mythical* account of American history. The two books

2. Segal, *Myth*, 4.

3. Ibid., 5.

4. Hooper, *The Collected Letters of C. S. Lewis*, 1:765.

5. Peretti, "The Modern Prometheus," 2.

6. Evangelical Protestant theologians continue to struggle with the concept and understanding of myth. For example, the prominent twentieth-century evangelical theologian Carl F. H. Henry writes: "The term myth has acquired a bewildering ambiguity of connotation in respect to religious thought. It has, in fact, become a 'tramp' word . . . To introduce the concept of myth in no way relieves us of the burden of asking what beliefs are literally true . . . and on what cognitive basis we affirm this to be the case. Contemporary neo-Protestant writers seem to employ the term myth as a linguistic device for evading the problem of truth" (Henry, *God, Revelation and Authority*, 59–69).

appear to have little in common and would likely appeal to two very different readers. Additionally, as the *Oxford English Dictionary* notes, "*Myth* is strictly distinguished from *allegory* and *legend* by some scholars, but in general use it is often used interchangeably with these terms."[7] This further complicates attempts to arrive at universal agreement. But must all uses of myth imply it is false? Two examples may serve to illustrate the challenge.

On September 11, 2001, al-Qaeda terrorists forced two commercial jet airplanes to crash into the Twin Towers of the World Trade Center in New York City, killing all passengers on board as well as thousands of workers in the buildings. No one remarking that it was a tragedy of "mythic proportions" would be understood to imply it is fantasy or make believe. "Mythic" in this context signifies a sense of magnitude or enormity, as well as the idea of the catastrophic. In this usage, "mythic" is used to describe a historical event. Lewis used the word this way when speaking of a book he desired, but found priced beyond his means. He commented that "the sum was to me almost mythological."[8] The price was not imaginary, it was factual; but it was beyond his means.

Myth scholar Robert Segal further illustrates this use of myth by referring to the phrase "rags to riches myth," a saying that he notes "uses the term myth positively yet still conveys the hold of the conviction."[9] In this case, while there is anecdotal and persuasive evidence of its veracity, it is not a universal truth; that is, while not everyone goes from rags to riches, there are people who do have this experience. This observation leads Segal to conclude, "I propose that, to qualify as a myth, a story, which can of course express a conviction, be held tenaciously by adherents. But I leave open-ended whether the story must in fact be true."[10]

Besides veracity, another challenge in defining myth are the presuppositions one has when approaching a story considered to be a myth. As C. S. Lewis notes in his essay "Religion without Dogma?," some people accept myths as literally true, some allegorically true, some as confused history, some as lies, and some as imitative of agricultural cycles.[11] Each category affects how one reads and interprets a myth. So the hermeneutical challenges raised by myth are many and complex. Myth is a word without clear definition or standardized use. Yet it has been a part of human thinking since ancient times and finds an accepted place in disciplines as varied

---

7. *Oxford English Dictionary* online, s.v. "Myth," italics in original.

8. Lewis, *Surprised by Joy*, 76.

9. Segal, *Myth*, 6.

10. Ibid.

11. Lewis, "Religion Without Dogma," 131–32.

as philosophy, psychology, history, literature, and religion. A myth may be fact or fantasy or a fantasy based on fact. It can be partially true, completely true, or completely false, or the content of the myth may not be as important as how it is received and understood by an audience. And there are some scholars who argue that technically myths do not exist, only variations on themes. Harvard Literature professor Reuben Brower writes,

> Although we commonly speak of "*the* Oedipus myth" or "*the* Hercules myth," and though anthropologists refer to mythical "archtypes" or "structures," it can be said that there are no myths, only versions. To put it another way, there are only texts for interpretation, whether the text is written or oral, a piece of behavior—a dance or a cockfight—a drawing or painting, a sculptured stone, or a terracotta pot.[12]

MYTH AS A RELIGIOUS PHENOMENON

As will be seen in later chapters, both Joseph Campbell and C. S. Lewis fully understood the difficulty of defining and conveying the nature of myth. For example, in responding to the interview question, "How would you define mythology?" Joseph Campbell answered, "My favorite definition of mythology: other people's religion. My favorite definition of religion: misunderstanding of mythology. The misunderstanding consists in the reading of the spiritual mythological symbols as though they were primarily references to historical events."[13] In this response Campbell blends together a number of disciplines including religion, history, epistemology, and mythology. But his response also draws attention to the tensions and differences between religion, history, and myth.

Similar tensions exist between reality and fantasy as well as between myth and knowledge, myth and history, and myth and reason. Questions arising from these tensions include: Can a religious doctrine have a historical component? Is religion simply a misunderstanding of mythology? Is religion synonymous with mythology? And what part, if any, can myth have within a religious belief system?

The joining together of myth and religion in interpreting myth has a long history. One of the earliest and most significant works in myth, and one known to both Campbell and Lewis, is Sir James George Frazer's

---

12. Brower, *Myth, Symbol, and Culture*, 155.
13. Campbell, *Thou Are That*, 111.

twelve-volume set, *The Golden Bough*,[14] a collection Joseph Campbell referred to as "the second of my long series of bibles."[15] In the introduction to this work, first published in 1890, the historian of science, Robert Temple, describes Frazer's thinking as

> man . . . progressing from a belief in magic as a means of controlling his environment to religious belief, which propitiated gods and spirits; to Frazer, the logical third stage in this process was scientific thought. His work made clear for the first time that matters of human belief are important, not so much for their content, as for their psychological significance.[16]

Here in one of the most influential scholarly contributions in the field of myth there is the merger of myth, religion, and psychology.

This merger of myth and religion has also resulted in a parallel discussion of theories of religion in which myth is a component. According to one theory, the myth-ritualist theory, "religion is primitive science: through myth and ritual, which operates together and constitute its core, religion magically manipulates the world."[17]

Further pointing out the influence of myth upon religion, and more specifically, upon Christianity, is French historian, literary critic, and philosopher Rene Girard's (b. 1923) observation, "Instead of reading myths in light of the Gospels, people have always read the Gospels in the light of myths."[18] Critical to understanding myth as a religious phenomenon is the question of hermeneutical order: Is one reading the Gospels in a context of myth or is one reading myth in a context of the Gospels? At stake is one's understanding of the historicity of the gospel accounts and their claims.

For purposes of this book Girard's reference to myth in relation to the Bible is significant not only because Campbell and Lewis often refer to the Bible in regards to myth, but also because the Bible speaks of myth with little ambiguity. Though there are no uses of "myth" or its lexical equivalent in either the Hebrew Old Testament or the Greek Septuagint, of the less than half a dozen uses of the Greek term μῦθος (mythos) in the New Testament, it is portrayed by the New Testament writers as containing no religious value

---

14. Frazer, *Illustrated Golden Bough*.

15. Larsen and Larsen, *Joseph Campbell*, 42.

16. Frazer, *Illustrated Golden Bough*, 6.

17. Segal, "The Myth-Ritualist Theory of Religion." For more discussion on theories of religion studies see Pals, *Eight Theories of Religion*.

18. Girard, *Things Hidden Since the Foundation of the Word*, 179.

and is placed in sharp contrast with history (2 Pet. 1:16), truth (2 Tim. 4:4), and godliness (1 Tim. 1:4; 4:7).[19]

But myth cannot and should not be dismissed too quickly from religion in general or from Christianity specifically for, as this study shows, the word has had an array of meanings and uses in history and literature since its first appearance. Its use in the Bible is a case of the word being used in a very specific way, one different from how contemporary thinkers such as Lewis and Campbell use it. In the Bible it is not the word or even the concept that poses the difficulty, but its interpretation by contemporary readers resulting in confusion and misunderstanding of myth's role in religion.

In a widely-used reference work in biblical studies edited by John Mc-Clintock and James Strong, the encyclopedia entry on the use of *myth* as used in the Bible makes this helpful distinction,

> . . . in the N. T. a myth is used in its latest sense to express a story invented as the vehicle for some ethical or theological doctrine, which, in fact, has been called in later times an ethopoeia or philosopheme. Yet the condemnation is *special* and not general, and cannot point with dissatisfaction to myths, which, like those of Plato, are the splendidly imaginative embodiment of some subjective truth, and which claim no credence for themselves, but are only meant to be regarded as the vehicles of spiritual instruction.[20]

According to this source, myths have a vital function in religious thought not because of their content or truthfulness, but because they are a means through which religious truth is expressed and conveyed. The distinction is one of whether the myth is used to *convey* doctrine or whether myth has *become* doctrine. This question is foundational in considering myth as a religious phenomenon. Another helpful question in this study is why myth is a *religious* phenomenon. What is it specifically about religion that makes it such a natural environment for myth?

Religious studies scholar Huston Smith (b. 1919) defines religion in both a wide and narrow sense, where a place for myth can be found in each definition. In its widest sense religion gives attention to personal conduct, to ethics and morality, to a "way of life woven around a people's ultimate concerns."[21] In this wider sense myth is able to provide a form of teaching that often corresponds to what is perceived in nature. In other words, what is experienced in everyday life, what is "real," is projected into the un-

19. Bromiley, *Theological Dictionary of the New Testament*, 762–95.

20. McClintock and Strong, *Cyclopedia*; italics in original.

21. Smith, *World's Religions*, 183.

known and in this way an ethical framework can be developed that rewards (perceived) good behavior and punishes (perceived) bad behavior.

Smith's second and more narrow definition is the concern to "align humanity with the transcendental ground of its existence."[22] Here, too, myth is able to provide concepts and convictions about the supernatural and the prehistoric events which lie beyond the scope of human research and understanding. So in this case myth is "neither fiction, history, nor philosophy; it is a spoken poetry, an uncritical and childlike history, a sincere and self-believing romance"[23] which is able to provide answers to the deepest questions of life and human existence. And whether the myth contains elements of historical fact or not, it becomes the means by which thoughts are projected into the spheres of history and reality in a way that, again, blends together a number of disciplines into a comprehensive worldview.

MYTH AS A CULTURAL PHENOMENON

The scope of myth is well stated by comparative religion historian Karen Armstrong as "Myths are universal and timeless stories that reflect and shape our lives—they explore our desires, our fears, our longings, and provide narratives that remind us what it means to be human."[24]

Myths, like their theories, "certainly go back at least to the Presocratics."[25] As a genre, myth appears to go back to the earliest time of writing though, as expected, it is used in a number of ways. The Greek poet Homer (ca. 8th century B.C.E.) used the term as an equivalent for the Greek *logos* ("word"), Plutarch (46–120 C.E.) used it for plausible fiction, and in Pindar (522–433 BCE) myth is used as "mentally conceived, rather than historically true," a meaning often ascribed to the word today.[26] It appears that myth goes as far back as human civilization. As Campbell observes, "Man apparently cannot maintain himself in the universe without belief in some arrangements of the general inheritance of myth."[27]

But myth is not only ancient, it is ubiquitous. Some form of mythology is found in every culture and civilization studied by anthropologists and students of myth. In an early and unpublished edition of *The Hero with a Thousand Faces*, Joseph Campbell, based on his lifelong study of the subject,

22. Ibid.

23. McClintock and Strong, *Cyclopedia*, 6:805.

24. Armstrong, *A Short History of Myth*, n.p.

25. Segal, *Myth*, 1.

26. McClintock and Strong, *Cyclopedia*, 6:805.

27. Campbell, *The Mythic Dimension*, 10.

explains how universally pervasive myths are: "All the religions of all time, the social forms of prehistoric and historic man, the arts, the philosophies, the prime discoveries in science and technology, the very dreams that blister sleep boil up from the simple basic, magic ring of myth."[28]

A similar view is argued by Karen Armstrong, a former Roman Catholic nun and the author of numerous works on comparative religion. Armstrong has devoted much of her academic career to the study of myth as both a religious and cultural phenomenon. In her book *A Short History of Myth*, Armstrong argues that mythology was essential to the early hunters and gathers of the Palaeolithic period (c. 20000 to 8000 BCE) since it served as a means whereby they could feel they had some control over their environment and were able to understand themselves and their predicaments in life.[29]

Armstrong notes that ethnologists and anthropologists have long recognized the influence and importance of the sacred or divine among cultures as one delves into human history. Prior to the rise of antiquity, humans had only nature and their own imaginations to help them understand their existence and find meaning or purpose for life. Scholars argue that, for the earliest humans, the spiritual world was as real and accessible as the physical and so similar mythical themes can be found throughout the world. A mountain, tree, or pole would serve as a link from earth to a heavenly realm, from a natural to a supernatural existence. But some disaster in the past would damage this bridge, thus setting up a universal longing for a lost paradise, a paradise as real as the physical realm and almost as close. But it's in this "almost" that myth arises. Armstrong notes: "The myth was not simply an exercise in nostalgia, however. Its primary purpose was to show people how they could return to this archetypal world, not only in moments of visionary rapture but in the regular duties of their daily lives."[30] Lewis explains it this way,

> Savage beliefs are thought to be the spontaneous response of a human group to its environment, a response made principally by the imagination. They exemplify what some writers call pre-logical thinking. They are closely bound up with the communal life of the group. What we should describe as political, military, and agricultural operations are not easily distinguished from rituals; ritual and belief beget and support one another.[31]

28. Larsen and Larsen, *Joseph Campbell*, 335.

29. Armstrong, *A Short History*, 12–13.

30. Ibid., 15.

31. Lewis, *The Discarded Image*, 1.

And in a personal correspondence (dated 1916) to Arthur Greeves prior to his conversion to Christianity, Lewis writes,

> Primitive man found himself surrounded by all sorts of terrible things he didn't understand—thunder, pestilence, snakes etc: what more natural than to suppose that these were animated by evil spirits trying to torture him. These he kept off by cringing to them, singing songs and making sacrifices etc. Gradually from being mere nature-spirits these supposed being[s] were elevated into more elaborate ideas, such as the old gods: and when man became more refined he pretended that these spirits were good as well as powerful. Thus religion, that is to say mythology grew up.[32]

Prior to advanced and abundant technology, in prescientific cultures humanity had a collective sense of beliefs that made few distinctions between thinking and believing.

Tied closely to the cultural universality of a paradise is an equally strong longing for transcendence. Even though the act of dying is a universal experience, throughout history humanity has been unable to fully understand, accept, or explain death in a satisfactory manner. Though death has been faced with bravado, heroism, acquiescence, and some individuals choose it over other alternatives, there often is still a sense of foreboding or fear in the face of death. Of all the human experiences, death is universal but perhaps the least understood.

In view of this mystery of death, myth has served as a way for humanity to experience a sense of transcendence by which they are able to elevate themselves beyond their own limited and sometimes tragic circumstances. Whether through prayer, ecstasy, or the services of a shaman or holy man, people have believed that if they could enter into a mythical world they would enter a realm far superior to their own.

This transitioning from the natural to the supernatural leads to another aspect of myth as a cultural phenomenon—myths are never wholly supernatural. For a myth to have any meaning or importance to a culture, it must be rooted in the culture and nature. Even though it may share similarities with others, each culture has its own ethos, a philosophy or worldview that is unique to that culture. Its philosophies may be the product of natural phenomena such as the weather (hot, cold, temperate), geography (mountainous, desert, forest), vocation (hunter, gatherer), relation to other cultures (conqueror, conquered, at peace), and technological differentiation (oral tradition or written languages). Each of these conditions greatly

---

32. Hooper, *The Collected Letters of C. S. Lewis*, 1:231.

influence the myths of a culture. Thus, while a desert region may have myths pertaining to rainfall, a more fruitful climate may have myths about an even greater harvest. Myths located in a mountainous region may have deities inhabiting the highest elevation, while peoples located along a river or near an ocean often have myths reflecting their geography.

But this cultural phenomenon of myth suffered perhaps its greatest setback at the onset of western modernity in the nineteenth and twentieth centuries. This movement had such an impact upon myth that Karen Armstrong states that "this new experiment [of western modernity] was the death of mythology."[33] As western culture made advancements in education, science, and reasoning, it was believed by many that there was little room left for the role of myth.

Prior to the rise of modernity, nature and agriculture were the primary means of interpreting the relationship of the physical to the spiritual. Human existence was contingent upon rain, sun, and soil. This reliance upon nature naturally led to a need for myths and, through them, upon the deities thought to control nature. The correlation was self-evident; there was a symbiotic cause-and-effect relationship between humans and the gods. But with the coming of the modern age and its reliance upon scientific research and verification, along with the need for efficiency and the demand for rational proof, the practical began to overthrow the spiritual, mysterious, and mythic. No longer were people dependent on the supernatural; they could now control their environment. Technology, with its standardized tools and techniques, frees people from their local environment. The ancient medicine man is replaced by medicine and the scientific and historical evidence takes the place of stories handed down by generations.

In reaction to this dominance of science and education over myth, scholars in the field of myth have suggested two approaches as ways to reconcile myth and modernity. The first approach is a re-characterizing of religion and therefore of myth. Under this approach one understands the stories of religion and of the Bible, especially the miraculous events, as mythical and therefore symbolic. Once a story is no longer read literally there is no longer any conflict with science. Science, like history, is concerned with facts and proofs, not symbols and meaning. So the Garden of Eden is symbolized as *representing* a perfect environment, a global flood serves to remind humanity of its existence in a chaotic universe, and a physical resurrection from death, such as Jesus Christ's, serves to offer some sense of hope in the face of death. Such deeper and symbolic meanings taking the place of historical

---

33. Armstrong, *A Short History*, 119.

readings removes interpretive and ideological conflicts between science and myth.

A second approach taken to reconcile myth to history and science is to reinterpret historical events or individuals in a way that elevates them to mythological proportions, but not so far as to become supernatural and thus contradict science. This approach allows the literal reading of the story while at the same time allowing some freedom for symbol and type to be applied.

As one example of this latter approach taken from American history, consider the life of George Washington.[34] His life and accomplishments have been taught to schoolchildren throughout American history, yet much of his life is mythical in stature. Stories of his skipping a silver dollar across the Potomac River at Mount Vernon and admitting that he chopped down his father's cherry tree have circulated since the early 19th century. Commemorative items such as coins bearing his image, sculptures, paintings, legends, songs, and poems have all given him a regal bearing. Naming states, cities, and towns after him and holding elaborate national celebrations of his birthday have resulted in his being referred to as the mythical "Founding Father" of the United States. And the famous advertisement "George Washington slept here" has elevated this otherwise common man close to deity.

So there are ways for myth to remain vital and meaningful as a cultural phenomenon, even in a highly technological and scientific age. It is possible to either revise religious stories to the status of symbol or elevate events and people in history to a status just below supernatural, yet above the ordinary, enough to inspire hope and aspiration. Both approaches allow myth to remain an essential part of culture while not challenging the authority of science.

MYTH AS A LITERARY GENRE

In commenting on how the myth-maker, and similarly, the teller of fairy tales speak to both the emotions and mind, philosopher Peter Kreeft writes:

> The human soul has intellect, will, and emotions; some knowledge of the truth, the good, and the beautiful. And God sent prophets to all three areas of the soul: philosophers to enlighten the intellect, prophets to straighten out the will, and myth-makers to tease and touch the emotions with the desire for himself. The philosophers have an analogue in the soul, a philosopher within: our understanding. The prophets have an analogue in

34. Segal, *Myth*, 57–60.

the soul too, a divine mouthpiece called conscience. And the myth-makers too have an analogue in the soul, a dreamer and poet and myth-maker within.[35]

However defined, myth forever enables imagination to be visualized and passed on from one generation to another.

From the French, *genre* is defined as a kind, sort, or style,[36] and is a term applied to a number of fields including literature, art, music, and culture. But while genre is a simple word to define, it is a difficult concept to understand and genres are numerous and complex since they are created, formed, changed, or disregarded based on cultural conventions and styles. Literary genres consist of a number of forms; these include anecdote, autobiography, ballad, didactic literature, epic, essay, myth, fantasy, and allegory, though there are dozens more.

The relationship between myth and religion is most commonly seen by its role in literature. Individuals, events, and mythical stories have been woven into literature from the time of the Christian faith, where myth was used to argue against paganism, through the greatest writers of literature such as Dante Alighieri (1265–1321), Geoffrey Chaucer (1343–1400), William Shakespeare (1564–1616), John Milton (1608–1674), to writers such as James Joyce (1882–1941) and T. S. Eliot (1888–1965).[37]

A matter of debate in the relationship of myth to literature is the order: Did myth originate from literature or is literature a product of myth? Scholars do not agree on an answer to this question, but they do agree on the focus of a common story line in myth. Where they differ is on the importance of the story. While some scholars argue the literary aspect is important, others contend *how* the myth is conveyed is unimportant to its role as a myth. No one argues myth is not a story, but they do question the importance of its form. And because there are so many kinds of myths including myths about gods, creation, floods, animals, and heroes, it is nearly impossible to find literary common ground even in a similarity in plot.[38]

Among the various literary genres to which myth is often compared, the two most common are fantasy and allegory. As a way of understanding the similarities and differences among myth, fantasy, and allegory, it is necessary to divide belief into two categories: *primary* and *temporary*. Primary belief is defined as belief in anything assumed to be ontologically real (that is, people, events, and activities believed to exist or to have existed).

---

35. Kreeft, quoted in Dickerson and O'Hara, *From Homer to Harry Potter*, 258.

36. *Oxford English Dictionary*, s.v. "genre."

37. Segal, *Myth*, 79.

38. Ibid., 85–90.

Temporary belief is the suspension of this primary belief and a "temporary acceptance of 'unreality'"[39] of events and people assumed not to be real. A second difference is that primary belief is permanent, it remains after the story ends (while temporary belief is short-lived, lasting only as long as the story is told).

With these two categories serving as a paradigm of belief, it is possible to see certain myths as those of permanent belief while other myths, along with fantasy and allegory, are seen as those of temporary belief. For example, one modern theory, serving for some also as a myth, that fits comfortably into a primary belief is the Big Bang theory. As a *theory*, it is a proposition or principle that attempts to explain an unverifiable phenomenon, the beginning of the universe. But this is conjecture and speculation, not scientific fact verified by empirical testing; so in this sense it is a myth. But because it is the logical conclusion of scientific evidence, it falls into the category of a primary belief. To many authorities in the earth sciences and astronomy, the Big Bang theory is a permanent, abiding principle that should be accepted until another theory with new and more persuasive evidence replaces it. These categories of permanent and temporary beliefs are not only seen in the sciences though; they often appear in fantasy literature as well.

One author considered by many as one of the leading scholars on the topic of fantasy and one who was instrumental in the writing career of C. S. Lewis was J. R. R. Tolkien. Tolkien has been described as "one of the greatest myth makers of the twentieth century—and arguably of all time."[40] In his *The Tolkien Reader: Stories, poems and an essay by the author of 'The Hobbit' and 'The Lord of the Rings,'"* Tolkien devotes a chapter to the topic of fantasy where he both explains and illustrates it.[41]

In this chapter Tolkien writes about fantasy and uses the same categories of primary and secondary belief.

> Fantasy . . . which combines with its older and higher use of an equivalent of Imagination the derived notions of 'unreality' (that is, of unlikeness to the Primary World), of freedom from the domination of observed 'fact,' in short of the fantastic. I am thus not only aware but am glad of the etymological and semantic connexions of *fantasy* with *fantastic*: with images of things that are not only 'not actually present,' but which are indeed not

39. Hammond, "Differences Between Myth."

40. Dickerson and O'Hara, *From Homer to Harry Potter*, 26.

41. Tolkien, *The Tolkien Reader*, 46–55.

to be found in our primary world at all, or are generally believed not to be found there.[42]

Tolkien's reference to our *primary* world implies there is another world beyond the primary one.

Tolkien explains that fantasy consists of a number of characteristics. First, fantasy consists of an "arresting strangeness,"[43] it meddles with the Primary World. Second, and this is for him a drawback with fantasy, fantasy is difficult to achieve, and it is hard to produce good fantasy without resorting to the fanciful. Third, fantasy is a natural human activity. To be good, fantasy depends on facts, evidence, and reason. "If men could not distinguish between frogs and men, fairy-stories about frog-kings would not have arisen."[44] Finally, good fantasy cannot be taken to excess. Like all literature, fantasy can be done badly or put to evil uses. "But of what human thing in this fallen world is that not true?"[45] Tolkien believed these principles are what make, or destroy, good fantasy.

Where myth, in the sense of a primary belief, and fantasy differ is that myth is a belief system that serves to explain the universe, social customs, religion, or social group. The myth offers an explanation of both how and why the universe and social structure works. On the other hand, fantasy does not serve as meta-narrative nor does it seek to explain "facts." Instead, it serves a purpose closer to the idea of imagination or entertainment. While certain myths are integrated into reality as a way of explaining it, fantasy offers an escape from reality by means of another universe that exists parallel to the world known by the culture. Both worlds are similar in ways but the differences within fantasy allow for a temporary escape or adventure from the normal existence.

Dickerson and O'Hara summarize Tolkien's approach to myth and fantasy stating:

> Another way to look at this is to note that the realm of myth is celestial, the realm of fantasy and heroic romance is an earthly kingdom (it doesn't matter which one), and the realm of fairy story is the local village. Likewise, there is a range of historical scope. Myth is timeless. To the extent that it is within time, it may span centuries. Most fairy tales, by contrast, take place in

---

42. Ibid., 47. Italics in original.

43. Ibid., 48.

44. Ibid., 55.

45. Ibid.

the matter of a few days. Works of fantasy and heroic romance typically span several months or even a few years.[46]

So even though the various genres have commonalities that overlap, there are also distinctions that should be made between them.

While there are no distinct boundaries to distinguish myth from fantasy, there are attributes that can be applied to help differentiate between them. Myths are broad and apply to events in the world or universe that affect history. Though the individual characters are important in myth, what the characters *do* is the critical point, since the principles arising from their actions are seen as explaining present life. Myths are comprehensive in nature and can be understood on many levels with each retelling.

Fantasy, on the other hand, is less ambitious, having simpler and more easily understood lessons and morals. While the myth may be interesting, the fantasy is enjoyable. The myth seeks to explain, while the fantasy entertains. This is not to say there are clear lines and categories to distinguish myth from fantasy, but only to say they are not the same thing.

Another genre separate from myth and fantasy, but often confused as one or both, is allegory. As Dickerson and O'Hara observe:

> If one mistake in approaching fantasy is to reject it altogether because of the presence of enchantment, and another is to reject it as untrue and devoid of meaning, and yet another error is to try too hard to force an allegorical meaning onto a particular work of fantasy. All three of these mistakes have been committed by well-meaning readers.[47]

So what is allegory and how does it differ from myth and fantasy?

Allegory is derived from the Greek word meaning to say something other than what one seems to say. In literature it can signify both an allegorical representation and an allegorical interpretation.[48] In the representation, the allegory is a way for the writer to present spiritual concepts in everyday physical events. In the interpretation, the allegorical approach allows the reader to see beyond the literal wording to find deeper, hidden, or mystical meanings not obvious from the words themselves. Similar to myth and fantasy, allegory is an ancient genre which first appeared in the Hellenistic period in Cynic-Stoic philosophy.[49]

---

46. Cited in Dickerson and O'Hara, *From Homer to Harry Potter*, 27. The quote is also found in the foreword in some editions of *The Fellowship of the Ring*.

47. Dickerson and O'Hara, *From Homer to Harry Potter*, 57.

48. Solen, *Handbook of Biblical Criticism*, 15.

49. Ibid.

One of the most influential writers in the 20th century on literary criticism and allegory was the literary theorist Northrop Frye (1912–1991). According to Frye, whenever someone comments on literature, they allegorize. Frye explains,

> It is not often realized that all commentary is allegorical interpretation, an attaching of ideas to the structure of poetic imagery. The instant that any critic permits himself to make a genuine comment about a poem (e.g., "In *Hamlet* Shakespeare appears to be portraying the tragedy of irresolution") he has begun to allegorize. Commentary thus looks at literature as, in its formal phase, a potential allegory of events and ideas . . . Allegory, then, is a contrapuntal technique, like canonical imitation in music.[50]

But not everyone understands allegory so broadly.

While Lewis had some positive things to say concerning allegory, and these will be discussed in due course, Tolkien did not like allegory and is frequently cited as declaring: "I cordially dislike allegory in all its manifestations, and always have done so since I grew old and wary enough to detect its presence;"[51] nevertheless his dislike of it did not prevent him from speaking about it at great length. Perhaps it's better to say that *because* of his dislike of it, he thought it important enough to study and understand. But what was it about allegory that Tolkien found so objectionable? The similarity of allegory to myth and fantasy would lead one to conclude that an author who enjoys one would naturally find the other two forms equally appealing. Why not Tolkien?

Tolkien had three criticisms of allegory. First, there was the question of degree. If X was being used allegorically, then why not Y? And Tolkien leveled this criticism against the writer as well as the reader. Not only did Tolkien see a danger in a reader interpreting something allegorically that the writer never intended, but he found it equally perilous for the writer to put in so much allegory that it left the reader confused about the true meaning.

The second concern Tolkien raised concerning allegory was how it risked simplifying a story. "Reducing a rich narrative to its (real or imagined) allegorical value is much like reducing a person to a mere label. Labeling a person . . . exposes us to the temptation of thinking we know everything there is to know about the person and that we are free from listening to them and engaging their ideas."[52] This was a great concern to

---

50. Frye, *Anatomy of Criticism*, 89–90.

51. Dickerson and O'Hara, *From Homer to Harry Potter*, 58.

52. Ibid.

Tolkien because the complexities of the drama or the theme of the story are then relegated to the shadows of the presumed allegorical meaning.

Tolkien's third criticism of allegory was that it often applied where it was never intended to do so. Despite critics insisting on an allegorical reading of *The Lord of the Rings*, Tolkien insists, "As for any inner meaning or 'message,' it has in the intention of the author none. It is neither allegorical or topical."[53]

Most people, in listening to a historical account or reading a narrative, would never think to look for allegorical meanings; that is not how one applies allegory. So Tolkien argues that myths and fantasies are not allegories, nor were they intended to be understood allegorically. Granted, such stories can make use of an occasional allegory, but even in these cases the allegory benefits or enhances the story, not the story enhancing the allegory. For Tolkien myth, fantasy, and allegory are three distinct genres that overlap at times.

As discussed earlier, myth defies definition, which is not to say it has not been defined, only that it has not been defined satisfactorily. Even Tolkien admits, "I will not attempt to define that, nor to describe it directly. It cannot be done. Faerie cannot be caught in a net of words; for it is one of its qualities to be indescribable, though not imperceptible."[54] Though distinctions are important, unlike many words or ideas, one cannot begin to understand myth by a dictionary definition and the same is true to some degree for fantasy and allegory as well. These are not matters of science or of reasoning, but are found instead in the imagination.

Taking this thought one step further, C. S. Lewis argued that myth is not only beyond the realm of facts and science, but it is even beyond words:

> Myth does not essentially exist in *words* at all. We all agree that the story of Balder is a great myth, a thing of inexhaustible value. But whose version—whose *words*—are we thinking when we say this? For my own part, the answer is that I am not thinking of any one's words. No poet, as far as I know or can remember, has told this story supremely well. I am not thinking of any particular version of it. If the story is anywhere embodied in words, that is almost an accident. What really delights and nourishes me is a particular pattern of events, which would equally delight and nourish if it had reached me by some medium which involved no words at all.[55]

---

53. Tolkien, *The Lord of the Rings*, foreword.

54. Tolkien, *Tolkien Reader*, 10.

55. Lewis, *George MacDonald*, xxvi–xxvii.

The story itself is sufficient, the means of communication is secondary.

Defining the Indefinable?

Myth, allegory, truth, and fantasy are grand concepts that at times overlap and at other times contradict. In his thesis on Lewis's epistemological thinking, Charlie Starr observes, "Myth is the beautiful pattern of being, truth is the beautiful known, and fact is the concrete beautiful."[56] How is one to understand and explain these terms and tensions? Is truth important when considering myth? How does myth differ from fantasy and both of them differ from allegory? Attention will now be turned to these questions.

First, myth, fantasy, and allegory should not be seen as truth or falsehood but as venues for truth, the "vehicles of spiritual instruction."[57] When understood this way myth and truth, including history, are seen as held in tension, instead of in conflict or contradiction. Read this way, the veracity of the story now includes two components, the characters and events *in* the story and the ideas or philosophy *of* the story. The reader no longer has to decide between absolute truth and falsehood or fact and fiction, since now both elements can delightfully be held together without conflict.

Second, if the explanation of myth and fantasy is not found in defining the terms, how can they be understood? The answer is in understanding how the concepts relate to one another.

Myth, fantasy, and allegory are best understood as one might define shades of color on a spectrum. On the one hand, there are some clearly defined blues and reds. So there are myths and fantasies where one can find almost universal agreement of the genre. But there are also areas of overlap where more than one shade can be discerned, and there are some stories that defy being understood in any one category as either myth *or* fantasy.

From this view, myth (and some would include fantasy) is the boldest and most significant story. Its scope is vast, encompassing the very limits of human imagination. Myth not only involves the world, but usually more than one world as it often transports one into a realm of gods and spirits. And myth not only pushes the boundaries of space, but also of time, playing itself out in an eternal setting, and typically involves eons when time is included. Finally, myth serves a philosophical purpose as it offers the culture spiritual, but seemingly plausible, answers to the great questions of humanity relating to the meaning of life, death, joy, and tragedy.

---

56. Starr, "The Triple Enigma," 310.
57. McClintock and Strong, *Cyclopedia*, 804; italics in original.

Fantasy, on the other hand, serves a different and less ambitious purpose. The scope of fantasy does not seek to bridge the realm of the gods to the world of humans, instead limiting itself to heroes below the heavens. This is not to say fantasy's scope is not vast, for it certainly is; it can involve an entire planet and more than one planet, but it limits itself to being under the heavens. While the activities of mythical gods create new worlds or alter the course of events, the heroes of fantasy influence only the lives of those around them.

Next, fantasy is typically more time conscious than myth. Whereas concern for time is not as common in myth, in fantasy time plays an important role as events play out over the course of months or years, typically within the lifetime of the main characters.

Finally, while it can certainly convey deep truths and moral lessons, fantasy is closer to a traditional story and serves to entertain while it instructs. Unlike myth, fantasy does not attempt to make sense out of tragedy or explain the creation of the human race, but rather serves to illustrate personal attributes such as courage, honesty, or wisdom on the individual level. While myth explains, fantasy confronts:

> For fantasy is true, of course. It isn't factual, but it is true. Children know that. Adults know it too, and that is precisely why many of them are afraid of fantasy. They know that its truth challenges, even threatens, all that is false, all that is phony, unnecessary, and the trivial in the life they have let themselves be forced into living. They are afraid of dragons because they are afraid of freedom . . . Children know perfectly well that unicorns aren't real, but they also know that books about unicorns, if they are good books, are true books.[58]

Thus while fantasy is not as grand as myth, like myth, it speaks of grand truths in ways where one not only learns the lesson, but sees it lived out in the every day life of the characters.

While allegory is one of the more difficult genres to identify, it is by far the most versatile. It can be found in both myth and fantasy, but its absence or presence does not affect the definition of either. And while myth and fantasy are forms of literature, allegory is also a mode of interpreting literature; a way of reading literature, including myth and fantasy, figuratively or symbolically, as opposed to a literal reading of words and sentences.

Even though allegory has seldom been controversial in regards to truth and falsity, myth and fantasy have long been at the center of such debates. And when religion enters the discussion and is mixed with myth, one can

---

58. Le Guin, quoted in Dickerson and O'Hara, *From Homer to Harry Potter,* 258–59.

anticipate that such debates will become even more heated. Complicating matters further is the role of logic and science upon the interpretation and purpose of myth and fantasy. Some scholars today argue that myths are useless, if not already extinct. But others, including J. R. R. Tolkien, C. S. Lewis, and Joseph Campbell counter that the relevancy and need for such stories have never been greater. In the opinion of fantasy author Ursula Le Guin,

> It has always been the case that there are people who claim myth and fantasy are outmoded, that the stories they tell are fantastic and therefore not relevant and not true . . . truth is not limited to that which has been proven by scientific experiment or deductive logic. If it were, we would never know any truth at all. Scientists need assumptions and logicians need premises to make their demonstrations relevant to life. Assumptions and premises come from our experience; they rest upon stories. We always have need of moral and other truth to be expressed in universal story, story that we can relate to and which is plastic enough to have relevance for our decisions.[59]

Tolkien, Lewis, and Campbell would perhaps agree with Le Guin's assessment; if not for myth and fantasy, there would be a greater difficulty in ascertaining truth.

As the "fixed" conclusions of science continue to change in light of research, and as theories are overthrown with the discovery of new evidence, the lessons of myth and fantasy remain unchanged and essentially eternal. Humans, whether they view themselves to be the product of evolution or the creation of a divine Creator, will continue to ask questions that lie beyond the purview of science and scientific evidence. And as long as these questions remain, myth and fantasy will give some individuals and groups frameworks, answers, and ways to live in the present age, regardless of the technological complexity of a culture.

59. Ibid., 258.

3

C. S. Lewis and Myth

D UE TO HIS PROLIFIC output of literature, C. S. Lewis holds many titles; terms such as Christian apologist, essayist, theologian, literary critic, medievalist, novelist, and academic often precede his name. But anyone who studies in the related fields of myth and fantasy finds that Lewis can also be described as a true mythologist. According to professor of theology, ministry, and education at King's College, London, Alister McGrath "While some popular Christian readers of Lewis, familiar only with the conceptually emaciated notion of myth as 'fiction,' regard this aspect of Lewis's thought with some apprehension and concern, it is seen by those familiar with the deeper meaning of the term as one of Lewis's most important and significant contributions, particularly to Christian theology and apologetics."[1]

In the estimation of computer science professor Matthew Dickerson and assistant professor of philosophy David O'Hara, C. S. Lewis (and J. R. R. Tolkien) are "arguably the two most important authors of fantasy in the twentieth century, and . . . will likely remain the most influential fantasy authors through the twenty-first."[2]

Lewis's intellectual and literary output is impressive, in addition to his over fifty books

> He saw to print more than 200 short pieces, nearly 80 poems, excluding those in the cycle *Spirits in Bondage* (1919). His essays range from critical, historical, and theoretical to religious, philosophical, and cultural. Devoted readers of his Narnia chronicles

---

1. McGrath, *The Intellectual World of C. S. Lewis*, 57.
2. Dickerson and O'Hara, *From Homer to Harry Potter*, 17.

for children may not have read, or even know of, *The Screwtape Letters* (1942), surely Lewis's second best-known work and the one that earned him a place on the cover of *Time* in 1947. Lewis the scholar is likely unknown to the readers of his Ransom trilogy of space fantasies. Those who know *Mere Christianity* (1952), based on the wartime BBC radio talks that made his voice the second-most recognized in Britain (after Churchill's), probably will not have read either the subtle *Problem of Pain* (1940) or the short analytical essays and of the sermons. Still fewer will have read Lewis's lyrical poetry. And almost no one is aware of his long narrative poems.[3]

Looking back on Lewis's life from his earliest childhood activities through his formal schooling, and from his interests and friends as an adult, this trajectory seemed almost inevitable. It was as if Lewis was being groomed to become one of the leading authors and scholars of myth. Attention in this chapter will be given to the influences, experiences, and people who instructed Lewis on myth, including the experiential, literary, and religious influences. Lewis's understanding of myth, the relation he saw between myth and Christianity, along with myth and spirituality, will also be explored.

SOURCES OF LEWIS'S VIEW ON MYTH

Although the line between outside influence and one's personal conclusions are often blurry, a study of Lewis's life and writings reveals some clearly identifiable experiences that shaped his thinking. Among many influences, the experiential, literary, and religious are three that are prominent.

Two key moments in Lewis's early life involve the imaginary world of Boxen, found in his early childhood writings, and the unfortunate death of his mother when Lewis was a child. And later, when he became an adult and an accomplished scholar, the necessity to read what he considered good mythology became a driving force behind his fantasy. He often admitted, especially to Tolkien who agreed with him, that there simply were no good mystical writings available in his day. In Lewis's words, "Tollers, there is too little of what we really like in stories. I am afraid we shall have to write some ourselves."[4]

Some of the literary influences that affected his thinking regarding myth included the works of Plato (424/423–348/347 B.C.E.), Samuel Taylor

3. Como, "Mere Lewis," 110.
4. Carpenter, *The Letters of J. R. R. Tolkien*, 378.

Coleridge (1772–1834), G. K. Chesterton (1874–1936), and Owen Barfield (1898–1997). And, as will be seen later, two significant influences were the writings of Scottish author George MacDonald (1824–1905), and the close, and at times tumultuous, friendship Lewis had with poet and university professor, John Ronald Reuel (J. R. R.) Tolkien.

Finally, consideration is given to the religious influence on Lewis's writings. From his childhood belief in a good God who could heal his mother but did not do so, to his years in boarding school as a confirmed atheist, and then to his conversion to theism and later to Christianity; each phase influenced his understanding of myth and how myth can exist with religious faith without either one destroying the other.

Experiential Influences

As Lewis testifies in the autobiographical volume of his first thirty-one years, *Surprised by Joy*, from his earliest years he was drawn to wonder and imagination. Writing about the close relationship he had with his older brother, Warren, Lewis alludes to this early interest, "Yet we were very different. Our earliest pictures (and I can remember no time when we were not incessantly drawing) reveal it. His were of ships and trains and battles; mine, when not imitated from his, were of what we both called 'dressed animals' — the anthropomorphized beasts of nursery literature."[5] In those early years came the unforgettable moment for Lewis when Warren walked into the nursery with "the lid of a biscuit tin which he had covered with moss and garnished with twigs and flowers so as to make it a toy garden or a toy forest." Lewis's first response to seeing that biscuit tin was that it was "the first beauty I ever knew . . . I do not think the impression was very important at the moment, but it soon became important in memory. As long as I live my imagination of Paradise will retain something of my brother's toy garden."[6] Even though other experiences would contribute to and influence Lewis's understanding of myth, those later events were simply building blocks placed upon a foundation Lewis had from childhood.

Another experience, and one closely tied to the first, was Lewis's appreciation of nature. As he shares, the nursery room where he and his older brother, Warren (Warnie), played with the biscuit tin garden overlooked the Green Hills of his home in Belfast. He wrote: "that is, the low line of the Castlereagh Hills which we saw from the nursery windows. They were not very far off but they were, to children, quite unattainable. They taught me

---

5. Lewis, *Surprised by Joy*, 6.
6. Ibid., 7.

longing—*Sehnsucht;* made me for good or ill, and before I was six years old, a votary of the Blue Flower."[7] Three things stand out from his observation.

First, and perhaps most noteworthy, is the age at which he had these sensations. For a child to be able to see into things so deeply *before* the age of six is remarkable. Granted, as Lewis recollects these events he does so as an adult and so can read adult ideas back into his childhood experience. Nevertheless, he is attempting to describe as honestly as he can what he experienced as a child. And even as an adult, what he remembers experiencing as a child is a sense of insight and imagination seldom heard from adults recalling a similar time in life.

Second, Lewis refers here to *Sehnsucht,* a term defined by one Lewis scholar as "that longing in every man, that ineluctable cry at the very roots of man's being which keeps man forever restless until he rest in God."[8] A German term for longing or craving, Lewis uses it as a synonym for what he commonly refers to as joy. In *The Cambridge Companion to C. S. Lewis,*[9] David Jasper offers this explanation of joy and Lewis's use of *Sehnsucht:*

> [A]n experience of inconsolable longing which [Lewis] describes as the 'central story of my life,' originating even before he was six years old. He also sometimes calls it *Sehnsucht,* the German word deliberately conveying the complex Romantic notion which Lewis distinguishes from both happiness and pleasure, for *Sehnsucht* is, rather, an 'unsatisfied desire which is itself more desirable than any other satisfaction.'[10]

And Alan Jacobs adds,

> Lewis thought that this mood of longing could be well or badly used. Indeed, one could say that, just as joviality is the mood of Jupiter and exhaustion that of Saturn, *Sehnsucht* is the mood of our world: the Silent Planet longs for connection, for a restoration of the music of the other spheres from which we have cut ourselves off.[11]

As can be seen from these observations, *Sehnsucht* is an experience of insight, something that takes place in the imagination and lies beyond description and is recalled differently from person to person. Though Lewis does not use the word often, this childhood experience so greatly influenced

---

7. Ibid.

8. Kilby, "The Creative Logician Speaking," 30.

9. MacSwain and Ward, *The Cambridge Companion to C. S. Lewis.*

10. Jasper, "The Pilgrim's Regress," 223.

11. Jacobs, "The Chronicles of Narnia," 278.

his thinking that the idea of *Sehnsucht* is found woven through much of his work.

A third observation is Lewis's mention of a votary of the Blue Flower. Like joy and *Sehnsucht*, the Blue Flower was a literary symbol for the elusive desire of some unknown object. The term was first coined by the German poet, Novalis (Friedrich von Hardenburg, 1772–1801), to describe a focus on emotions instead of theory.[12]

In seeking to identify experiential influences in an author's thinking, one would expect to find seminal ideas forming during the college years when a young person is first exposed to new and contrary ideas that challenge traditional thinking, or in early adulthood when one is able to assess and critique ideas and opinions with the advantages of study and life experiences. But these earliest influences on Lewis's thinking took place years before such events. And a biscuit tin, nature, and longing for the unknown would not be the only experiences to leave a lifelong impression upon the young Lewis.

Lewis turned six years old on November 28, 1904, and in four short years, when he was almost ten (August 28, 1908), his loving mother, Flora, passed away from cancer at the age of forty-six. No event affected Lewis's world and thinking as deeply as the death of his mother. This moment became the watershed event around which Lewis would refer to himself by either "boyhood" or "childhood"; all events were categorized as happening before or after his mother's death.

In describing how he came to the realization of his mother's condition, Lewis wrote:

> There came a night when I was ill and crying both with headache and toothache and distressed because my mother did not come to me. That was because she was ill too, and what was odd was that there were several doctors in her room, and voices and comings and goings all over the house and doors shutting and opening. It seemed to last for hours. And then my father, in tears, came into my room and began to try to convey to my terrified mind things it had never conceived of before. It was in fact cancer and followed the usual course; an operation (they operated in the patient's house in those days), an apparent convalescence, a return of the disease, increasing pain, and death. My father never fully recovered from this loss.[13]

---

12. Downing, *The Most Reluctant Convert*, 29.
13. Lewis, *Surprised by Joy*, 18.

The senior Lewis was not the only one who failed to fully recover from this loss. Later, in his autobiography, Lewis bares the heartache he experienced as he came to grips with the finality of his mother's death. He wrote:

> We lost her gradually as she was gradually withdrawn from our life into the hands of nurses and delirium and morphia, and as our whole existence changed into something alien and menacing, as the house became full of strange smells and midnight noises and sinister whispered conversations. This had two further results, one very evil and one very good. It divided us from our father as well as our mother. They say that a shared sorrow draws people closer together; I can hardly believe that it often has that effect when those who share it are of wildly different ages. If I may trust my own experience, the sight of adult misery and adult terror has an effect on children which is merely paralyzing and alienating. Perhaps it was our fault. Perhaps if we had been better children we might have lightened our father's sufferings at this time. We certainly did not.[14]

The heartache and loss of his mother in death and his father in grief would never be forgotten by Lewis. When one considers that Lewis published this account in 1955 when he was fifty-seven, a mere eight years before his own death, the abiding influence this experience had on his entire life is unmistakable.

A final influence upon Lewis was an experience in adulthood when he was thirty-six, but it was *the* seminal event that propelled him to write myth and fantasy. Quoting from *The Letters of J. R. R. Tolkien*,[15] Martha Sammons describes the moment involving Lewis and Tolkien:

> In 1936, Lewis said "Tollers, there is too little of what we really like in stories. I am afraid we shall have to write some ourselves." Tolkien writes that the type of literature he wanted to read was scarce and "heavily alloyed." Lewis compares what they wanted to write and read to *The Hobbit*. They agreed to each write a story: one on time and one on space, flipping a coin to decide.[16]

While his childhood imagination was positively influenced by the wonder of make-believe and his love of nature, and tragically impressed by the loss of his mother and emotional separation from his father, it was a desire to read the kind of stories he enjoyed that prompted Lewis (and Tolkien) to

---

14. Ibid., 19.

15. Humphrey, *The Letters of J. R. R. Tolkien*, 378, 211 respectively.

16. Sammons, *War of the Fantasy Worlds*, 4.

begin writing stories that would result in C. S. Lewis being regarded one of the most influential authorities on myth and fantasy.

Literary Influences

Besides life experiences there were also literary and social events that affected Lewis's thinking on myth,

> The student of Lewis the critic must immediately be struck by the *social* context of his literary thought. He was a man of deep intellectual friendships, and he enjoyed the good fortune of having friends who were great in more senses than one, men who shared broad sympathies and imaginative powers.[17]

As professor of English literature at Oxford and Cambridge universities and recognized as a formidable Christian apologist and an acclaimed writer of science fiction and children's literature, C S. Lewis wrote extensively on a wide number of topics. He was not only a prolific author but also a voracious and fluent reader in Greek, Latin, and French. From the moment he learned how to read, he fell in love with reading and much of what he read is evidenced throughout his writings. Further enhancing his ability to integrate what he read into his writings was a memory that was nothing short of photographic. As one of his pupils, English theater critic and writer Kenneth Tynan (1927–1980) would testify, "He had the most astonishing memory of any man I've ever known. In conversation I might have said to him, 'I read a marvelous medieval poem this morning, and I particularly liked this line.' I would then quote the line. Lewis would usually be able to go on to quote the rest of the page. It was astonishing."[18] At gatherings at his house he would boast of forgetting nothing he read. When this boast was met with incredulity from his guests Lewis

> would solicit a series of numbers from the most skeptical guest, which he would then apply to a bookcase, a shelf within that case, and a book upon that shelf. The guest would then fetch the specified volume (which could be in any number of several languages), open to a page of his own choosing, read aloud from that page, and stop where he pleased. Lewis would then quote the rest of that page from memory.[19]

---

17. Fleming, "Literary Critic," 25; italics in original.

18. Hooper, *C. S. Lewis: Companion and Guide*, 42.

19. Como, "Mere Lewis," 109–10.

Lewis was also as comfortable critiquing popular thinkers he disagreed with as he was in supporting those he enjoyed. His criticism of some authors were as clear as his praise of others. For instance, in speaking of the work of Sigmund Freud, Lewis remarks, "And furthermore, when Freud is talking about how to cure neurotics he is speaking as a specialist on his own subject, but when he goes on to talk general philosophy he is speaking as an amateur . . . I have found that when he is talking off his own subject and on a subject I do know something about . . . he is very ignorant."[20]

An avid reader, Lewis sometimes read as a student, at times as a teacher, and often for pleasure. Some authors he read addressed his own particular fields of interest and these obviously influenced his thinking, while others he read simply because he enjoyed them, but these, too, often appear in his writings.

In the book, *From the Library of C.S. Lewis: Selections From Writers Who Influenced His Spiritual Journey*,[21] James Stewart Bell and Anthony Dawson have compiled over 200 selections of quotes and references that appear in Lewis's writings from over a hundred authors as ancient as Augustine (354–430) and Dante (1265–1321) to more contemporary writers such as Dorothy L. Sayers (1893–1957) and J. R. R. Tolkien. Bell points out the debt Lewis owed to such authors:

> Lewis would later admit that without these and other profound spiritual influences he could not be the kind of Christian he was, nor could he have the impact he had on the world with his own writings. If that is so, these writings should have intrinsic value for all of us, as well as help us better understand the spiritual formation of C.S. Lewis himself.[22]

Further explaining the influence such authors had on Lewis's thinking Bell writes,

> To truly understand Lewis and his works we need to get behind his role as Christian apologist to his interest in philosophy and literature, in reason and romanticism. Lewis was not a one-dimensional reader. His eclectic tastes range over a wide variety of genres and time periods. He was a fan of science fiction and fantasy writers as well as Aristotle, Shakespeare, and Augustine. In Lewis's world, myth and allegory mix with precise logic in philosophical debate. Scholars continue to explore how these influences fit together, but there is no magic formula; Lewis

20. Lewis, *Mere Christianity*, 84.
21. Bell and Dawson, *From the Library of C. S. Lewis*.
22. Ibid., 1.

was a complete figure who didn't quite fit the trends of his own generation and is able to speak to the needs of each succeeding one.[23]

While an introduction of every writer who influenced Lewis's thinking is not necessary and beyond the scope of this book (excluding the influence of J. R. R. Tolkien which has been discussed earlier), three authors are specifically important to this study: Plato, George MacDonald, and Owen Barfield.

Among the ancient philosophers who influenced his thinking, Lewis greatly admired Plato. As he testifies in his *Reflections on the Psalms,* "We do of course find in Plato a clear Theology of Creation in the Judaic and Christian sense,"[24] later referring to Plato as "an overwhelming theological genius."[25] Though his origins are shrouded in mystery, Plato is not only considered the founder of the first institute of higher learning in the Western world, the Academy in Athens, but along with his mentor Socrates and his student Aristotle, he is considered one of the founding fathers of Western philosophy and science. Colin Duriez points out that "[Plato's] work provided much imaginative inspiration for C. S. Lewis, though Lewis was not a Platonist as such . . . some forms of Platonism were deeply influential during the medieval period, which was C. S. Lewis's great love and which was the object of much of his scholarship."[26]

Because Plato is synonymous with ancient philosophy and science, his love and involvement in myth is not always readily apparent, but as Dickerson and O'Hara observe:

> Just as myths helped to shape the way nations and peoples understood themselves, they also spurred the rise of philosophy and science. Plato and Aristotle, the great Athenian philosopher-scientists, spent considerable time dwelling on the myths, and Plato wrote and retold a number of myths in his philosophic writings. Aristotle devoted one of his treatises, *The Poetics,* to a study of dramatic mythopoeisis. Aristotle spent his life studying the rational principles of the cosmos and wrote extensively on medicine, theology, political science, ethics, physics, astronomy, biology, and metaphysics. His thought and Plato's have become deeply wedded to modern theology and serve as much of the basis of modern science. Yet when he retired to his estate at Chalcis, he wrote to a friend that as he became older and more

23. Ibid., 1–2.

24. Lewis, *Reflections on the Psalms,* 79.

25. Ibid., 80.

26. Duriez, *The C. S. Lewis Encyclopedia,* 166.

alone, he became fonder of myths, which provided for him a solace that other texts apparently could not.[27]

As early as the time of Plato, the blending of "medicine, theology, political science, ethics, physics, astronomy, biology, and metaphysics" and myth is evident, a point not lost on Lewis who admitted he had "a delighted interest in, and reverence for, the best pagan imagination, who loved Balder before Christ and Plato before St. Augustine."[28]

Plato's influence on Lewis can be seen in direct quotes from Plato as well as in Lewis's ability to weave Platonic thought into his writings. For instance, in his first extensive work of fiction, *The Pilgrims Regress* (1933), Lewis opens each of the ten books with an epigraph and the first is a quote from Plato. Then he opens the second book with another quote from Plato. To this second quote "Lewis adds in a footnote, truly enough, that many deny the ascription to Plato; whether or not it is genuine, this text, like its predecessor, exemplifies what Lewis called the Romantic strain in Greek philosophy."[29]

Platonic thought can be found scattered throughout Lewis's works. For instance, in the science fiction work *Perelandra* (1943), the world is portrayed as a shadow of reality and, as Sammons points out, "Lewis's view of reality, involving man's separation from his heavenly potential, can be described as Platonic."[30] As Sammons explains,

> Lewis's Platonism is perhaps most obvious in *The Last Battle* when Aslan's followers go to his country. The children notice that things are "like" but "not like" things in Narnia. Professor Kirke explains, "It was only a shadow or copy of the real Narnia . . . just as our own world, England and all, is only a shadow or copy of something in Aslan's real world." It is as different as things being different from shadows or as being awake is different from a dream. "It's all in Plato." Walter Hooper suggests that this is a reference to Plato's *Republic* and *Phaedo* in which he describes the "immortality and unchanging reality of changing forms." The children find the real Narnia and real England, of which the others were only a shadow or copy. In fact, Aslan calls England the "Shadow-Lands."[31]

27. Dickerson and O'Hara, *From Homer to Harry Potter*, 106.

28. Lewis, *God in the Dock*, 132.

29. Duriez, *C. S. Lewis Encyclopedia*, 65.

30. Sammons, *War of the Fantasy World*, 110.

31. Ibid., 113.

None of this is to say that all of Lewis's thinking was steeped in Platonic thought, for it clearly was not, and in places he even reverses certain Platonic ideas. For instance, in *The Great Divorce,* Lewis "reverses the shadowy Platonic conception of Heaven,"[32] by describing things in Heaven as "solider" or harder than things on earth. In Lewis's paradise, the Platonic shadowy ideal becomes concrete. Not surprisingly, scholars continue to debate the effect Platonism had on Lewis's fiction,[33] but anyone looking for authors who influenced Lewis finds Plato an early first choice.

But if asked who influenced him the most, Lewis's answer would not be Plato. In his preface to *George MacDonald* Lewis confesses, "I have never concealed the fact that I regarded [George MacDonald] as my master; indeed I fancy I have never written a book in which I did not quote from him."[34] Lewis regarded his debt to MacDonald as inestimable. According to Dickerson and O'Hara:

> Considering just how many books C. S. Lewis wrote, it is easy to assume he was exaggerating. When you begin to read Lewis carefully, however, you quickly realize that he was not. We cannot think of one major work of Lewis in which there is not a clearly discernible trace—and often a direct quote—of MacDonald's thought.[35]

And Dickerson and O'Hara ask, "Where would Lewis and Tolkien be without MacDonald?"[36]

Best known for his fairy tales and fantasy novels, George MacDonald (1824–1905) was a Scottish Christian minister whose writings influenced many fantasy authors who came after him.

> Whereas the Grimm's fairy tales remain to this day the most famous—the name *Grimm* is synonymous with fairy tale—and Hans Christian Andersen is also a household name, the influence of the lesser-known George MacDonald on the genre of modern fantasy is arguably equally great or even greater, and is also easier to trace than any of his fellow nineteenth-century writers.[37]

---

32. Ibid.

33. Ibid., 114.

34. Dickerson and O'Hara, *From Homer to Harry Potter,* 129, brackets in original.

35. Ibid., 150.

36. Ibid., 260.

37. Ibid., 148; italics in original.

In many ways the lives of Lewis and MacDonald parallel one another. Like Lewis, who lost his mother at age nine, MacDonald lost his mother when he was eight, an event never far from his thinking. Tolkien went so far as to say that "death is the theme that most inspired George MacDonald";[38] and death would weigh heavily in Lewis's writings as well. Despite their mothers' untimely deaths, each boy enjoyed a simple and pleasant childhood.

> He never lost sight of his humble childhood and adolescence, spent living in a cottage so small that he slept in the attic. He was a happy boy, writing, climbing, swimming, fishing, and reading while lying on the back of his beloved horse.[39]

But to say MacDonald had a pleasant childhood is not to say he had a happy adult life. He lived much of his life in poverty, suffered ill health (spending the last twenty years of his life in Italy for lung disease), and most of his eleven children died at an early age.[40]

> Depending on how you count the publications, MacDonald wrote 51 books. By my reckoning I count thirty novels, two fantasies for adults, five children's fantasy books, five collections of sermons, six poetry collections, and three books of literary criticism. He is most well remembered for his adult and children's fantasy and his sermons, but the 30 novels represent the majority of his output, these semi-realistic novels are often further classified as either Scottish or English depending on the location of the story.[41]

Considering the state of his health and difficulty of his life, his literary output was remarkable.

Lewis was still a child when MacDonald died; although they never met, MacDonald strongly influenced him. MacDonald was a true kindred spirit for Lewis in every sense of the term, serving not only as a literary mentor, but as someone who was able to put in words ideas that Lewis previously thought inexpressible.

Lewis's initial exposure to MacDonald is described as an insignificant part of a typically routine afternoon for the sixteen-year-old boy. It was a cold October day and Lewis was at a train station in Leatherhead, a town in the county of Surrey, England. He writes:

---

38. Tolkien, *The Tolkien Reader*, 68.
39. Duriez, *C. S. Lewis Encyclopedia*, 123.
40. For a full biography of George MacDonald, see Hein, *George MacDonald*.
41. Trexler, "George MacDonald," 2.

> The glorious week end of reading was before me. Turning to the
> bookstall, I picked out an Everyman in a dirty jacket, *Phantastes,
> a faerie Romance*, George MacDonald. Then the train came in.
> I can still remember the voices of the porter calling out the vil-
> lage names, Saxon and sweet as a nut—'Bookham, Effingham,
> Horsley train.' That evening I began to read my new book.[42]

The impression was nothing short of astonishing,

> But now I saw the bright shadow coming out of the book into
> the real world and resting there, transforming all common
> things and yet itself unchanged . . . that night my imagination
> was, in a certain sense, baptized; the rest of me, not unnaturally,
> took longer. I had not the faintest notion what I let myself in for
> by buying *Phantastes*.[43]

His enthusiasm for MacDonald is evident in a letter to his good friend Arthur Greeves, "As for Macdonalds, no need to urge me to read any I can get
hold of"[44] and in a later note, "I know nothing that gives me such a feeling
of spiritual healing, of being washed, as to read G. Macdonald."[45]

Perhaps no author and no single book had a greater influence over
Lewis's understanding of myth as much as MacDonald's *Phantastes*. Colin
Duriez writes "MacDonald's sense that all imaginative meaning originates
with the Christian Creator became the foundation of C. S. Lewis's thinking
and imagining."[46] Similarly, Dickerson and O'Hara conclude:

> We could show the influence of George MacDonald on many
> other modern authors as well, but perhaps in no other case quite
> so clearly as with C. S. Lewis. However, if once we acknowledge
> the influence of Tolkien and Lewis on the rest of modern fan-
> tasy, then this is unnecessary.[47]

As Lewis remarked to Arthur Greeves about his recent purchase of a number of MacDonald books, "Lucky devil to come on a deposit of Geo. Macdonalds. I will buy any you don't like—at any rate don't let any go till I've
seen them."[48]

---

42. Lewis, *Surprised by Joy*, 179.

43. Ibid., 181.

44. Hooper, *The Collected Letters of C. S. Lewis*, 1:885.

45. Ibid., 1:936.

46. Duriez, *C. S. Lewis Encyclopedia*, 123.

47. Dickerson and O'Hara, *From Homer to Harry Potter*, 156.

48. Hooper, *The Collected Letters of C. S. Lewis*, 1:883.

Lewis even has MacDonald making a personal appearance in one of his books. In *The Great Divorce*,[49] a fantasy tale of individuals in hell taking a bus ride to heaven where they are invited (and implored) to stay,[50] Lewis bestows upon MacDonald a great honor by making him Lewis's personal guide throughout heaven. As they meet Lewis says,

> 'I don't know you, Sir' said I, taking my seat beside him.
> 'My name is George,' he answered. 'George MacDonald.'
> 'Oh,' I cried. 'Then you can tell me! You at least will not deceive me.' Then, supposing that these expressions of confidence needed some explanation, I tried, trembling to tell this man all that his writings had done for me. I tried to tell how a certain frosty afternoon at Leatherhead Station when I first bought a copy of *Phantastes* (being then about sixteen years old) had been to me what the first sight of Beatrice had been to Dante: *Here begins the New Life.*[51]

Since Beatrice was Dante's conception of the ideal woman, Lewis could bestow no greater tribute upon MacDonald than to place him as his escort through the heavenly realm.

MacDonald's style was unlike many others, but it was his approach to writing fairy tales that captivated Lewis and opened up new venues of looking at the craft. In addition to writing several fairytales of traditional length, MacDonald, who was also a prolific and successful Victorian novelist, took some of the usual devices of the fairy tale genre and spun from that material several book-length works of Faeri. That is, he blended the fairy tale with the novel—two forms with which he was very familiar—and in crossing that frontier the predecessor of the modern fantasy romance was born. In many ways the nineteenth-century became *the* century of the fairy tale, as well as an important time in the development of modern fantasy.[52] By blending the fairy tale with the novel, MacDonald brought together for Lewis the two ideas necessary to ignite the spark of his own imagination. As Sayer observes, "We shall not understand Jack unless we can appreciate his gift for being utterly absorbed in the imaginative world of a great writer, artist, or musician. It is not easy to think of other British writers of similar sensibility."[53]

49. Lewis, *The Great Divorce*.

50. MacSwain and Ward, *The Cambridge Companion to C. S. Lewis*, 251.

51. Ibid., 66; italics in original.

52. Dickerson and O'Hara, *From Homer to Harry Potter*, 132.

53. Sayer, *Jack*, 77. "Jack" or "Jacks" was a nickname Lewis gave to himself "before he was four years old" (Hooper, *C. S. Lewis: Companion and Guide*, 4).

Another aspect of MacDonald's work that Lewis later came to appreciate, and one that grew over the years, was the theological, since, like MacDonald, Lewis believed that only God can create out of nothing; all an author can do is work with the raw materials God provides.

> MacDonald and Lewis share a conservative view of the artist, claiming it is better to use the word *creation* for "that calling out of nothing which is the imagination of God." Only God can create from nothing. "Everything of man must have been of God first." The creation is "divine art" that humans can view with awe. But humans, created in God's image, receive creativity as a gift. Man simply rearranges and recombines elements God has made. However, by using materials from our world and drawing on reality, the author can express Truths that cannot be expressed or explained in other ways. For MacDonald, man may invent new worlds with their own laws because he delights in "calling up new forms," the nearest he can come to creation. If they are mere inventions, they are Fancy. If they are new embodiments of old Truths, they are products of the imagination.[54]

Sammons shows that distinctions are important in distinguishing myths.

Lewis concurred with MacDonald on this rearranging of creation to produce works of Fancy. Since such a genre afforded the opportunity for an author to subtly embed the great doctrines of Christianity into his fictional novels,

> Lewis writes that "any amount of theology can now be smuggled into people's minds under cover of romance without their knowing it." A Christian writer does not need to write moral or theological works. In fact, if the Christianity is less obvious, it may reach some audiences more effectively. For example, he describes books by G. K. Chesterton and George MacDonald as traps for atheists. George MacDonald's *Phantastes* "baptized" his imagination; similarly, Chad Walsh says that when he read *Perelandra,* "I got the taste and smell of Christian truth. My senses as well as my soul were baptized."[55]

Although no one would say that Lewis's thinking was thoroughly Platonic, Lewis would admit his indebtedness to the literary influence of George MacDonald, a mythmaker he once called "the greatest genius of this kind whom I know."[56]

54. Sammons, *War of the Fantasy Worlds,* 72; italics in original.

55. Ibid., 161.

56. Lewis, *George MacDonald,* 14; italics in original.

But not all the influences upon Lewis's life came from people who preceded him and whose ideas he could only read about. A third person to significantly persuade Lewis's approach to myth was his good friend and fellow Inkling, Owen Barfield (1898–1997).[57]

Owen Barfield was a British author, poet, and philosopher who met Lewis in 1919 when they were both twenty-one. Barfield would outlive Lewis by thirty-four years and Tolkien by twenty-four. In the fall of 1919 the two men met and immediately became best friends and remained so until Lewis's death. In 1923, Barfield married stage designer Maud Douie and they adopted three children whose names Lewis would make famous: Alexander, Lucy, and Geoffrey. Fans familiar with Lewis's science fiction and fantasy writings know that he wrote his 1949 children's classic *The Lion, the Witch and the Wardrobe* for Owen's daughter Lucy and dedicated his 1952 book *The Voyage of the Dawn Treader* to her brother Geoffrey.

Unlike the influence of Plato and MacDonald that came by reading their works, Barfield's influence on Lewis's literary views was through personal friendship and rigorous academic debate. Duriez explains,

> In 1929 Barfield moved back to London to train in his father's firm of solicitors. He would visit Oxford once a term, and this sometimes coincided with an Inkling's meeting, and he would then attend. He always saw himself as a fringe member. About 1930 he had finished his "metaphysical argument" with Lewis, the "great war." This roughly coincided with the process of Lewis's conversion to Christianity. After the "war" he had jokingly said to Lewis that while Lewis had taught him to think, he had taught Lewis what to think. Lewis undoubtedly forced him to think systematically and accurately, passing on hard-won skills he had acquired from his tutelage under W. T. Kirkpatrick. Barfield in his turn helped Lewis to think more imaginatively, to combine his imagination with his formidable intellect. This was a "slow business," remembered Barfield.[58]

In spite of their differences of opinion, "Lewis's debt to Owen Barfield was enormous. He paid tribute to him in *Surprised by Joy* and earlier in *An Allegory of Love* ('the wisest and best of my unofficial teachers')."[59]

Even though Lewis and Barfield were close friends it was a friendship as described in Proverbs 27:17, "Iron sharpens iron, and one man sharpens another." In *Surprised by Joy* Lewis describes Barfield as

---

57. For more on Owen Barfield, see De Lange, *Owen Barfield*.

58. Duriez, *C. S. Lewis Encyclopedia*, 28.

59. Ibid.

. . . the man who disagrees with you about everything. He is not so much the *alter ego* as the antiself. Of course he shares your interests; otherwise he would not become your friend at all. But he has approached them all at a different angle. He has read all the right books but has got the wrong thing out of every one. It is as if he spoke your language but mispronounced it. How can he be so nearly right and yet, invariably, just not right? He is as fascinating (and infuriating) as a woman. When you set out to correct his heresies, you find that he forsooth has decided to correct yours! And then you go at it, hammer and tongs, far into the night, night after night, or walking through fine country that neither gives a glance to, each learning the weight of the other's punches, and often more like mutually respectful enemies than friends. Actually (though it never seems so at the time) you modify one another's thought, out of this perpetual dogfight a community of mind and a deep affection emerge. But I think he changed me a good deal more than I him. Much of the thought which he afterward put into *Poetic Diction* had already become mine before that important little book appeared. It would be strange if it had not. He was of course not so learned then as he has since become; but the genius was already there.[60]

So it was their differences and disagreements that played a major role in their becoming close friends.

Barfield would never become as well known as Lewis because, unlike Lewis, most of his work remains unknown and unavailable.[61] But both authors began with the same literary interests.

Both he and C. S. Lewis began their literary careers with the expectation of writing primarily poetry. Both published some poetry early on and sporadically throughout their writing careers, but both also gradually gave up the hope of being recognized as important poets. Both also published fiction, but only Lewis would gain popularity in this area and that not for more than two decades after their undergraduate years. Barfield's most ambitious work of fiction, a novel entitled "English People" has remained unpublished. He continued to write but not publish poetry throughout his career. Nevertheless, the lifelong concern with what has come to be called creative writing, and which Barfield prefers to call "forgetive writing," worked to keep his focus literary and his philosophy humane. He never ceased to be responsive to the "felt change of consciousness" that only

60. Lewis, *Surprised by Joy,* 199–200; italics in original.

61. Tennyson, *A Barfield Reader,* xx.

literature can bring that he first described in *Poetic Diction* in the nineteen-twenties.[62]

But even though not as well known as Lewis, Barfield had no small influence on Lewis's thinking in ways both private and public.

The most public way Barfield influenced Lewis was through what came to be called the "Great War," an exchange Barfield described as "'an intense interchange of philosophical opinions' and Lewis described as 'an almost incessant disputation, sometimes by letter and sometimes face-to-face, which lasted for years.'"[63] While hard to pinpoint the exact timing of the beginning of this exchange, it started not long after Barfield's acceptance of anthroposophism (1922) and lasted until Lewis's conversion to the Christian faith (1931).

Anthroposophism was a mixture of eastern and western philosophies close to ancient Gnosticism and was sometimes referred to as a "spiritual science" and founded by Hungarian philosopher, Rudolf Steiner (1861–1925). Both Steiner and Barfield believed anthroposophism was compatible with Christianity. "Anthroposophists recognize that the being they call the Christ is to be acknowledged as the center of life on earth. [Steiner's] claim was no less than that 'the Christian religion is the ultimate religion for the Earth's whole future.'"[64]

But it wasn't the theological differences between Christianity and anthroposophism that sparked debate between Barfield and Lewis, it was the role of imagination as a vehicle of truth. Lewis believed that myth, as a way of understanding the world, came before language and that language grew out of mythological understandings.[65] Barfield on the other hand argued that one is able to understand human consciousness by studying language, that words originally contained both a metaphorical and literal meaning that became separated in time. This meant one could study human consciousness by studying language:

> Barfield's theory holds that myth, language, and humanity's perception of the world are interlocked and inseparable. The word *myth* in this context must be taken to mean that which describes humankind's perception of its relationship to the natural and supernatural worlds. Words are expressed myths, the embodiments of mythic concepts and a mythic worldview. Language in

62. Ibid., xxi.

63. Ibid., 83

64. Ibid., 20.

65. Dickerson and O'Hara, *From Homer to Harry Potter,* 33.

its beginnings made no distinction between the literal and the metaphoric meaning of a word, as it does today.[66]

Commenting on this observation Dickerson and O'Hara observe,

> This agrees with and articulates more clearly Lewis's ideas that myths exist apart from words. Lewis also wrote, "In myth the imagined events are the body and something inexpressible is the soul: the words, or mime, or film, or pictorial series are not even clothes—they are not much more than a telephone" (*Preface*, xvii–xviii). More important to our present discussion, it also presents myth as a *vehicle* for truth even more powerful than are language and propositional speech—indeed, even as an *embodiment* of truth.[67]

It was this distinction between concepts and words that so intrigued Lewis about Barfield's thinking, for Lewis agreed that the source of meaning was imagination. To illustrate his idea, Barfield referred to two seventeenth-century inventions, the wind harp and the camera obscura.

> The harp's medium is air, which is both inside and outside us. It is thus similar to inspiration. The camera's medium is light, which does not enter the body. The camera can only present a replica or internal reproduction of the world. Thus the Aeolian wind harp is an "emblem" for the Romantic movement, and the camera is an "emblem" for the Renaissance. These two symbols contrast two types of perception: inspiration and a caricature of imagination. Barfield asks, "Is it fanciful . . . to think of a sort of mini-harp stretched across the window of the eye—an Apollo's harp if you will—as perhaps not a bad image for the joy of looking with imagination?" Barfield identifies this joy with the Joy Lewis spent his life searching for.[68]

It was for this discovery of joy that Lewis would be in the debt of Owen Barfield, but even though influenced by Barfield, just as he was with Plato and MacDonald, Lewis would not be thoroughly captivated by all of Barfield's thinking. The two men remained convinced of their own understandings of the nature of reality and of the role and importance of mental images. And in time, Lewis would come to embrace a very different Christian faith from what Barfield envisioned. Nevertheless, Barfield helped Lewis to articulate

---

66. Flieger, *Splintered Light*, 37–38; italics in original.

67. Dickerson and O'Hara, *From Homer to Harry Potter*, 33. *Italics in original*

68. Sammons, *War of the Fantasy Worlds*, 38–39.

his belief that myths could exist apart from words and could serve as a vehicle for truth, "indeed, even as an *embodiment* of truth."[69]

A final literary influence on Lewis, and one to be discussed later in this chapter, was the concept of "Northernness" that grew up out of his reading of Norse myths. Northernness was an idea that swept Lewis up into what he described as "huge regions of the northern sky."[70] He once referred in a private correspondence to his "whole Norse complex—Old Icelandic, Wagner's *Ring*, and (again) Morris."[71] Upon a chance reading of Longfellow's *Saga of King Olaf*, a twenty-two part poem that follows the adventures of King Olaf of Norway, spurred to avenge his slain father and reclaim his kingdom by the Norse god Thor, Lewis testified, "I desired with almost sickening intensity something never to be described (except that it is cold, spacious, severe, pale, and remote) and then . . . found myself at the very same moment already falling back out of that desire and wishing I were back in it."[72]

This idea of Northernness became an innate response for Lewis, a kind of longing that overtook him as he read myths and became such a passion for him that he likened it to his childhood experience and lifelong ambition of finding Joy,

> Pure "Northernness" engulfed me: a vision of huge, clear spaces hanging above the Atlantic in the endless twilight of Northern summer, remoteness, severity . . . and almost at the same moment I knew that I had met this before, long, long ago . . . And with that plunge back into my own past there arose at once, almost like heartbreak, the memory of Joy itself, the knowledge that I had once had what I had now lacked for years, that I was returning at last from exile and desert lands to my own country; and the distance of the Twilight of the Gods and the distance of my own past Joy, both unattainable, flowed together into a single, unendurable sense of desire and loss, which suddenly became one with the loss of the whole experience, which, as I now stared round that dusty schoolroom like a man recovering from unconsciousness, had already vanished, had eluded me at the very moment when I could first say *It is.* And at once I knew

---

69. Dickerson and O'Hara, *From Homer to Harry Potter*, 33; italics in original.

70. Lewis, *Surprised by Joy*, 17.

71. Hooper, *The Collected Letters of C. S. Lewis*, 2:630. Wagner is German composer and poet Richard Wagner (1813–83); Morris is poet and fiction writer William Morris (1834–96).

72. Lewis, *Surprised by Joy*, 17.

(with fatal knowledge) that to "have it again" was the supreme and only object of desire.[73]

Lewis once described Northernness as "essentially a desire and implied the absence of its object,"[74] and it was a desire he lived with throughout his life. As Starr points out, this "Joy-as-longing" was "a confirmation of myth's origin and purpose. It comes from God to draw humanity to Himself."[75]

Religious Influences

In addition to the influences on Lewis by the loss of his mother and the closeness of his brother, as well as by the philosophical and literary giants he read or knew personally, another significant influence was his religious beliefs.

There may have been no deeper influence on Lewis's personal and professional life than his conversion to, and personal faith in, Jesus Christ. He would describe it with this powerful analogy, "I believe in Christianity as I believe that the sun has risen, not only because I see it but because by it I see everything else."[76] Just as all of Western history can be divided between BC, (Before Christ) AD (Anno Domini, "year of our Lord"), or more broadly B.C.E. and C.E., so all of Lewis's thinking and writing concerning myth must be understood in light of it occurring before or after his Christian conversion. To Lewis, Christianity enabled him to fuse together heart and mind, logic and fiction. Following his conversion Lewis

> could now reexamine mythology and anthropology and conclude, in opposition to Frazer, not that man created God but rather that mythology is the result of "gleans of celestial strength and beauty" moving upon the minds even of pagan and sinful men . . . the world, including its evil, is neither a duality nor an absurdity, but rather the particular sort of world described by St. Paul and Jesus Christ.[77]

To many readers C. S. Lewis is best known for books addressing matters of the Christian faith. For these readers, though they are aware that he wrote science fiction and essays on literature, his preeminent contribution is his writings concerning the Christian faith. Throughout his life Lewis

73. Lewis, *Surprised by Joy*, 73. *Italics in original.*

74. Ibid., 82.

75. Starr, "The Triple Enigma," 173.

76. Lewis, *They Asked for a Paper*, 165.

77. Kilby, "The Creative Logician Speaking," 30.

admitted he was not a trained theologian. His goal was always to a·
topics and doctrines common to most denominations. "There is no m;
about my own position. I am a very ordinary layman of the Church of England, not especially 'high,' nor especially 'low,' nor especially anything else."[78]
He clearly states his future trajectory in his *Preface:*

> Ever since I became a Christian I have thought that the best,
> perhaps the only, service I could do for my unbelieving neigh-
> bors was to explain and defend the belief that has been common
> to nearly all Christians at all times . . . I got the impression that
> far more, and more talented, authors were already engaged in
> such controversial matters than in the defense of what Baxter
> calls 'mere' Christianity. That part of the line where I thought I
> could serve best was also the part that seems to be thinnest. And
> to it I naturally went."[79]

Lewis made no pretenses about being a theologian; nevertheless, he is quite
articulate on many aspects of theology, especially regarding his own spiritual experience (what he came to believe was true about God and Christianity
based on a plain, but educated, reading of the Bible). And this experience,
combined with his academic acumen, resulted in his being a recognized
spokesperson for Christianity.

Lewis was occupied with explaining and defining the Christian faith,
something he combined with his understanding that mythology could be a
conduit to explain Christian doctrine. Not only did religion influence his
understanding of myth, but he saw myth as having a vital and vibrant role
to play in religion. As Starr observes, "The role that myth played in Lewis'
conversion cannot be overstated. It was central because myth was central to
his life."[80] Mythology served as a means of bringing together the natural and
the supernatural, the literary and the spiritual. Those familiar with Christian theology and with Lewis's series, such as *The Chronicles of Narnia,* have
long recognized his use of the literary genre to express religious beliefs and
values in ways not obvious to others unfamiliar to religious teaching. As
Lewis admitted concerning his reading of Chesterton and MacDonald prior
to his Christian conversion,

> I did not know what I was letting myself in for. A young man
> who wishes to remain a sound Atheist cannot be too careful of
> his reading. There are traps everywhere — "Bibles laid open,

78. Lewis, *Mere Christianity*, 6.

79. Ibid.

80. Starr, "The Triple Enigma," 172–73.

millions of surprises," as Herbert says, "fine nets and strata-gems." God is, if I may say it, very unscrupulous.[81]

Lewis knew personally how myth could serve to convey spiritual truth in non-religious language.

Lewis was able to bring together myth and Christian doctrine by means of transcendence, i.e., the notion that doctrine transcended myth. As mentioned earlier, in his essay entitled "Myth Became Fact" Lewis observes:

> Now as myth transcends thought, Incarnation transcends myth. The heart of Christianity is a myth which is also a fact. The old myth of the Dying God, *without ceasing to be myth* comes down from the heaven of legend and imagination to the earth of history. It *happens* — at a particular date, in a particular place, followed by definable historical consequences. We pass from a Balder or an Osiris, dying nobody knows when or where, to a historical person crucified (it is all in order) *under Pontius Pi-late*. By becoming fact it does not cease to be myth: that is the miracle.[82]

It was this tension of *myth being fact* that broke down a wall in Lewis's think-ing and enabled him to reconcile ideas that up to that point were alternative and, at times, conflicting ways of looking at the world. As Alistar McGrath, Senior Research Fellow at Harris Manchester College at Oxford summarizes:

> Who indeed could achieve such a fusion, reconciling what many would see as polar opposites? At the intellectual level, Lewis was searching for a true marriage of reason and imagination—some-thing that eluded him totally as a young man. It seemed to him then that his life of the mind was split into two disconnected hemispheres . . . Lewis's later discovery of the Christian faith of-fered him a synthesis of reason and imagination which he found persuasive and authentic till the end of his life.[83]

Prior to this stage in his thinking, Lewis believed there was fact and there was myth, and each had its place, but one always needed to distinguish between them; myth was not fact nor was a fact myth. This separation of ideas troubled Lewis deeply. He wrote:

> Such, then, was the state of my imaginative life; over against it stood the life of my intellect. The two hemispheres of my mind

81. Lewis, *Surprised by Joy*, 191.
82. Lewis, "Myth Became Fact," 66–67; italics in original.
83. McGrath, *C. S. Lewis*, 74.

were in sharp contrast. On the one side a many-islanded sea of poetry and myth; on the other a glib and shallow "rationalism." Nearly all that I loved I believed to be imaginary; nearly all that I believed to be real I thought grim and meaningless. The exceptions were certain people (whom I loved and believed to be real) and nature herself . . . Hence at this time I could almost have said with Santayana, "All that is good is imaginary; and all that is real is evil." In one sense nothing less like a "flight from reality" could be conceived. I was so far from wishful thinking that I hardly thought anything true unless it contradicted my wishes."[84]

Myth becoming fact enabled Lewis to fuse together these two previously irreconcilable ideas in his thinking. He also came to understand that his struggle was not unique; other thinkers and writers long before him tried to find a way to bridge these two worlds and, in fact, he sensed this longing was universal, as is evident in a sermon he gave at the Church of St. Mary the Virgin at Oxford on June 8, 1942:

> In speaking of this desire for our own far-off country, which we find in ourselves even now, I feel a certain shyness. I am almost committing an indecency. I am trying to rip open the inconsolable secret in each one of you—the secret which hurts so much that you take your revenge on it by calling it names like Nostalgia and Romanticism and Adolescence[85]

Lewis observed that even though people use different names for this desire such as Nostalgia, Romanticism, and Adolescence, the desire is the same and is in everyone.

By his own admission a key component that helped Lewis understand myth was his struggle with the Christian doctrine of redemption through faith in the death and resurrection of Jesus Christ. What clarified his thinking regarding myth in this context was an observation made by two fellow Inkling members[86], J. R. R. Tolkien and Oxford English professor, H. V. D. "Hugo" Dyson (1896–1975), who pointed out that the teaching Lewis found impossible to believe in the Bible was perfectly plausible when considered as myth. Lewis wrote:

84. Lewis, *Surprised by Joy,* 170–71.

85. Lewis, "The Weight of Glory," 363.

86. The Inklings were a group of writers who met weekly in Lewis's room at Magdalen College and at the Eagle and Child Pub throughout the mid-1930s to the end of the 1940s to read and discuss writing projects.

> My puzzle was the whole doctrine of Redemption: in what sense
> the life and death of Christ 'saved' or 'opened salvation' to the
> world . . . Now what Dyson and Tolkien showed me was this:
> that if I met the idea of sacrifice in a Pagan story I didn't mind
> it at all: again, that if I met the idea of a god sacrificing himself
> to himself (cf. the quotation opposite the title page of *Dymer*
> ["Nine nights I hung upon the Tree, wounded with the spear
> as an offering to Odin, myself sacrificed to myself." *Havamal*] I
> liked it very much and was mysteriously moved by it . . . Now
> the story of Christ is simply a true myth: a myth working on us
> in the same way as others, but with this tremendous difference
> that *it really happened*: and one must be content to accept it in
> the same way, remembering that it is God's myth where the oth-
> ers are men's myths.[87]

The distinction in the closing sentence, "God's myth" and "men's myth,"
clinched the concept for Lewis. Men have myths and God has a myth, and
while the veracity of men's myths is important and open to question, God's
myth *"really happened."* As White observes, "The idea that Christianity is
a true myth lies at the heart of what Lewis went on to spend the rest of his
literary career describing."[88]

This admission reveals that Lewis did not hesitate to use classical and
mythological ideas to buttress his Christian faith, even when the myths deal
with the human instead of the divine. His quote from the chief Norse god,
Odin, taken from *Havamal*, a collection of ancient Norse poems attributed
to Odin, next to the title page in his narrative poem, *Dymer,* shows that
Lewis is not a foe of mythology but an advocate—yet an advocate with a
different interpretation. He is not anti-mythology.

What surprised Lewis was the recognition that the very same idea he
found reasonable in a myth, he considered astonishing and beyond belief in
a "religious" context even though the adherents of that religion considered
the event historical. Unable to resolve that contradiction, Lewis had to rethink his presuppositions and, instead of seeing the two sources as opposites
as he originally thought, he began to think of them as having much in common. Critical to understanding the influence of religion on his thinking of
myth is the importance of noticing that he does not simply let religion dic-
tate his understanding of myth; he is also careful to allow myth to persuade
his understanding of religion. He argues for this balance in "Myth Became
Fact" declaring:

87. Hooper, *They Stand Together*, 427, italics and brackets in original.
88. White, *C. S. Lewis*, 148.

> We must not be ashamed of the mythical radiance resting on our theology. We must not be nervous about 'parallels' and 'Pagan Christs': they *ought* to be there—it would be a stumbling block if they weren't. We must not, in false spirituality, withhold our imaginative welcome.[89]

In Lewis's mind the seemingly irreconcilable ideas of fact and myth not only came together and made peace, but they were able to build an entirely new coalition that recognized and respected myth in a way that he believed could bring glory to God.

As a devout follower of Jesus Christ and the author of many apologetic works on behalf of the Christian faith, Lewis knew all too well the harm that is done in the cause of religion. The closing sentiments of the devil in Lewis's "Screwtape Proposes a Toast" put it well:

> All said and done, my friends, it will be an ill day for us if what most humans mean by 'religion' ever vanishes from the Earth. It can still send us the truly delicious sins. The fine flower of unholiness can grow only in the close neighborhood of the holy. Nowhere do we tempt so successfully as on the very steps of the altar.[90]

Lewis believed that the closer myth came to the steps of the altar, the more likely the religious individual would be tempted to disparage it as unholy and deny it any positive contribution to religion. Instead of taking an either/or approach to myth and religion, Lewis took a more conciliatory and/so approach that allowed him to move freely between the two without fear of contradiction while earning the respect of devout followers of both endeavors.

Statement of Lewis's View of Myth

Myth was a faith and life-sustaining religious element for Lewis. It provided vitality for faith and an ability to comprehend the world in which one lives. In fact, Lewis likened myth to the life-giving sustenance provided to the Israelites wandering in the wilderness sustained by miraculous nourishment from heaven—manna (Ex 16:14). So, for Lewis, was myth. He writes: "Myth

---

89. Lewis, "Myth Became Fact," 67; italics in original.

90. Lewis, "Screwtape Proposes a Toast," in Lewis, *Complete C. S. Lewis Signature Classics*, 296.

is . . . like manna; it is to each man a different dish and to each the dish that he needs."[91]

The more one becomes familiar with Lewis, the more apparent it becomes that he was not only an *authority* on myth, as a teacher of a topic, but myths had a devotional quality to them as well. He simply enjoyed reading myths. They had a transcendent, spiritual quality to them. Anglican theologian J. I. Packer writes of this significance of myth on Lewis:

> Myths, to Lewis, were a class of stories that impact receptive souls as reflecting and pointing to transcendent realities which are felt without as yet being focused. Myths triggered what Lewis called "Joy," that is, delightful desire for that which they, so to speak, smell of; and Lewis's theology as a place for pre-Christian myths in various cultures as "good dreams" of God, holiness and heaven, God-given dreams that bring awareness of the sort of life that we need and want and do not have and so prepare minds and hearts for the gospel.[92]

For some Christians the idea that myths are "God-given dreams" is not persuasive and raises a number of theological questions. But the idea that such dreams could conceivably "bring awareness of the sort of life that we need and want and do not have and so prepare minds and hearts for the gospel," that myth engages the imagination, is certainly a sentiment most Christians can appreciate.

His observation that "Myth is . . . like manna" is close to a technical definition of myth by Lewis for the illustration provides the components needed to understand what myth meant to Lewis, what a myth is, and what it does. Like the manna, myth is concrete, it exists in this world of the physical senses; it is spoken, heard, and often written down. But like the heaven-sent bread, myth has an abstract, other-world nature about it. The manna came from the realm of the invisible and supernatural into the visible and natural to provide nourishment for anyone who would take and eat. Likewise, myth can be viewed as a provision, as the food needed for someone to live in this world of chaos and pain. Myths provide people with what is needed to sustain the heart, mind, and soul. "It is only while receiving the myth as a story that you experience the principle concretely."[93]

Lewis's views and statements about myth are scattered throughout his works, without there being any single exhaustive presentation of his views; his brief essay "Myth Became Fact" (1944) was one of the most direct

---

91. Lewis, "Shelly, Dryden, and Mr. Eliot," in Lewis, *Selected Literary Essays*, 205.

92. McGrath, *The J. I. Packer Collection*, 272.

93. Lewis, "Myth Became Fact," 66.

treatments. Here he advocates for a balance of myth and the historical Christian faith. He writes,

> Those who do not know that this great myth became Fact when the Virgin conceived are, indeed, to be pitied. But Christians also need to be reminded . . . that what became Fact was a Myth, that it carries with it into the world of Fact all the properties of a myth. God is more than a god, not less; Christ is more than a Balder, not less. We must not be ashamed of the mythical radiance resting on our theology.[94]

But not even this essay is extensive and so one needs to canvass Lewis's other writings to get a sense of how he understood myth. Since he taught and lectured on numerous topics and wrote dozens of essays and books, one can find him discussing myth where least expected. In one place he argues myth can serve as a "partial solution" to the problem of pain,[95] while in another he contends that myth is not a religion or a philosophy, but a "summing up and actuality of them all."[96] Regarding the effect of myth, "It gets under our skin, hits us at a level deeper than our thoughts or even our passions, troubles oldest certainties till all questions are reopened, and in general shocks us more fully awake than we are for most of our lives."[97]

But in personal correspondence to Owen Barfield sometime during 1927–1928, when Lewis was around thirty and a few years before his conversion to Christianity, he explains his understanding of myth as

> a description or a story introducing supernatural personages or things, determined not, or not only, by motives arising from events within the story, but by the supposedly immutable relations of the personages or things: possessing unity: and not, save accidentally, connected with any given place or time.

Then Lewis contrasts this definition of myth with his definition of a legend:

> (A *Legend* is a story attached to a context, in a place and time series accepted as real by the teller, itself believed by the teller to be true, but departing from truth unconsciously, or without full consciousness, in the interests of greatness, the marvellous, or of edification.)[98]

94. Ibid., 67.

95. Ibid., 66.

96. Lewis, *Surprised by Joy*, 6.

97. Lewis, *George Macdonald*, 16–17.

98. Hooper, *The Collected Letters of C. S. Lewis*, 3:1619, italics and parenthesis in original.

A definition of myth, even his own, was not sufficient to Lewis for explaining what a myth is or how it should be understood. That would take far more thought and explanation, but that was a challenge Lewis was happy to engage.

In 1961, over thirty years after his explanation to Barfield and just two years before his death, Lewis's work *An Experiment in Criticism*[99] was published. In it Lewis devotes an entire chapter to correcting common misunderstandings and makes clear his own understanding of myth as well as addressing the challenges of reading myth. His fuller explanation later in life shows very little change from his brief earlier definition.

He begins the chapter by expressing his dissatisfaction with the very term "myth," to him myth is in many ways an unfortunate word. He states:

> In the first place we must remember that Greek term *muthos* does not mean this sort of story but any sort of story. Secondly, not all stories which an anthropologist would classify as myths have the quality I am here concerned with. When we speak of myths, as when we speak of ballads, we are usually thinking of the best specimens and forgetting the majority.[100]

But as he concludes, "In spite of these inconveniences I must either use the word *myth* or coin a word, and I think the former the lesser evil of the two."[101]

Following this apology, Lewis gives six characteristics that identify a myth. First, a myth is comprised of what he refers to as the extra-literary; there is a mythical experience common to all myths. Lewis contends that myth is not limited to a literary style such as a poem or essay. It is something that touches the human experience.

Second, enjoying myth is not contingent on narratives such as suspense or surprise; the contemplative aspect is what is important and that does not require a specific form of telling. By this Lewis means a myth is not a "who-done-it?" In fact a myth may reveal the end of the story at the outset, it does not need the element of surprise.

Third, sympathy is kept to a minimum in myth so we don't "project ourselves at all strongly into the characters. They are like shapes moving in another world."[102] The reader does not need to enter into the joy or sadness of the individual characters to understand their triumph or tragedy.

99. Lewis, "On Myth," in Lewis, *An Experiment in Criticism*, 40–49.
100. Ibid., 42.
101. Ibid., 43.
102. Ibid., 44.

Fourth, a myth is characterized as fantastic, dealing with the impossible. A myth is not simply an exaggeration of the natural order; myths take place where the uncommon and bizarre occur. When myths occur in the natural world things are influenced and changed by the supernatural.

Fifth, in myth there is a sense of the grave or serious; there are no comic myths. Where humor occurs in a myth it is not there for the sake of being funny. The reader is to experience solemnity and have a sense that something holy or other-worldly is happening.

And finally, "The experience is not only grave but awe-inspiring. We feel it to be numinous. It is as if something of great moment has been communicated to us."[103] The reader will feel as if something of great importance has been conveyed and that life as presently experienced, while true, remains incomplete.

One final but critical observation to understanding Lewis's explanation of myth is his concern for effect; his interest is in myths

> as we experience them: that is, myths contemplated but not believed, disassociated from ritual, held up before the fully waking imagination of a logical mind . . . Since I define myths by their effect on us, it is plain that for me the same story may be a myth to one man and not to another. This would be a fatal defect if my aim were to provide criteria by which we can classify stories as mythical or non-mythical. But that is not my aim. I am concerned with ways of reading . . .[104]

This concern with "ways of reading" is essential to understanding Lewis's view of myth, otherwise one will accuse him of the "fatal defect." To understand his six point criteria, one has to also understand his objective as well as all that lies behind his reservation with the term myth and why he thinks it important to identify the characteristics of a myth. McGrath summarizes, "For Lewis, a myth is a story which evokes awe, enchantment, and inspiration, and which conveys or embodies an imaginative expression of the deepest meanings of life—meanings that prove totally elusive in the face of any attempts to express them abstractly or conceptually."[105]

103. Ibid., 44.
104. Ibid., 45–46.
105. McGrath, *The Intellectual World of C. S. Lewis*, 63.

MYTH: MANY WAYS TO STATE THE SAME TRUTH

Another component of myth that Lewis carefully considered is the universal similarities found throughout myths. For instance, most pagan mythologies tell of a god who is killed and rises again, a narrative similar to the Christ story. This was a similarity Lewis found most interesting. As he observes, "The odd thing is that here those anthropologists who are most hostile to our faith would agree with many Christians in saying 'The resemblance is not accidental.'"[106] Lewis posed three solutions to the question, one anthropological and two Christian.

The anthropological answer is that myth originates in the human heart or imagination and so "the likeness is a family likeness."[107] Since early humanity lived in an agricultural context it should not be surprising that myths reflect cycles or seasons similar to the sun rising and setting or the planting and harvesting of crops.

The Christian answer is twofold: one diabolical and one godly. Some Christians would attribute the similarities to Satan, "a liar and the father of lies."[108] These Christians maintain that in seeking to lead humanity away from God, Satan imitates the truth in every conceivable way including the world of myth. They reason, "The resemblance of Adonis to Christ is therefore not at all accidental; it is the resemblance we expect to find between a counterfeit and the real thing, between a parody in the original, between imitation pearls and pearls."[109]

A second answer by Christians, and one Lewis would include as his own, is that the thematic similarities in myth are the result of their containing elements of humanity (the need of story), divinity, and evil all pointing toward God. Since God's grand truth for humanity is the death and resurrection of his son, Jesus Christ, all of creation, including the rising and setting of the sun and the seeding and harvesting of crops, point toward that great truth.

> The resemblance between these myths and the Christian truth is no more accidental than the resemblance between the sun and the sun's reflection upon a pond, or that between a historical fact and the somewhat garbled version of it which lives in popular

---

106. Lewis, *Reflections on the Psalms*, 106.
107. Ibid.
108. John 8:44.
109. Lewis, *Reflections on the Psalms*, 106.

report, or between the trees and hills of the real world and the trees and hills in our dreams.[110]

Lewis argues the similarities are there, they have to be there because God exists and human nature and myth reflect that existence. But one needs to be cautious concluding that, since these similarities exist, one can call into question the veracity of Christian doctrine simply because it resembles pagan myth. Lewis asks, "What light is really thrown on the truth or falsehood of Christian Theology by the occurrence of similar ideas in Pagan religion?" and answers,

> Supposing, for purposes of argument, that Christianity is true; then it could avoid all coincidence with other religions only on the supposition that all other religions are one hundred percent erroneous . . . The truth is that the resemblances tell nothing either for or against the truth of Christian theology. If you start from the assumption that the Theology is false, the resemblances are quite consistent with that assumption . . . But if you start with the assumption that the Theology is true, the resemblances fit in equally well. Theology, while saying that a special illumination has been vouchsafed to Christians and (earlier) to Jews, also says there is some divine illumination vouchsafed to all men . . . We should, therefore, expect to find in the imagination of great Pagan teachers and myth makers some glimpse of that theme which we believe to be the very plot of the whole cosmic story—the theme of incarnation, death, and rebirth. And the differences between the Pagan Christs (Balder, Osiris, etc.) and the Christ Himself is much what we should expect to find.[111]

So questions of truth and falsehood are not simply resolved by whether the lesson is derived from myth or Christian theology, for the two can have much in common without having everything in common.

But Lewis admits these similarities are not necessarily intentional on a human level and in some cases apparent similarities may be little more than mere coincidence or the result of someone reading them into a story. But this does not explain all similarities.

> But when I meditate on the Passion while reading Plato's picture of the Righteous One, or on the Resurrection while reading about Adonis or Balder, the case is altered. There is a real connection between what Plato and the myth-makers most deeply were and meant and what I believe to be the truth. I know that connection

---

110. Ibid., 107.

111. Lewis, *The Weight of Glory,* 127–28.

and they do not. But it is really there. It is not an arbitrary fancy
of my own thrust upon the old words . . . Thus, long before we
come to the Psalms or the Bible, there are good reasons for not
throwing away all second meanings as rubbish.[112]

The truth in myth must be distinguished from the myth conveying truth.
To Lewis's thinking, the truth of Christianity, not its mythical element, is
what makes it believable. He admits, "If Christianity is only a mythology,
then I find the mythology I believe in is not the one I like best. I like Greek
mythology much better, Irish better still, Norse is best of all."[113]

But Lewis did not allow the similarities among myths to swallow up
the distinctives of Christian truth. Although pagan myths prefigured Christianity, they were incomplete or at best a partial revelation of the nature of
God. God is a being, the creator and sustainer, but He is not a mere force
or impersonal spirit. God not only made humanity, he loves humanity, a
truth that sets Christianity apart from the world of story and myth. "Hence
I think that nothing marks off Pagan theism from Christianity so sharply
as Aristotle's doctrine that God moves the universe, Himself unmoving, as
the Beloved moves a lover. But for Christendom 'Herein is love, not that we
loved God but that he loved us.'"[114]

Myth and Creativity

Lewis was familiar with myth and creativity not only because he was a reader and admirer of myth, but because he also wrote myth. His most famous
piece in this genre turned out to be his last work of fiction and a book not
originally well received by the reading public (but the one Lewis considered
his best), the novel aptly entitled *Till We Have Faces: A Myth Retold*.[115] As
Lewis once wrote to a correspondent (August 26, 1960), "You gave me great
pleasure by what you said about *Till We Have Faces*, for that book, which I
consider far and away the best I have written, has been my one big failure
both with the critics and with the public."[116] Shultz and West summarize the
book's influence,

In retelling the myth on which the novel is based, Lewis creates
a new myth, one that develops more completely and in a more

112. Lewis, *Reflections on the Psalms*, 108.

113. Lewis, *The Weight of Glory*, 119.

114. Lewis, *The Problem of Pain*, 45.

115. Lewis, *Till We Have Faces*.

116. Hooper, *The Collected Letters of C. S. Lewis*, 3:1181.

satisfactory way meanings that earlier narrators of the myth were unable to grasp. But the result makes demands beyond those of Lewis's other works, demands many readers have found puzzling and daunting.[117]

Lewis's *Till We Have Faces* offers an example of how Lewis thought myth should be written, but it does so in a way that is difficult to interpret. "The main charge against the novel when it first appeared was obscurity. 'What is he trying to say?'"[118] "In many cases, readers come to Lewis's works looking for answers and explanations. Perhaps one reason *Till We Have Faces* is his least popular story is because it doesn't provide easy answers or explanations."[119]

The myth Lewis retold was explained by him in a "Note" in the first American edition of the novel. "The story of Cupid and Psyche first occurs in one of the few surviving Latin novels, the *Metamorphoses* (sometimes called *The Golden Ass*) of Lucius Apuleius Platonicus, who was born about 125 A.D."[120] *Metamorphoses* is the only Latin novel known to have survived in its entirety and is an amusing work describing the adventures of one Lucius who, through magic, is accidently turned into an ass. From the vantage point of the ass he shares his many and varied adventures including the story of Cupid and Psyche.

Briefly, the tale concerns Psyche, the most beautiful woman in the world, who is envied by her family and by Venus, the Roman goddess of love. When Cupid, the Roman goddess of desire and affection, is sent to destroy her he instead falls in love with her and takes her to his castle. She is told she can never look upon his face though he visits and makes love to her in the dark of the night. Eventually, Psyche's sisters, jealous of her, demand she identify her husband; she does that night, but accidently wakes him resulting in his leaving and banishing her from the castle.

In hopes of atoning for her crime, Psyche offers herself as a slave to Venus who assigns her four impossible tasks: sort through a hill of mixed grains; gather wool from a dangerous golden sheep; get water from a cleft beyond human reach; and seek beauty from Persephone, Queen of the

---

117. Huttar, "*Till We Have Faces*," 403. For more see Christopher, "Archetypal Patterns"; Donaldson, *Holy Places*; Gibson, *C. S. Lewis*; Glover, *C. S. Lewis*; Holyer, "Epistemology"; Howard, *The Achievement of C. S. Lewis*; Kilby, "*Till We Have Faces*"; Manlove, *C. S. Lewis*; Reddy, "*Till We Have Faces*"; Schakel, *Reason and Imagination*; Starr, *C. S. Lewis's*; Ulrech, "Prophets, Priests, and Poets"; Urang, *Shadows of Heaven*; Van Der Weele, "From Mt. Olympus to Glome."

118. Hooper, *C. S. Lewis: Companion and Guide*, 243.

119. MacSwain and Ward, *The Cambridge Companion*, 290.

120. Lewis, *Till We Have Faces*, 311.

underworld. With the help of animals and gods she completes the tasks. Later she is put in a coma, Cupid rescues her, begs Zeus, the father of the gods, that she may become immortal, and the two are forever united.

In speaking of Lewis's version of the myth, English professor Peter Schakel summarizes,

> The opening paragraphs indicate that this story will deal with some of the deep, universal issues that all human beings face: whether gods exist and, if so, what they are like, and why bad things happen to good people. Lewis had contemplated such questions in his expository works, such as *The Problem of Pain*, *Mere Christianity* and *Miracles*, trying to supply answers that would help readers understand what they needed to know. In *Till We Have Faces*, instead of abstract meaning . . . Lewis offers an imaginative experience which gives readers a taste of reality.[121]

Lewis first read the tale in 1916 but it took him forty years to bring his rework to fruition, not finishing the project until 1955.[122]

The genesis of the idea came to Lewis when he was a twenty-three year old undergraduate at Oxford. He wrote in his diary for November 23, 1922, "After lunch I went out for a walk up Shotover, thinking how to make a masque or play of Psyche and Caspian."[123] About a year later (September 9, 1953), he writes

> My head was very full of my old idea of a poem on my own version of the Cupid and Psyche story in which Psyche's sister would not be jealous, but unable to see anything but moors when Psyche showed her the Palace. I have tried it twice before, once in couplet and once in ballad form.[124]

Growing up with Greek and Norse mythologies, Lewis was familiar with the story and convinced it could be retold and re-interpreted. In the spring of 1955, during a visit of his future wife, Joy Gresham, Lewis finally understood what he wanted his version to say and with Joy's help the story developed quickly.[125]

One aspect of the book Lewis was especially proud of is found in a letter,

---

121. MacSwain and Ward, *The Cambridge Companion*, 289.
122. Ibid., 281.
123. Lewis, *All My Road Before Me*, 142.
124. Ibid., 266.
125. Hooper, *C. S. Lewis: Companion and Guide*, 247.

> My new book went to press last week. It is the story of Cupid &
> Psyche told by one of the sisters—so that I believe I've done what
> no mere male author has done before, talked thro' the mouth of,
> & lived in the mind of, an *ugly* woman for a whole book.[126]

Lewis's creativity in the rewriting is evident in his disagreement with the
original author and with his earlier understanding as to why the lead character, Orual, could not see Psyche's palace when she visited her or why, when
given wine, she could taste only water. At his first reading, Lewis concluded
the elder sister could not see or taste these things because these things did
not exist. "Thus he [Lewis] believed the elder sister was in the right because
there was no palace for her to see and no wine for her to taste."[127]

But after his conversion to Christianity, Lewis came to a very different conclusion to explain Orual's inability to experience what she was told.
"Lewis recognizes now that it is because 'spiritual things are spiritually
discerned.'[128] Psyche's sisters could not have seen the god's palace because
they did not believe in divine mysteries."[129] Walter Hooper identified two
changes to the story as a result of Lewis's conversion,

> (1) Psyche has two half-sisters, but the story is told by Orual (or
> 'Maia' as Psyche calls her), who, when visiting Psyche, cannot
> see her palace; (2) Lewis now knows *why* the palace is invisible
> to Orual.[130]

Lewis explains his revision this way:

> The central alteration in my own version consists in making
> Psyche's palace invisible to normal, mortal eyes—if "making" is
> not the wrong word for something which forced itself upon me,
> almost at my first reading of the story, as the way the thing must
> have been. This change of course brings with it a more ambiva-
> lent motive and a different character for my heroine and finally
> modifies the whole quality of the tale. I felt quite free to go be-
> hind Apuleius, whom I suppose to have been its transmitter, not
> its inventor. Nothing was further from my aim then to recapture
> the peculiar quality of the *Metamorphosis*—that strange com-
> pound of pictaresque novel, horror comic, mystagogue's tract,

126. Hooper, *The Collected Letters of C. S. Lewis*, 3:716.

127. Schakel, "Till We Have Faces," in MacSwain and Ward, *The Cambridge Companion*, 282.

128. An allusion to 1 Cor. 2:14.

129. Schakel, "Till We Have Faces," in MacSwain and Ward, *The Cambridge Companion*, 283.

130. Hooper, *C. S. Lewis: Companion and Guide*, 248–49; italics in original.

> pornography, and stylistic experiment. Apuleius was of course a
> man of genius: but in relation to my work he is a "source," not an
> "influence" nor a "model."[131]

In saying "I felt quite free to go behind Apuleius," one should not think
Lewis is simply looking at the myth through a different lens, nor as simply
modifying it or giving it a different interpretation. In Lewis's thinking he
was correcting the "transmitter" Apuleius.

> My version of Cupid & Psyche. Apuleius got it all wrong. The el-
> der sister (I reduce her to one) couldn't *see* Psyche's palace when
> she visited her. She saw only rock & heather. When P. said she
> was giving her noble wine, the poor sister saw only spring water.
> Hence her dreadful problem: 'is P. mad or am I blind?' As you
> see, tho' I didn't start from that, it is the story of every nice, af-
> fectionate agnostic whose dearest one suddenly 'gets religion,' or
> even every luke warm Christian whose dearest gets a Vocation.
> Never, I think, treated sympathetically by a Christian writer be-
> fore. I do it all thro' the mouth of the elder sister. In a word, I'm
> v. much 'with book': *Juno Lucina fer opem*."[132]

Though other authors have been influenced by the story, making reference
to it in their own works,[133] and a few authors have put it in verse,[134] poetry,[135]
and adapted for the story for children,[136] Lewis was unique in his approach
of correcting Apuleius and giving the perspective of a sister.

What Lewis does in his version is remarkable. He makes certain ideas
acceptable in story form that might otherwise not be understood if presented didactically. And it illustrated what Lewis said about religion being
"thick" or "clear,"

> We may . . . divide religions, as we do soups, into 'thick' and
> 'clear.' By Thick I mean those which have orgies and ecstasies
> and mysteries and local attachments: Africa is full of Thick re-
> ligions. By Clear I mean those which are philosophical, ethical
> and universalizing: Stoicism, Buddhism and the Ethical Church
> are Clear religions. Now if there is a true religion it must be
> both Thick and Clear: for the true God must have made both
> the child and the man, both the savage and the citizen, both the

131. Lewis, *Till We Have Faces*, 313.

132. Hooper, *The Collected Letters of C. S. Lewis*, 3:590; italics in original.

133. Milton, *Milton's Comus*.

134. Morris, *The Earthly Paradise*.

135. Tighe, *Psyche with Other Poems*.

136. Peabody, *Old Greek Stories Told Anew*.

head and the belly . . . Christianity breaks down the wall of the partition. It takes a convert from central Africa and tells him to obey an enlightened universalist ethic: it takes a twentieth-century academic prig like me and tells me to go fasting to a Mystery, to drink the blood of the Lord. The savage convert has to be Clear: I have to be Thick. That is how one knows one has come to the real religion.[137]

As Lewis scholar and trustee of the Lewis estate, Walter Hooper explains, in *Till We Have Faces*, Lewis was trying to show

> a contrast between the 'Thick' dark idolatry of Ungit and the 'Clear' pale enlightenment represented by Greek thought and religion during that period. To make the contrast and sharper still, he asked the publisher, Jocelyn Gibb, to design a cover for the book that would reflect the two. The cover was to show a Stone representing Ungit and a Statue representing Psyche. In a letter to Gibb of 11 April 1956 he said the Stone should be 'Billowy, Indefinite, Ugly, Suggestive of life, Dark, Sexy, Old and Barbarous' while the Statue should be 'Rigid, Definite, Pretty-pretty, Dead as a Dutch doll, Light, New, Thinks of itself very civilized and Up-to-date.' The artist attempted this on the cover of the English edition, but the result was not entirely satisfactory.[138]

Till We Have Faces also serves as an example of an observation Lewis makes in his essay "Meditation in a Toolshed,"[139] that a distinction be made between analyzing something from the outside (contemplation) and experiencing it from the inside (enjoyment). Lewis could have simply presented the same lessons in a textbook and reached the point of contemplation (as any good professor), but by using myth the reader is able to *enjoy* as well as *learn* the lessons. As he says in his essay "Myth Became Fact," "What flows into you from the myth is not truth and reality (truth is always *about* something, but reality is that *about which* truth is), and, therefore, every myth becomes the father of innumerable truths on the abstract level."[140] For Lewis this is true of all myths and not specifically those within Christianity. But unlike others, Christianity is the myth that became fact.

The origin and source of Lewis's creativity was his imagination:

---

137. C. S. Lewis, "Christian Apologetics" in *God in the Dock*, 102–3.
138. Hooper, *C. S. Lewis: Companion and Guide*, 253–54.
139. Lewis, "Meditation in a Toolshed," 212–15.
140. Lewis, "Myth Became Fact," 66; italics in original.

> It could be urged that the theme of imagination constitutes the
> taproot of Lewis's entire work (excepting the Christian faith
> itself). There is scarcely a line in any work of his—theological
> treaties, literary criticism, topical essay, fiction, or poetry—that
> does not bespeak some vast assumption on Lewis's part as to
> the inevitable and crucial place that imagination must be given
> among us mortals in all of our discourse.[141]

For Lewis, imagination expressed through myth was the corpus callosum
that brought together what he knew was true with what he knew was real.
"Both faculties [logical and romantic] were of great importance, not only to
his development, but also, when he eventually brought them into harmony,
to his achievement as a creative writer and literary critic."[142]

As seen earlier, Lewis would describe this tension and its resolution in
Surprised by Joy,

> Such, then, was the state of my imaginative life; over against it
> stood the life of my intellect. The two hemispheres of my mind
> were in the sharpest contrast. On the one side a many-island city
> of poetry and myth; on the other a glib and shallow "rational-
> ism." Nearly all that I loved believed to be imaginary; nearly all
> that I believed to be real I thought grim and meaningless."[143]

Once Lewis understood myth as something beyond folklore and legend,
or as something limited to the nonexistent, and began seeing it as stories
of people and places of uncommon significance that embodied a way of
thinking or feeling, a theme or moral, it afforded him a way to express the
imaginative in ways that appealed to the rational. According to Alister
McGrath "The young Lewis increasingly found himself torn between the
intellectually parsimonious and the imaginatively rich — between a purely
rational and historical account of things, which dismissed myths as primitive superstitions, and an awareness of their compelling imaginative power
and beauty."[144]

In *Surprised by Joy,* Lewis shares an incident that took place when he
was twenty-eight years old that turned out to be a watershed event for his
understanding of myth. He had recently finished reading G. K. Chesterton's
The Everlasting Man[145] when he found himself sitting across from an athe-

---

141. Carnell, "Imagination," 214.

142. Sayer, *Jack,* 95; brackets not in original.

143. Lewis, *Surprised by Joy,* 170.

144. McGrath, *The Intellectual World of C. S. Lewis,* 55.

145. Chesterton, *The Everlasting Man.*

ist who was discussing the gospel accounts in light of mythologist James Frazer's concept of the "Dying God." He recounts the story:

> Then I read Chesterton's *Everlasting Man* and for the first time saw the whole Christian outline of history set out in a form that seemed to me to make sense. Somehow I contrived not to be too badly shaken. You will remember that I already thought Chesterton the most sensible man alive "apart from his Christianity." Now, I veritably believe, I thought—I didn't of course *say*; words would have revealed the nonsense—that Christianity itself was very sensible "apart from its Christianity." But I hardly remember, for I had not long finished *The Everlasting Man* when something far more alarming happened to me. Early in 1926 the hardest boiled of all the atheists I ever knew sat in my room on the other side of the fire and remarked that the evidence for the historicity of the Gospels was really surprisingly good. "Rum thing," he went on. "All that stuff of Frazer's about the Dying God. Rum thing. It almost looks as if it really happened once." To understand the shattering impact of it, you would need to know the man (who has certainly never since shown any interest in Christianity). If he, the cynic of cynics, the toughest of the toughs, were not—as I would still have put it—"safe," where could I turn? Was there no escape?[146]

And so Lewis found himself surrounded by logical persuasions of the Christian faith not only in his reading but by his conversations as well. What he observed about reading, "A young man who wishes to remain a sound Atheist cannot be too careful of his reading. There are traps everywhere,"[147] now applied to his conversations as well. Lewis was faced with the proposition that one of the most ardent atheists he ever met was willing to concede, at least theoretically, that the gospel message of Christ's death and physical resurrection "looks as if it really happened once." Suddenly, and yet also gradually, he realized matters of faith, of the supernatural, could be accepted as having happened in the natural. Real water could become real wine, a few real fish could feed thousands of real people, and a dead and buried body could come to life and walk out of the tomb. All of a sudden Lewis was faced with the prospect that "the evidence for the historicity of the Gospels was really surprisingly good." What could he do?

As it turned out there would be "no escape" for Lewis and he later argued that Frazer's story of the Dying God really did happen, the myth did become fact. And so it followed for Lewis that myth was the genre perfectly

146. Lewis, *Surprised by Joy*, 223–24; italics in original.
147. Ibid., 191.

suited to express what happened when the two hemispheres of his mind merged, the side of myth and joy and the side of the intellect. As Starr points out, "Lewis led a bifurcated mind for years . . . He describes his younger self in terms of split halves."[148] Now what he thought of as real was no longer grim and meaningless and what he loved and imagined was possible.

Myth and Spirituality

Just as thought needs some mode of expression if it is to be shared, so spirituality needs some way to be expressed if the concept or experience is to be known beyond the individual. For Lewis, myth served that means well, but he also realized that communication was not enough. Irrespective of what one experiences or how precisely and honestly one communicates it to another, the philosophy of the listener will determine how the person hears what is said.

Lewis begins his classic work *Miracles* with a story that illustrates and explains the challenge in speaking of spiritual concerns:

> In all my life I have met only one person who claims to have seen a ghost. And the interesting thing about the story is that the person disbelieved in the immortal soul before she saw the ghost and still disbelieves after seeing it. She says that what she saw must have been an illusion or a trick of the nerves. And obviously she may be right. Seeing is not believing. For this reason, the question whether miracles occur can never be answered simply by experience. Every event which might claim to be a miracle is, in a last resort, something present to her senses, something seen, heard, touched, smelled, or tasted. And our senses are not infallible. If anything extraordinary seems to have happened, we can always say that we have been the victims of an illusion. If we hold a philosophy which excludes the supernatural, this is what we always shall say. What we learn from experience depends on the kind of philosophy we bring to experience. It is therefore useless to appeal to experience before we have settled, as well as we can, the philosophical question.[149]

To simply teach that the spiritual is true is inadequate and even experiencing it is not enough since "Seeing [or experiencing] is not believing." It ultimately comes down to trusting. One must allow for the supernatural and miraculous or the divine is not considered a possibility.

148. Starr, "The Triple Enigma," 176.
149. Lewis, *Miracles*, 2.

In *Miracles*, Lewis describes two basic attitudes toward life, a materialistic naturalism and a theistic supernaturalism. He also discusses the commonly held belief that "primitive" people were gullible and thus prone to accept a supernatural answer for what is now known to be a natural event and a second approach whereby moderns see the miraculous stories as myths in need of being de- or re-mythologized.[150] But Lewis goes beyond such views to discuss where they come from, one's world view, and he argues that things such as conscience and reason lend evidence to the reality of a supernatural world.

Because Lewis was an atheist until he was almost thirty, for the first half of his life he was comfortable with a rationalistic and naturalistic view that did not need the idea of God. His "God" was philosophical and not a personal being.

> I distinguished this philosophical "God" very sharply (or so I said) from "the God of popular religion." There was, I explained, no possibility of being in a personal relation with Him. For I thought He projected us as a dramatist projects his characters, and I could no more "meet" Him, than Hamlet could meet Shakespeare. I didn't call Him "God" either; I called Him "Spirit." One fights for remaining comforts.[151]

But Lewis realized this view posed a problem since philosophy and reason, like religion, were not part of the "physical." The question became: if one can have a non-physical idea, why can't there also be a God above and beyond the physical universe?

Although Lewis would not grapple with the question of spirituality in the Christian sense until later in life, he did struggle with something similar in his younger years as an atheist. Instead of trying to find God or understand spirituality though, he longed to attain what he what would refer to as Joy or, in a term reminiscent of myth, "Northernness." As he explains,

> One caution must be repeated. I have been describing a life in which, plainly, imagination of one sort or another played the dominant part. Remember that it never involved the least grain of belief; I never mistook imagination for reality.[152]

At this stage in his life such a distinction between imagination and reality made sense to Lewis, but further reflection would cause him to question

---

150. Duriez, *The C. S. Lewis Encyclopedia*, 132.

151. Lewis, *Surprised by Joy*, 223.

152. Ibid., 82.

his definition of each and the distinctions he made between them. As Sayer points out,

> This idea of northernness was an early reason that caused Lewis to pursue myth. Since his earlier experiences with joy, he had loved 'northernness.' This was one of the most important loves of his life; it became a description of a particular imaginative world. Perhaps the passion for northernness predates his first acquaintance with Norse mythology."[153]

Evidence of this passion for "northernness" is seen in his description of it as something to be experienced but not explained. In reflecting on an experience at age nine after reading *Tregner's Drapa* in Henry Wadsworth Longfellow's (1807–1882) *Sage of King Olaf,* the tale of the death of the Norse god, Balder, Lewis says,

> . . . instantly I was uplifted into huge regions of northern sky, I desired with almost sickening intensity something never to be described (except that it is cold, spacious, severe, pale, and remote) and then, as in the other examples, found myself at the very same moment already falling out of that desire in wishing I were back in it . . . it is that of an unsatisfied desire which is itself more desirable than any other satisfaction. I call it joy, which is here a technical term and must be sharply distinguished from both happiness and from pleasure.[154]

In Lewis's mind this realm of northernness was the place where imagination, joy, satisfaction, and desire converged and myth was the means by which one could describe it to others.

Once this northernness idea took form, it, in his words, "engulfed" Lewis and became the one thing he sought most of all. "This bent to 'Northern' things is quite real and one can't get over it — not that I ever thought of trying."[155] And although attaining it would remain elusive to him until he converted to Christianity, he knew it had to be pursued. He experienced it in the past and knew it could be experienced again if he kept searching. As noted earlier, he wrote in his autobiography:

> Pure "Northernness" engulfed me: a vision of huge, clear space is hanging above the Atlantic in the endless twilight of the Northern summer, remoteness, severity. and almost at the same moment I knew that I met this before, long, long ago (it hardly

153. Sayer, *Jack*, 76.
154. Lewis, *Surprised by Joy*, 17–18; italics in original.
155. Hooper, *The Collected Letters of C. S. Lewis*, 2:171.

seems longer now) in *Tegner's Drapa*, that Siegfried (whatever it might be) belonged to the same world as Balder and the sunward-sailing cranes. And with that plunge back into my own past there arose at once, almost like heartbreak, the memory of Joy itself, the knowledge that I had once had what I had now lacked for years, that I was returning at last from exile and the desert lands to my own country; and the distance of the Twilight of the Gods in the distance of my own past Joy, both unattainable, flowed together into a single, unendurable sense of desire and loss, which suddenly became one with the loss of the whole experience, which, as I now stared round the dusty schoolroom like a man recovering from unconsciousness, had already vanished, and eluded me at the very moment when I could first say *It is*. And that once I knew (with fatal knowledge) that to "have it again" was the supreme and only important object of desire.[156]

This "supreme and only important object of desire" would be a major impetus for Lewis's understanding and expression of myth and spirituality.

C. S. Lewis was author of an impressive array of books both scholarly and popular. From the childhood loss of his mother to his early delight with the works of George Macdonald on through his friendship with literary giant J. R. R. Tolkien and to his teaching at Oxford and Cambridge and many books in the fields of science fiction and Christian apologetics, what continues to make Lewis so intriguing to many readers is his uncanny ability to "see through" things. While many writers are content to simply convey information or make a point, Lewis always wants to do more. He wants his readers to distinguish what is read from what is meant. He explains:

> The books or the music in which we thought the beauty was located will betray us if we trust to them; it was not in them, it only came through them, and what came through them was longing. These things—the beauty, the memory of our own past—are good images of what we really desire; but if they are mistaken for the thing itself they turn into dumb idols, breaking the hearts of their worshippers. For they are not the thing itself; they are only the scent of a flower we have not found, the echo of a tune we have not heard, news from a country we have never yet visited.[157]

---

156. Lewis, *Surprised by Joy*, 73. Siegfried is a reference to a character in Richard Wagner's (1813–83) last of four operas, *Gotterdammerung*, or *Twilight of the Gods*.

157. Lewis, "The Weight of Glory," 363.

It was this longing, this seeking of beauty, that spurred Lewis to never stop searching or to cease imagining. He knew there was a country yet to be visited and the search prompted him to continue looking.

In *An Experiment in Criticism*, Lewis characterizes "Dryasdust" critics by saying "Find out what the author wrote and what the hard words meant and what the allusions were to, and you have done far more for me than a hundred new interpretations or assessments could ever do."[158] This chapter has attempted to survey what Lewis wrote concerning myth and how he came to his conclusions by considering the people and events that influenced his thinking.

Among the early influences in his childhood were his love of nature, his vivid imagination as he played with his older and beloved brother, Warren, and the sudden and shocking death of his mother. This early loss, compounded by the strain it put on his relationship with his father, left a lifelong impression upon Lewis. But the pleasant memories of that childhood also left him with a longing for something he called Joy, something he would spend his entire life trying to understand, define, and, if possible, regain.

As Lewis matured, his love for the "Northernness" of Wagner's music and Norse mythology grew while his Christian faith became little more than a childhood memory. As he studied Latin, Greek, French, German, and Italian his love of language and learning grew resulting in a scholarship to University College, Oxford. Yet his academic achievements did not so much replace his childhood experiences as much as they complemented them and gave him perspective on how to further explore and explain them.

This love of reading introduced Lewis to authors who would further influence his thinking regarding myth. Men such as Plato, George MacDonald, and his close friend, J. R. R. Tolkien, all challenged Lewis to find ways to combine what he felt and hoped with what he knew.

But not only did his reading and relationships challenge his thinking, they also challenged his faith and beliefs and in his early thirties Lewis abandoned his atheism and converted first to theism and later to Christianity. This was a significant change that influenced how he understood myth since he discovered myth to be a way to bridge the worlds of the natural and supernatural as well as his "deep and vivid imagination . . . and a profoundly analytical mind."[159] The two conflicting worlds of materialistic naturalism and theistic supernaturalism could now be brought together and discussed with others of similar interests.

---

158. Lewis, *An Experiment in Criticism*, 121.
159. Kilby, "The Creative Logician Speaking," 19.

To anyone familiar with both authors, it is not hard to discern striking similarities and vivid contrasts between C. S. Lewis and Joseph Campbell when it comes to the meaning, role, and place of myth in a technological society. But where they may differ the most is in their understanding of myth as it relates to Christian belief. While both men were raised in homes where Christianity was taught, they both, like many in similar situations, abandoned the faith in early adulthood. Where Campbell came to explain Christianity as myth, Lewis came to explain myth by Christianity as the myth that became fact.

4

Joseph Campbell and Myth

WIDELY KNOWN AND RESPECTED in academia and popular culture for his study and presentation of myth, Joseph Campbell's extensive writings offer both breadth and depth on the subject of mythology. For many contemporary students of the subject his work is foundational and the standard against which other approaches are compared.

But in spite of Campbell's popular appeal there is no succinct treatment of his definition of myth and the authors and movements that influenced his thinking are scattered throughout his many writings, interviews, and lectures. This chapter will address Campbell's understanding of myth by investigating the key religious and academic influences upon his thinking. Also discussed is his life-long motto "Follow your bliss" since this maxim best sums up in a practical way much of his understanding of myth, religion, and philosophy.

CAMPBELL'S DEFINITION OF MYTH

Myth, as seen earlier, is a difficult concept to define. "One may muse that no term in the English language carries a range of meaning so seemingly antithetical as does myth."[1] And in the case of Joseph Campbell, a clear definition is no less elusive. A dizzying array of definitions are found throughout his extensive works, including the following: "A myth is the imaging of a

1. Hein, *Christian Mythmakers*, 6.

conception, or realization of truth."[2] "Myths are the masks of God."[3] "Myths, like dreams, are products of the imagination."[4] And "This I would regard as the essentially religious function of mythology—that is, the mystical function, which represents the discovery and recognition of the dimension of the mystery of being."[5] As he travelled on publicity tours for his books, he was often asked to define myth. In responding to the question once put to him by an argumentative radio talk show host, Campbell said,

> So I replied with my definition of myth. "No, myth is not a lie. A whole mythology is an organization of symbolic images and narratives, metaphorical of the possibilities of human experience and the fulfillment of a given culture at a given time."[6]

And the definition that would become Campbell's best known and personal favorite, "Mythology may, in a real sense, be defined as other people's religion. And religion may, in a sense, be understood as a popular misunderstanding of mythology."[7] Though succinct and memorable, this definition gives evidence of circular reasoning and a lack of specificity.

Not only is a definition hard to come by, but the meaning and purpose of myth are equally difficult to identify in Campbell's works. Consider, for example, his comments from *Thou Art That:*

> For example, when disaster strikes, when you meet with a great calamity, what is it that supports you and carries you through? Do you have anything that supports you and carries you through? Or does that which you thought was your support now fail you? That is the test of the myth, the building myth, of your life.[8]

So one purpose of myth is to sustain an individual during tragedy or loss. During such times our first reaction is to look for answers, for reasons that explain such difficulty. But since answers are impossible, and if found, seldom satisfy, we next seek a way to maintain our composure and not give in to despair. Myth, at least enduring myths, provide such comfort and strength by casting the personal tragedy on a grand scale where one no longer feels alone and hopeless.

2. Larsen and Larsen, *Joseph Campbell,* 415.

3. Ibid., 425.

4. Campbell, *Thou Art That,* 24.

5. Ibid., 3.

6. Ibid., 1–2.

7. Ibid., 8.

8. Ibid., 24.

In another place Campbell observes,

> The "monstrous, irrational and unnatural" motifs of folktale and myth are derived from the reservoir of a dream and vision. On the dream level such images represent the total state of the individual dreaming psyche. But clarified of personal distortions and profounded—by poets, prophets, visionaries—they become symbolic of the spiritual norm for Man the Microcosm.

> Mythology is psychology, misread as cosmology, history and biography. Dante, Aquinas and Augustine, al-Ghazali and Mahomet, Zarathustra, Shankaracharya, Nagarjuna, and T'ai Tsung, were not bad scientists making misstatements about the weather, or neurotics reading dreams into the stars, but masters of the human spirit teaching a wisdom of life and death.[9]

Here Campbell makes a number of comments that shed light on his understanding of myth. First, he states that mythology is psychological. Second, he equates folktale with myth, something he hesitates to do elsewhere. When Bill Moyers comments "So when we talk about folk tales, we are talking not about myths but about stories that ordinary folks tell in order to entertain themselves . . ," Campbell responds, "Yes, the folk tale is for entertainment. The myth is for spiritual instruction."[10]

A third point is that Campbell lumps together two of the most prominent theologians in Christian history, Aquinas and Augustine, along with a poet and moral philosopher, Muslim theologians and Eastern mystics, and refers to all of them as authors of myth. An assimilation of such diverse scholars blurs a tremendous amount of history and religious beliefs and leaves one wondering how such diversity and complexity can be remedied simply by applying myth?

In another excerpt, this one taken from a journal Campbell kept during the years of World War II, he writes,

> . . . I learned that the essential form of the myth is a cycle, and that this cycle is a symbolic representation of the form of the soul, and that in the dreams and fancies of modern individuals (who have been brought up along the lines of a rational, practical education) these myth-symbols actually reappear—giving

---

9. Joseph Scharl, Joseph Campbell, and Padriac Column, *The Complete Grimm's Fairy Tales*, 860, cited in Larsen and Larsen, *Joseph Campbell,* 329.

10. Campbell, *The Power of Myth,* 59.

testimony of a persistence, even into modern times, of the myth power.[11]

Here one sees the depth, breadth, and authority of myth. It is cyclical, it represents "the form of the soul," and it contains a power that enables it to transcend time and culture. There is a timelessness to myth. Myth is human, it springs from the imagination, so wherever and for however long humans exist there will be myths. This realization of myth's power caused him to write later in the same journal,

> With this the emphasis of my studies shifted from the historical to the mythological. I began to read, with fresh understanding, the novels of Thomas Mann and *Ulysses* of James Joyce. The role of the artist I now understood as that of revealing through the world-surfaces the implicit forms of the soul, and the great agent to assist the artist in this work was the myth.[12]

This insight on myth is significant since it broadens the meaning to include non-religious literature implying that religion may not be the central aspect of myth.

So, myth sustains one in tragedy. Myth is similar to, but evidently not synonymous with, folktale. Myth permeates all religions and may be what is called "religion," yet myth springs from the human imagination and so does not need to be thought as religious the way the term is traditionally understood. Myth originates in the human heart and yet has a power all its own.

After summarizing a number of definitions offered by earlier scholars, Campbell concludes:

> Mythology has been interpreted by the modern intellect as a primitive, fumbling effort to explain the world of nature (Frazer); as a production of political fantasy from prehistoric times, misunderstood by succeeding ages (Muller); as a repository of allegorical instruction, to shape the individual to his group (Durkheim); as a group dream, symptomatic of archetypal urges within the depths of the human psyche (Jung); as the traditional vehicle of man's profoundest metaphysical insights (Coomaraswany); and as God's Revelation to His Children (the Church). Mythology is all of these. The various judgments are determined by the viewpoints of the judges. For when scrutinized in terms not of what it is but of how it functions, of how it has served mankind in the past, of how it may serve today, mythology

11. Larsen and Larsen, *Joseph Campbell*, 226.

12. Ibid.

shows itself to be as amendable as life itself to the obsessions
and requirements of the individual, the race, the age.[13]

Though Joseph Campbell understood myth as a universal phenomenon that
served to explain the great mysteries of life such as birth, growth, tragedy,
and death, he clearly realized that myth's magnitude was greater than what
the mind could comprehend or language could adequately explain. By saying "Mythology is all of these. The various judgments are determined by the
viewpoints of the judges," Campbell seems averse to answering questions of
meaning or purpose in a definitive way. Although there are certain themes
that can be identified in the myths of various cultures, with no outside authority to give guidance, what an individual makes of these themes is apparently up to him or her.

Campbell's diversity of definitions and range of explanations is not
surprising to those who knew him personally. Husband and wife coauthors
Stephen and Robin Larsen, students and friends of Campbell for over twenty years, explain his philosophical approach:

> Never simple or monolithic, Joseph Campbell's philosophy
> shows itself to have been an open system, constantly integrating
> new information from whatever field of life he encountered. But
> what most distinguished him, even at this early stage, seems to
> have been his sense of destiny, his determination to welcome
> as appropriate—as food for the soul—whatever came to him;
> and his immediate willingness to convert his experiences into
> communicable hypotheses.[14]

Campbell's open system allowed him to integrate new discoveries made
from philosophy, religion, morality, and cultural ritual wherever he found
them. Such an approach gave him a worldview that truly took in the whole
world. And if someone happens to believe in an absolute, the *belief* was
Campbell's focus, not the absolute. His interest wasn't in defining or defending any one truth, it was in comparing and contrasting all truths to show
that what they had in common far outweighed what separated them. But as
will be seen, this lack of specificity makes him vulnerable to criticism.

Sources of Campbell's View of Myth

Joseph Campbell's "open system" of philosophy regarding myth was not
simply the result of his student days at Canterbury prep school (New

13. Campbell, *The Hero*, 382.

14. Larsen and Larsen, *Joseph Campbell*, 102.

Milford, Connecticut) where his favorite subject was biology, or from his experiences at Dartmouth College where he studied biology and mathematics, or from Columbia University where he entered the English Department and earned his Bachelor of Arts degree and later a Masters thesis with his paper *The Dolorous Stroke* about the Grail legend.[15]

Complementing his academic studies was Campbell's insatiable desire for reading, traveling, and exploring the imagination. Between 1927–1934 he travelled widely and studied for a time at the University of Paris where he immersed himself in modern art and literature and later transferred to the University of Munich to study Sanskrit literature and Indo-European philology along with the works of Austrian psychotherapist Sigmund Freud, Swiss psychiatrist Carl Jung, German novelist Thomas Mann (1875–1955), and the genius of modern German literature, Johann von Goethe (1749–1832).

Two weeks prior to the stock market crash Campbell returned to the United States, giving up work on his doctorate to live in a cabin in Woodstock, New York, with his sister, Alice Marie, where he immersed himself in an extended period of reading and self-reflection. "His early years proved to Joseph that he could do whatever he wanted to do without having to be a slave to money—one of the characteristics associated with those courageous enough to truly follow their bliss as he did."[16] After traveling across the country by himself he became friends with John and Carol Steinbeck and their neighbor, biologist Ed Ricketts. Ricketts and Campbell travelled up the coast of British Columbia to Alaska where Campbell further explored ideas about the relationship between mythology and biology.

In 1933 he returned to Canterbury prep to teach history and English and pursue his own studies in the works of philosopher Oswald Spengler (1880–1936), Thomas Mann, Carl Jung, and one of the most influential writers of the twentieth century (and one of Campbell's literary heroes), James Joyce (1882–1941). After a year of teaching at Canterbury, Campbell resigned and returned to Woodstock to read and write. In the following year (1934), he was invited to teach at the recently founded Sarah Lawrence College (Bronxville, NY) where he remained in the Literature department for thirty-eight years until his retirement.

One must appreciate that Joseph Campbell's understanding of mythology came from more than his classroom participation as either student or teacher. Long before he picked up his first textbook or heard his first lecture on myth or legend, Campbell was significantly impressed by two religious influences that would serve as foundations for all his thinking and writing.

---

15. Ibid., 61–78.
16. Maher and Briggs, *An Open Life*, 15.

RELIGIOUS INFLUENCES

Native American Spirituality

Two experiences that forever changed Joseph Campbell's life and determined the trajectory of his lifetime of study in mythology happened long before Sarah Lawrence College, University of Munich, Columbia University, or Canterbury preparatory school. These influences were the spiritual beliefs of Native Americans and his religious upbringing in Roman Catholicism.

In response to a question on how he became interested in mythology he stated:

> I'd have to say it was due to having been brought up a Roman Catholic, and having taken it very seriously as a boy. Then my father used to take me to see Buffalo Bill when he brought his Wild West shows to Madison Square Garden, which was exciting. And we used to go to the Museum of Natural History, where I was tremendously impressed by the great room full of totem poles. My father was very generous in helping me find books about the American Indians—George Bird Grinnell's books, *Indian Lodge Tales* [sic], the reports of the American Bureau of Ethnology, and so on. I eventually became a sort of little walking scholar in the field of American Indians.
>
> Meanwhile, I was being educated by the nuns in the Roman Catholic religion and it didn't take me very long to realize that there were virgin births, deaths and resurrections, in both mythological systems. So very early on I became interested in this comparative realization, and by the age of eleven or twelve, I was pretty well into the material.[17]

Unforeseen at the time, this childhood experience of attending a Wild West show, similar to one experienced by hundreds of children, left an indelible impression on Campbell and set a course for his future understanding of myth and religion. So powerful was this early encounter with Native Americans that Campbell later wrote in his personal journal, "I early became fascinated, seized, obsessed, by the figure of a naked American Indian with his ear to the ground, a bow and arrow in his hand, and a look of special knowledge in his eyes."[18]

But as captivating as this encounter was, it also prompted Campbell to consider deeper existential questions. Even at this young age Campbell, like C. S. Lewis, was trying to understand his experience. Unlike most children

17. Ibid., 119.
18. Cited in Larsen and Larsen, *Joseph Campbell,* 3

who go through an average day pretending, exploring, and wondering, Campbell, even at an early age, was curious as to *why* this encounter with the American Indians so captivated him.

> Such was the force of this life-shaping obsession that in his later years Campbell himself wondered at its nature. Was it some primordial memory that had been lurking beneath his commonsense little-boy concerns, or a premonitory symbol of some of the major themes that were to occupy him as an adult? Was the boy, in some way he didn't yet understand, to grow into the pathfinder?[19]

Such was some of the earliest thinking of Joseph Campbell.

After this definitive moment in his childhood, Campbell started on a personal journey of exploration paired with sympathy for, and fascination with, the Native Americans. Two books from grade school that he recalled as significant were Lewis Henry Morgan's *League of the Iroquois*[20] and Earnest Thompson Seton's *Book of Woodcraft*.[21] Of the second book he said "I read and reread it until it fell apart."[22] Concerning a chapter in *Book of Woodcraft* entitled, "The Spartans of the West," that described an army campaign against Native Americans, Campbell recalls thinking,

> When General Crook set off in deep winter to hound the Dakota patriots to their death, and to slaughter their women and babies, he admitted, as we have seen, that it was a hard campaign to go on. "But," he added, "the hardest thing is to go and fight those whom we know are right."[23]

Even at this early age Campbell had a desire to live what he learned. This was evident when, at about 12 years of age while watching a classic cowboy-and-Indian movie from the early 1900s, Campbell was indignant as the audience of children and adults cheered a Caucasian cowboy chasing a Native American. Angrily he stood up and yelled at the audience "You don't know what you're doing! You wouldn't cheer if you knew!"[24] Larsen notes:

> He recorded his memory of the event twenty-five years later, when he was tormented about whether to enter the armed

19. Larsen and Larsen, *Joseph Campbell*, 3–4.

20. Morgan, *League of the Iroquois*.

21. Seton, *Woodcraft and Indian Lore*.

22. Larsen and Larsen, *Joseph Campbell*, 4; Morgan, *League of the Iroquois*; Seton, *Book of Woodcraft*.

23. Cited in Larsen and Larsen, *Joseph Campbell*, 4.

24. Ibid.

services or become a conscientious objector. In contemplating his twelve-year-old protest, he wrote "My line from that moment to this has been without essential change!!"[25]

As a youth, Campbell was deeply impressed by the beliefs and culture of the Native Americans. Their belief systems, their "myths," would serve as a template as he reflected on the reasons for his own personal compulsions as well as the beliefs and religious systems of others outside the Native American culture and the Roman Catholicism in which he was raised. He had many questions. Were there patterns or similarities in the major world religions that paralleled the belief system of the Native Americans? Could the major beliefs of all religions be as similar as the questions and problems faced by all humanity concerning birth, growth, tragedy, and death? Could the "Great Spirit" of native Americans, the Muslim's Allah, the Jew's Jehovah, the Christian's triune God or a state of Eastern Nirvana all be the same idea with its name and character being determined by the culture? Are the people in the East who face tragedy and death simply projecting their cultural ideals of hope and afterlife (if any) as do people in the West? Is the modern Westerner, in spite of technological advances, simply following the same belief patterns as his or her primitive ancestors and grappling with the same existential dilemmas?

The more Campbell studied other faiths the more similar they became,

> Campbell's exhaustive readings in the dozens of culture matrices he had selected were evident at this time. He couldn't think of Osiris or a Jesus now without summoning their brothers, the dismembered and resurrected gods of Polynesia, the Yucatán, or for that matter of the Indian shamans of North America.[26]

And so this melding of Native American spirituality with the beliefs of the major world religions began very early for Campbell and was the genesis of his thinking that the *sine qua non* behind all religious beliefs and ideas of spirituality was myth.

In response to a question by Bill Moyers concerning the idea of a "Chosen People," a title often used of the Jewish people, Campbell used the example of the "oneness" he saw permeating all belief systems by comparing the cultural similarities among Native Americans to that of the Jews to conclude that *all* people are "Chosen People." He explains:

> The woman from the sky originally comes from a hunting-culture base, and the woman of the earth comes from the planting

25. Ibid.
26. Ibid., 336.

culture. The twins represent two contrary principles, but quite different contrary principles from those represented by Cain and Abel in the Bible. In the Iroquois story, one twin is Sprout or Plant Boy, and the other is named Flint. Flint so damages his mother when he is born that she dies. Now, Flint and Plant Boy represent the two traditions. Flint is used for the blade to kill animals, so the twin named Flint represents the hunting tradition, and Plant Boy, of course, represents the planting principle.

In the Biblical tradition, the plant boy is Cain and the flint boy is Able, who is really a herder rather than a hunter. So in the Bible, you have the herder against the planter, and the planter is the one who is abominated. This is the myth of hunting people or herding people who have come into a planting-culture world and denigrate the people whom they have conquered.[27]

As he would share throughout this interview, the patterns he discerned in Native American spirituality became for him, at their core, indistinguishable from those evident in the second early religious influence in his life, his Roman Catholic upbringing.

Roman Catholicism

The second great influence in Campbell's life was his childhood exposure to Roman Catholicism. "I was born and grew up a Catholic, I was a very devoted Catholic."[28] As mentioned earlier, as an adult Campbell reflected:

> I was brought up in terms of the seasonal relationships to the cycle of Christ's coming into the world, teaching in the world, dying, resurrecting, and returning to heaven. The ceremonies all through the year keep you in mind of the eternal core of all that changes in time. Sin is simply getting out of touch with that harmony. . . It wasn't long before I found the same motifs in the American Indian stories that I was being taught by the nuns at school.[29]

During these formative years his Roman Catholic upbringing, as well as his respect and fondness for Native American culture, merged in his thinking to produce a worldview that identified similarities in the various religions of the world. Suddenly, instead of many opposing voices all claiming absolute truth, Campbell found a single "taproot" below the surface out of which

27. Campbell, *The Power of Myth*, 105.

28. Campbell, *Thou Art That*, 59.

29. Campbell, *The Power of Myth*, 10.

all religions sprang. To him, the concept of myth served as the central core belief that not only reconciled the differences that seem to plague religionists but also served to provide answers to many of the difficult questions that arose between the world of science and the humanities.

But in spite of the myriad of questions it answered and the problems it solved for him, by its nature, myth was challenged to resolve other problems posed by religion regarding absolute truth and the historical arguments made by certain major religions such as Judaism and Christianity. In both religions, miracles actually happened in a specific time and place. Moses received the Ten Commandments "written with the finger of God,"[30] and Jesus Christ physically rose after three days in the tomb and then literally ascended in the presence of eye witnesses, "as they were looking on, he was lifted up, and a cloud took him out of their sight."[31] For Campbell, these narratives, recorded as history, posed a problem.

The way Campbell presented the problem was as one of emphasis. Believers in the West, primarily Christians and Jews, put the focus on a personal relationship with a living being, God, while adherents in Eastern religions put the focus on the divinity within each individual.

> We in our tradition do not recognize the possibility of such an experience of identity with the ground of one's own being. What we accent, rather, is the achievement and maintenance of her relationship to a personality conceived to be our Creator. In other words, ours is a religion of relationship: a, the creature, related to X, the Creator (aRX). In the Orient, on the other hand, the appropriate formula would be something more like the simple equation, $a=X$.[32]

This distinction between the divinity without and the divinity within sets up a paradigm of exclusivity in the Western religions. Instead of everyone being born a god or as having god within, Judaism and Christianity maintain one is born alienated from God and in need of a relationship with Him. According to Campbell, each belief offers a way of admittance:

> According to Jewish thought, one does so by being born of a Jewish mother. God, in a certain period, which is difficult to date precisely, contracted a Covenant with the Jewish race, requiring circumcision and a number of other ritual attentions, in return for which they were to enjoy forever His exclusive regard. In the Christian tradition, no less exclusively, the historical character,

30. Exod 31:18.

31. Acts 1:9.

32. Campbell, *Thou Art That*, 27.

Jesus, is regarded as the one and only incarnation on earth of the Godhead, the one true-God-and-true-Man. This avatar we are taught to regard as a miracle. In the Orient, on the other hand, everyone is to realize this truth in himself, and such an incarnation as Krsna Rama, or the Buddha is to be thought of simply as a model through which to realize the mystery of the incarnation in oneself.[33]

What further troubled Campbell was that once the divine was located outside the individual and a relationship was necessary to connect to the deity, a specific set of beliefs, what Campbell calls a "a sanctified social context," was put in place and the focus shifted from universal inclusivity to claims of exclusivity of one belief superior over others.

Further bolstering such religious hubris was the claim that these beliefs were verified in time and space by the miraculous.

How do *we* achieve, however, the required relationship to Jesus? Through baptism and thereby membership in his Church—that is to say, within and by means of a sanctified social context stressing certain exclusive claims. These claims depend for validation upon the historicity of certain specific miracles. The Jewish tradition depends on the notion of a special revelation to a singular "chosen" people, in a certain place, and all these circumstances in historical time. The documentation, however, is questionable. Likewise, the Christian tradition is based on the idea of a single incarnation, the authentication of which is in the evidence of certain miracles, followed by the founding of a Church and the continuity of this Church through time: every bit of this dogma is also *historical*.[34]

This was a great concern for Campbell, the idea that certain followers of myths, myths common to all humanity, would remove them from their universal setting and place them in a limited (and limiting) context and so move the emphasis from the message to one of the messenger (i.e., the church or dogma). This transference was devastating and self-serving and it removed the influence of myth from anyone outside the specific religious context.

That is why our symbols have all been so consistently and persistently interpreted as referring not primarily to our inner selves but to supposed outer historical events. This emphasis may be good for the institution of the Church or the prosperity of the

33. Ibid., 27–28.
34. Ibid., 28; italics in original.

synagogue, but may not at all contribute to the spiritual health of the unconvinced individual.[35]

For myth and organized religion to coexist the unique religious characteristics must be subservient to the greater mythical principles.

But this approach was making it difficult, if not impossible, for Campbell to reconcile Catholicism with the universal principles found in myth. To resolve this dilemma and find a way forward he concluded that specific convictions of Roman Catholicism (and other major religions) served as a hindrance to a more enlightened worldview provided by myth, and this resulted in his finally leaving the Catholic Church.

> Joseph Campbell's own religious heritage was Roman Catholic. He formally abandoned the Church when, as a student of mythology, he felt that the Church was teaching a literal and concrete faith that could not sustain an adult. By the age of twenty-five, Campbell like others of his time had moved out of the structures of Catholicism. Campbell later softened what at one point seemed to be bitter feelings toward Catholicism, acknowledging the pedagogical need to teach children through concrete interpretations, rather than through metaphors they could not understand. He never, however, returned to attending Mass, although he understood and profoundly underscored its potent symbolism in many of his lectures.[36]

At the point where myth and religion could not be reconciled, Campbell concluded that such doctrines were divisive and based on a misreading of a text by taking it literally as opposed to symbolically, and such beliefs had to be set aside for beliefs more amiable to myth and its application to daily life. As times change so beliefs need to change and moral orders must change as well.

> On this immediate level of life and structure, myths offer life models. But the models have to be appropriate to the time in which you are living, and our time has changed so fast that what was proper fifty years ago is not proper today. And many of what were thought to be the vices of the past are the necessities of today. The moral order has to catch up with the moral necessities of actual life in time, here and now. And that is what we are not doing. The old-time religion belongs to another age, another

---

35. Ibid.
36. Eugene Kennedy in Campbell, *Thou Art That*, xvii.

people, another set of human values, another universe. By going
back you throw yourself out of sync with history.[37]

The great advantage of myth over traditional religion is its absence of any
final authority such as doctrine, creed, Church, or holy book. Myth is more
pliable than religion so it can adapt easily to any culture, and with little concern for absolute truth or claims of historicity, myth has a chameleon-like
nature allowing it to thrive among any people.

But for Campbell this inability to reconcile myth with the historical
claims of certain religions was no trivial point. Though his conclusions
seemed reasonable and even necessary to him, they did not satisfy everyone; critics and supporters alike were quick to point out this lacuna. One
critic, Mortimer Adler, a philosopher, educator, Catholic spokesperson and
former editor of *Encyclopedia Britannica,* caustically remarked, "From what
Campbell himself wrote on the subject [Catholicism], I can only conclude
that his understanding of the Christian creed and its theology was puerile.
In that field he was an ignoramus."[38]

And even Campbell's closest allies felt a need to address his turbulent
relationship with Catholicism in light of mythology. Dr. Sam Keen, editor
of *Psychology Today,* an admirer and seminar partner with Campbell wrote:

> You don't get light without a shadow. Joseph was a man who had
> a single enthusiasm for a lifetime. He paid certain things for it.
> We all do. I think, he jumped out of Roman Catholicism without
> psychiatric help and never looked at it psychologically, and what
> he jumped into was individualism. And so when he deals with
> Roman Catholicism, and the Judeo-Christian tradition, he's do-
> ing it from a point of view where he's still got stuff he hasn't quite
> dealt with about it . . You have to remember that Joseph grew up
> loving mythology and loving the plurality of the stories. So he
> was naturally offended by that single instance in human history
> [the Judeo-Christian tradition] where plurality is taken as idola-
> try. In the last years he grew to a point where he would be very
> critical about the literalism of the Judeo-Christian tradition, and
> then he would laugh and say, "There I go again."[39]

Though Campbell would later laugh dismissively at such criticisms, they
nevertheless point to his challenge of trying to integrate myth, religion, and
specific faith traditions. In many cases the very nature of certain religions

37. Campbell, *The Power of Myth,* 13.

38. "That Campbell Fellow." http://www.radicalacademy.com/adlercampbell.htm.

39. "Man and Myth," quoted in Larsen and Larsen, *Joseph Campbell,* 490–91. Brackets in original.

does not allow for such integration without redefining the religion into something else entirely, a major problem for Campbell and the adherents of those religions.

It isn't surprising that Campbell found similarities between religion and myth. The abstract nature of each discipline, the lack of a role for science, and the melding of thoughtful reasoning with belief, makes it difficult to distinguish where religion ends and myth begins. But Campbell's journey was not his alone; others before him also noticed points of similarity, and even in his day there were scholars teaching and writing on similar themes. Campbell popularized for his generation what others had said to earlier generations. In that sense, he shared an activity with C. S. Lewis—the popularization of strongly held positions with respect to religion. While Lewis did this through radio broadcasts and the publication of books, Campbell did it through lectures, television, and the publication of books. Three earlier scholars in particular whom Campbell admired were social anthropologist and mythologist Sir James Frazer, the father of modern psychoanalysis, Sigmund Freud (1856–1939), and the founder of analytical psychology, Carl Jung.

ACADEMIC INFLUENCES

Sir James Frazer

For the first twenty years of his life, Campbell wrestled with what appeared to be two disparate approaches to matters of belief or faith. Though raised Roman Catholic, he grew to find it narrow and authoritarian. While he acknowledged the Bible provided answers to the great questions of life, the answers came from a single book and a Church that claimed to speak for God while not allowing for other answers to satisfactorily serve the needs of those outside the Church. For instance, Native Americans came to their own answers to the same questions by observing nature and noting the patterns and cycles of human existence. The questions remain the same but the answers were different. Why did humanity have similar questions but different answers? Was there a way to harmonize such worldviews while still respecting the unique characteristics? Was there a common thread running through not only Roman Catholicism and Native American spirituality, but through all world religions? Was there any way to tie all these disparate components together in one universal belief system?

In 1924, at the age of twenty and while a senior at Columbia University, Campbell walked into a New York bookstore and picked up a volume that dramatically closed the gap in his thinking between the lure of Native American spirituality and the global influence of Roman Catholicism. Stephen and Robin Larsen explain what happened,

> At around this time he went down to Scribner's and found another life-changing book: Sir James Frazer's *Golden Bough*. "It became the second of my long series of Bibles," he wrote.[40]

Sir James George Frazer was a Scottish social anthropologist who influenced the early stages of the modern studies of comparative religion and myth, and he is often considered one of the founding fathers of modern anthropology. His most famous work, *The Golden Bough*,[41] traced the evolution of human behavior, primitive myth, magic, taboo, religion, and ritual, along with their parallels to Christianity. The book first appeared in two volumes in 1890 and finally in twelve volumes in 1911–15. The book's title came from the golden bough in the sacred grove at Nemi, near Rome. Frazer's contention was that human belief progressed through three stages. First there was primitive magic, followed by religion, replaced later by the most mature stage, science.

Frazer's *Golden Bough* provided Campbell an early but fundamental clue for identifying the common thread running through the maze of world religions. Religion was simply a way to explain human existence and was part of an evolutionary mental process involving magic and myth.

Where Frazer differed from other mythologists was at the root level of cause, i.e., to why myth was invented. While others perceive myth as a way to explain the world, Frazer's approach was more personal. People need to eat and so magic, myth, and later, religion, were invented as a way to appease the powers and secure food. But magic only involved impersonal, mechanical forces; it was in the stage of myth and religion where gods were introduced. As mythology scholar Robert Segal explains,

> On its own every society invents first magic and then religion. Every society invents its myths as part of its religion. As with [Edward] Tyler, so with Frazer: similar causes are bound to yield similar effects, so that gods and therefore myths are bound to prove similar worldwide. Frazer puts the point in a line that Campbell repeatedly invokes as the clearest statement of independent invention through experience: ". . . the resemblance which may be traced in this respect between the religions of the East and West is no more than what we commonly, though

---

40. Larsen and Larsen, *Joseph Campbell,* 48.

41. Frazer, *The Golden Bough.*

incorrectly, call a fortuitous coincidence, the effect of similar causes acting alike on the similar constitution of the human mind in different countries and under different skies."[42]

As Segal observes, Campbell was persuaded by Frazer's insights since they gave him a new way of looking at myth and religion that no longer kept the two disciplines apart but did not make them synonymous or rendered either one useless. Instead, everything fell into place and made sense. Fraser's work serves as a catalyst of correlation and twenty year old Campbell was on his way to seeing the necessary linkage of magic, myth, religion, and science.

Briefly, Frazer addresses the right of the Year King, or King of the Wood, in the sacred grove at Nemi. Renewal of the land was achieved by slaying the King and Frazer contends this theme is found throughout the world's religions and myths. Sometimes it appears as Osiris, Adonis; or Baldur of Norse mythology, "even in the burning of men in effigy in the British Isles, as on Guy Fawkes Day or the leafy 'Jack' of May Day rites."[43]

> About fifteen years later Campbell wrote: "At this time, following the rationalism of Frazer and my teachers, the church's connection with the primitive seemed to me a point decidedly against it [he criticized the church for being just a transformation of an older form], but I was fascinated by the primitive, and the problem of honestly correlating my fascination and my criticism never quite occurred to me." The analogy of the sacrificed Year King to the sacrificial theme of the Christian story was irresistible to Campbell, but at this point he didn't quite know what to do with it, especially since, on the face of it, "mythology" somehow was being compared with the forms of "religion." (Later he would eliminate that distinction in his thoughts, lightly defining mythology as "other people's religion.").[44]

Suddenly everything Campbell was wrestling with regarding the similarities and universal themes of religion and spirituality was starting to congeal. Even the unique characteristics among the world religions began to find their place in myth. The more Campbell studied Frazer and considered his assumptions, the wider he drew his circle for what myth could encompass.

As Campbell studied, he began to see connections between works such as *Beowulf*, ancient myths, primitive folktales, and what he was now reading in Frazer. He began to notice similar social patterns in each culture and

---

42. Segal, *Joseph Campbell*, 248–49, brackets added. Frazer quote reference, Frazer, *The Golden Bough*, esp. chs. 3–4.

43. Larsen and Larsen, *Joseph Campbell*, 48.

44. Ibid., 48–49, brackets in original.

that each religion and myth made similar ethical assumptions. He began to think of himself as "a student of social psychology"[45] and would conclude,

> To offer an image of the universe that is in accord with the knowledge of the time, the sciences and the fields of action of the folk to whom the mythology is addressed; and to validate, support, and imprint the norms of a given specific moral order, that namely of the society in which the individual is to live.[46]

Campbell would later describe this process of correlation by what he called a magic word, Mythos.

> From now on Campbell's eyes were open in a new way. His newfound vision seemed to transform whatever he beheld; that was why he referred to it as the "florescent" eye, the eye of the Mythos.[47]

In Campbell's thinking, the works of Frazer provided the first critical key to understanding myth by affecting two critical areas of his life: the personal and the professional.

On a personal level, reading Frazer mellowed some of the animosity Campbell felt toward Roman Catholicism while professionally Frazer became a dominant theme in Campbell's teaching. In 1955, Campbell wrote his wife Jean, who had Catholic missionaries in her family, that a trip to India had softened his attitude toward all missionaries. Referring to Frazer, he admitted that he repented of a patronizing attitude toward the Christian missionaries in her family and had started to view missionaries as people of courage. "'Christian benefits cannot be shrugged away,' he admitted. He was ready, he said, to re-embrace the notion of Sir James Frazer that magic, religion, and science were 'an advancing series.'"[48]

On a professional level Frazer's writings were becoming central in his classes. By 1937 he confesses that Mythos was starting to loom large in his studies and lectures,

> I had . . . dropped my course in Backgrounds to Literature, and was experimenting with a course in Folklore and Myth. I was rereading Fraser's *Golden Bough* and was studying Durkheim's *Forms elementaires de la vie religieuse*, but my principal emphasis has been on the writings of Freud and Jung. Now the Indian formulae came back to me with great meaning. I was struck by

45. Ibid., 48.
46. Ibid., 48–49.
47. Ibid., 227.
48. Ibid., 395–96.

the idea of life-activities as rights symbolical of transcendental import.[49]

By October of that year his classes at Sarah Lawrence were going strong and he admitted to having "the best group of students" ever. *The Golden Bough* was now an integral part of his curriculum and he impressed himself "by his own powers of exposition."[50]

Campbell would gradually disagree with Frazer on certain details of interpreting myth. For instance, where Campbell assumed that in the East all humanity was considered divine, Frazer believed such divinity was limited only to the king. This led the two men to disagree on the scope of certain practices such as the ritualistic killing of kings to ensure the health of the god of vegetation. While Frazer thought this practice universal, Campbell limited it to the East.[51]

In spite of later differences that distinguished his views from Frazer, Campbell would always consider that fortuitous trip into Scribner's bookstore a life-changing experience. But Frazer was not alone in influencing Campbell's thinking on myth. Equally significant were Sigmund Freud and Carl Jung.

Sigmund Freud

Sigmund Freud was an Austrian neurologist who became known as the father of psychoanalysis. He developed theories about the unconscious mind and the mechanism of repression, and established the field of verbal psychotherapy by creating a clinical method for treating psychopathology through dialogue between patient and psychoanalyst.

Campbell's introduction to Freud and psychoanalysis took place in 1924 when he was twenty years old. He was just learning to read French when he purchased a French copy of Freud's book, *Totem et Tabu.*[52] At this point myth was not his primary interest, though the title of the book no doubt caught his attention. He would later pinpoint his formal introduction to psychoanalysis to his German studies in Munich in 1927.[53]

---

49. Ibid., 235.

50. Ibid., 253.

51. Segal, *Joseph Campbell*, 114–15.

52. Freud, *Totem and Taboo.*

53. Larsen and Larsen, *Joseph Campbell*, 582.

While not a mythologist in the traditional understanding of the word, and "only in passing does Freud himself analyze myth,"[54] Freud did allude to myth and understood the role it played in the mind and culture. As Freudian scholar Christine Downing, who, as the first woman president of the American Academy of Religion, gave her presidential address on "Sigmund Freud and the Mythological Tradition," points out, Freud was familiar with myth but understood it in his own terms.

> These forces—sex, death, and society—act on man both from outside and from within his own head. Of course, Freud does not call them "gods" but rather "instincts." The instincts, especially the sexual instinct, are irreducible for Freud; they are ultimate terms, self-explicable. He himself admits: "The theory of the instincts is so to say in our mythology."[55]

As Frazer and Campbell believed, Freud realized myth was human; it developed in the mind or imagination. Myth lives in the unconscious and so the characters of myth, the gods and demons, heroes and villains, all live within each individual, and by extension, in each culture as well. But reconciling the individual source of myth and the universality of mythical themes proved to be a challenge for Freud.

> Freud's project was to reawaken us to the mythological memories still alive in our unconscious, and also to that capacity for mythopoeic thought reflected in the form of unconscious processes. Oedipus and other archetypal figures live in us. They are symbols in our dreams whose meaning seems not to derive from our own personal history nor to be accessible through free association, universal symbols which mean in my dreams what they mean in yours and what they meant in the myths of long ago. Like Jung, Freud toyed for a time with the notion of some kind of biological inheritance of cultural acquisitions to explain the presence of such "archaic content," though he never really found an explanation that satisfied him. Explanation in any case seemed less important than recognition.[56]

Freud recognized the convergence of myth, dreams, and thought upon the human psyche, but he was not able to explain the role of each or the common themes found in universal symbols. But he did realize the importance of myth in modern civilization and he recognized the importance of finding

54. Segal, *Theorizing About Myth*, 118.

55. Downing, "Sigmund Freud," 5.

56. Ibid., 12.

the deeper meanings of myths, meanings that could lead to the consciousness necessary for a healthy mental state.

When Campbell first discovered Freud he was impressed with his interpretation of the infant psyche and the role symbolism played in raising children, not only in the West but throughout all cultures. So impressed was he that he opens his Preface of *The Hero with a Thousand Faces* with a quote from Freud's *The Future of an Illusion*:[57]

> The truths contained in religious doctrines are after all so distorted and systematically disguised . . . that the mass of humanity cannot recognize them as truth. The case is similar to what happens when we tell a child that new-born babies are brought by the stork. Here, too, we are telling the truth in symbolic clothing, for we know what the large bird signifies. But the child does not know it. He hears only the distorted part of what we say, and feels that he has been deceived; and we know how often his distrust of the grown-ups and his refractoriness actually take their start from this impression. We have become convinced that it is better to avoid such symbolic disguising of the truth in what we tell children and not to withhold from them a knowledge of the true state of affairs commensurate with their intellectual level.[58]

Campbell later quotes Freud, "I recognized the presence of symbolism on dreams from the very beginning. But it was only by degrees and as my experience increased that I arrived at a full appreciation of its extent and significance"[59]

Freud's research led him to see not only the importance of symbolism in dreams but in other manifestations as well, including myth:

> This symbolism is not peculiar to dreams, but is characteristic of unconscious ideation, in particular among the people, and is to be found in folklore, myths, legends, linguistic idioms, proverbial wisdom and current jokes, to a more complex extent than in dreams.[60]

Though originally impressed with his work, Campbell later had a falling out with Freud's approach when he came across the work of the Swiss psychiatrist, Carl Jung. He now noticed an entirely different approach to

---

57. Freud, *The Future of an Illusion*, 44–45.

58. Campbell, *The Hero with a Thousand Faces*, vii.

59. Ibid., 19; Freud, *The Interpretation of Dreams*, 350–51.

60. Ibid.

interpreting myth, one he found to be more persuasive. As he explained it in an interview,

> When I wrote *The Hero with a Thousand Faces*, they [Freud and Jung] were equal in my thinking: Freud served in one context, Jung in another. But then, in the years following, Jung became more and more eloquent to me. I think the longer you live, the more Jung can say to you. I go back to him every so often, and things that I've read before always say something new. Freud never says something new to me anymore; Freud tells us what myths mean to neurotics. On the other hand, Jung gives us clues as to how to let the myth talk to us in its own terms, without putting a formula on it.[61]

It was Freud's negative approach to myth, his attributing it to neurosis, which Campbell found troubling. He believed Jung's approach of myth as metaphor gave a fuller understanding to the role myth could play in modern life and psychology. When Freud spoke about myth he always looked backwards to an individual's birth and early upbringing, myth was simply reflective of one's childhood. But Jung saw myth speaking to each phase of life, from youth to old age.

> Personally, I find Jung as an interpreter of myths far more impressive than Freud. Freud projects a Viennese family romance of Papa, Mamma, and their boy-child into every mythology on earth, regarding myths not as symbolic of adult insights, but as symptomatic of an infantile pathology; not as revelatory, but as concealing; not as progressive, leading to maturity, but as regressive, pointing back to childhood. Jung's view, on the other hand, is that the figurations of myth are to be read as the metaphors of a necessary, almost pedagogical discipline, through which the powers of the psyche are led forward to mature relationships, first to the responsibilities of adulthood and then to the wisdom of age.[62]

Generally speaking, Freud saw sex as the main determinant in psychology. As such, he saw the acting out of sexual urges as central to all human behavior, including the invention and interpretation of myth. On this point Campbell could not agree. But Jung understood sex, and all organs of the body, along with myth and religion, as positive, and myth was a means for people to get back in touch with these inner forces. As Campbell summarized, "Our outward-oriented consciousness, addressed to the demands of

61. Cited in Maher and Briggs, *An Open Life*, 121.
62. Campbell, *The Mythic Dimension*, 5.

the day, may lose touch with these inward forces; and the myths, states Jung, when correctly read, are the means to bring us back in touch."[63]

So while Sigmund Freud introduced Campbell to the important role psychology and psychoanalysis played in understanding myth, it was Carl Jung who opened up a new dimension of dream and mythological consciousness in a positive way that brought together myth and religion so they made sense in a technological age.

Carl Jung

Scattered throughout his many books, articles, and interviews, Joseph Campbell often refers to authors with whom he differed and credits those he admired for the way they challenged and stimulated his thinking regarding myth. Of the three men he often refers to with great respect, James Frazer, Sigmund Freud, and Carl Jung, he credits Jung as having made an unusual impact and offering a persuasive alternative to Freud on the origin and purpose of myth.

> In our time, Joseph Campbell has done much to popularize a generally Jungian view of myth by suggesting that the source of myth is the human psyche. Impressed with such a reservoir of archetypal images within, he counsels us to submit to ourselves and find solution to the perplexities and problems of life within the human mind.[64]

Recalling his early encounter with Jung, Campbell stated:

> Now, my own discovery of Jung happened when I was a student in Germany in the 1920s. I was interested in mythology at that time. But I had never found any relationship of psychology to mythology in the literature that I was introduced to in college or graduate school. But, my god, when I began reading Jung's works—particularly the work that's been translated as *Symbols of Transformation*! That was just one of those things that sends all the lights up in all directions! I knew that a whole new dimension of understanding of what mythology was all about had come to me. So as far as the psychological interpretation of mythology and elucidation and evaluation go, I find Jung the

---

63. Campbell, *Myths to Live By*, 14.
64. Hein, *Christian Mythmakers*, 7.

base. Others who interest me now also relate to him positively: Stanislav Grov, and R. D. Laing.[65]

The discovery of Jung also caused Campbell to further consider and compare Freud's understanding of myth. It was during his year as a graduate student in Germany (1928–1929) that Campbell discovered both authors who, in his words, "opened up a psychological dimension to the field of mythology. Suddenly I realized why the subject was interesting to me, and a lot of new mysteries and wonders came through."[66]

As he wrestled with each scholar's approach, he started to find Jung's explanations not only more comprehensive in explaining myth, but more relevant and adaptable to changes in culture. To a certain degree, Campbell found Freud enveloped in the theory of Jung: "I think the psychology of Freud tends more to relate to what Jung calls the personal unconscious. When you break past that into realms that cannot be interpreted in terms of personal experience, you're in the field of mythic forms. And if you're acquainted with the mythic forms, you understand where you are in a way that's impossible if you have no previous acquaintanceship."[67] Campbell concluded that Freud's theory was severely limited since Freud spoke of myth as it applied to neurotics while Jung spoke broadly and in ways that could benefit each generation. As Campbell once commented, "As I say, he brings more and more to me. But he's not the final word—I don't think there is a final word; his work has opened up prospects and vistas, however."[68]

In *Myths to Live By*, Campbell presents a contrast of the views of Freud and Jung. Freud was a critic of myth, believing myth was infantile, something that served humanity in its primitive stages that needed to be displaced by a more enlightened understanding of the human condition. To Freud myths were public dreams while dreams were private myths and both myth and dreams were symptoms of neurosis, an illness, a repression of infantile incest wishes and something to be treated and cured. Campbell concludes Freud's view as,

> The person with a neurosis feels ashamed, alone and isolated in his illness, whereas the gods are general projections onto a universal screen. They are equally manifestations of unconscious, compulsive fears and delusions. Moreover, all the arts, and particularly religious arts, are, in Freud's view, similarly pathological; likewise, all philosophies. Civilization itself, in fact, is

65. Cited in Maher and Briggs, *An Open Life*, 50.
66. Ibid., 121.
67. Ibid., 50.
68. Ibid., 121.

a pathological surrogate for unconscious infantile disappointments. And thus Freud, like Frazer, judged the worlds of myth, magic, and religion negatively, as errors to be refuted, surpassed, and supplemented finally by science.[69]

Campbell found such criticism of myth, magic, and religion harsh and wrong. Not only was such an approach unnecessary, but it prevented one from attaining the very mental health Freud advocated. Instead of looking at myth as an illness to be treated, Campbell believed myth should be promoted and embraced. Myth is human and contains what humanity needs to live a full and satisfying life. Myth only needs to be better understood.

In contrast to Freud, Jung saw myth as timeless, because myth originates in the psyche and speaks to the human condition; nothing in the outside worlds of environment, culture, or science can lessen the role or importance of myth.

An altogether different approach is represented by Carl G. Jung, in whose view the imagery of mythology and religion serve positive, life-furthering ends. According to his way of thinking, *all* the organs of our bodies—not only those of sex and aggression—have their purposes and motives, some being subject to conscious control, others, however, not. Our outward-oriented consciousness, addressed to the demands of the day, may lose touch with these inward forces; and the myths, states Jung, when correctly read, are the means to bring us back in touch. They are telling us in picture language of powers of the psyche to be recognized and integrated in our lives, powers that have been common to the human spirit forever, and which represent that wisdom of the species by which man has weathered the millenniums. Thus they have not been, and can never be, displaced by the findings of science, which relate rather to the outside world than to the depths that we enter in sleep. Through a dialogue conducted with these inward forces through our dreams and through a study of myths, we can learn to know and come to terms with the greater horizon of our own deeper and wiser, inward self. And analogously, the society that cherishes and keeps its myths alive will be nourished from the soundest, richest strata of the human spirit.[70]

---

69. Campbell, *Myths To Live By*, 14.

70. Ibid., 14–15; italics in original.

Jung's method of understanding myth by tapping into these "inward forces," dreams, and the psyche, opened up a life-affirming perspective for Campbell that brought together the best of psychology, religion, and myth.

The son of a pastor, Carl Gustave Jung was a Swiss psychiatrist and psychologist who influenced not only his own chosen fields but the fields of philosophy, anthropology, and theology as well. Having an early interest in spirituality and mythology, he went on to work closely with Sigmund Freud until differences caused them to go their separate ways. Believing Freud put too much emphasis on human sexuality, Jung developed the idea of a *collective unconscious*. As Nicole B. Barenbaum notes:

> The collective unconscious includes thought patterns and behavioral responses called *archetypes*, which have developed through the centuries. Jung believed that archetypes enable people to react to situations in ways similar to their ancestors. He also believed that the collective unconscious contains wisdom that guides all humanity.[71]

Jung's hypothesis provided a way for Campbell to resolve the dilemma concerning the origins of common myths. Just as James Frazer helped Campbell understand *universal similarities* in myth, so Carl Jung helped him by pointing out *how* such similarities can be explained. Indeed, the critical contribution Jung made to Campbell's thinking was an explanation of how vastly different cultures can arrive at myths with similar themes that address the great questions of human existence.

Because Jung and "Jungian" have become common terms, distinctions are often lost. Today these terms are used to refer to anyone simply interested in myth or who considers myth an important contribution in the study of anthropology. But these are imprecise uses of the terms and do not adequately explain the contribution Jung made to myth generally and to Campbell's thinking specifically.

Technically, it's not a mere interest in myth or even in the similarities found among myths that defines "Jungian." As Segal explains:

> What *is* distinctively Jungian is the *explanation* of the similarities. There are, once again, two possible explanations: diffusion and independent invention. Diffusion means that myth originates in a single society and spreads elsewhere from it. Independent invention means that every society invents myth on its own.[72]

---

71. Barenbaum, "Jung, Carl Gustav," 5; italics in original: http://www.worldbookonline.com/advanced/article?id=ar292580&st-carl+jung.

72. Segal, *Joseph Campbell*, 246; italics in original.

Anthropologists and mythologists have long realized that although myths among differing cultures are seldom identical in every point, they often have similar themes and story lines and this commonality has presented a challenge.

In response to an interviewer's observation that other cultures have their own texts with similar motifs, Campbell responds:

> Well, there's no doubt about it. The great German anthropologist, Adolph Bastian [1826–1905], was the first to note that, with very few exceptions, there are themes that occur in all mythologies and all the religions of the world. He called these *elementary ideas.* Where do they come from? They don't come from the fact-world; they come from the psyche, just as fairy tales do. Then he also observed that, in the different provinces of mankind, they occur in different inflections, according to place and time. These he called *ethnic* or *folk ideas.*
>
> There are the two sides to our subject. The folk idea is a historical problem: why do we have this form here and that one over there? At the elementary idea is a very deep psychological one. In India there are two words that refer to the two aspects of mythology: *desī*, which means local or provincial; and *marga,* meaning the path. And, by casting off the shell of the local, historical inflection, one comes to the elementary idea which is the path to one's own innermost heart. The word *marga* comes from the root word meaning the trail or path of an animal. So you follow the animal of the spiritual guide to your own inwardness. That's what myths are good for. And all the great traditions are talking to the same point.[73]

But how can cultures separated by continents and advancements in technology, and with nothing more than the human experience in common, arrive at similar ways to explain those experiences?

In seeking an answer to this dilemma two explanations have been offered, the approach of the Diffusionists and that of the Inventionists. Neither explanation contends that myths of any two societies are identical; they only recognize that certain myths are similar enough to suggest springing from a common cause. Diffusionists, who notice too many similarities for independent invention, admit that no two societies are alike while inventionists must admit the similarities to be more than coincidence. Neither side is seeking to deny differences; they are only trying to account for the similarities.

---

73. Cited in Maher and Briggs, *An Open Life,* 68; italics in original, brackets added.

> If the prime argument of diffusionists is that the similarities are too precise to have arisen independently, the prime argument of independent "inventionists" is that diffusion, even when granted, fails to explain either the origin of myth by the societies to which it spreads.[74]

As Campbell studied Jung's "independent invention," he found it a satisfactory explanation of myth and religion. Jung enabled Campbell to see the big picture of world religions and to realize that, instead of religion needing a divine origin (where each divine origin conflicted with the divine origin of other religions), religion and myth had human origins. The supernatural did not come down from above and outside human existence, it came up from deep within the human psyche. Campbell found this psychological origin of myth convincing and it set Jung apart from his contemporaries and even from other scholars who, like him, believed in independent invention.

Attributing the similarities in myths to independent invention wasn't just a Jungian idea. Other theorists of myth such as Edwin Tyler, James Frazer, and Sigmund Freud also attributed the similarities to invention. But what made Jung's contribution unique was the form of independent invention he advocated.

Two possibilities for the source of invention are experience and heredity. Independent invention as *experience* understands every society as inventing myth for itself, while independent *invention* as heredity means that every society inherits myth. Such invention does not mean each person in the society creates myth, but that every member may have the experience that leads to its creation while only a few people create the myth.

Invention as heredity means that each person is born with the experience to create myth. All people have the same elements or similarities to make myth, what Jung calls archetypes. And, as in independent invention, only certain members create the actual myths; in heredity their roles are far more limited since they are working with the innate archetype and turning it into myth. Where Tyler, Frazier, and Freud attributed the independent invention to experience, it was Jung who attributed it to a psychological and not biological heredity.

This inherent psychological source of myth is what made Jung's approach truly "Jungian." While other scholars were teaching independent invention, Jung rooted the genesis of this invention in heredity instead of the more commonly held understanding of experience.

> He claims that everyone is born not just with the need of some kind that the invention of myth fulfills but with the myths, or

74. Segal, *Joseph Campbell*, 246–47.

the contents of myths, themselves. More precisely, everyone is born with the contents of myths already elevated to the level of myth.[75]

To Jung, the human mind was self-contained with everything needed for myth; it not only felt the needs and posed the questions, but it also contained the raw materials for the myths.

Jung's influence in Campbell's thinking was apparent in a second way. He not only helped Campbell understand the origins of myth, but he also drew attention to the critical role of the hero. For Jung, the true subject is the archetype and his or her adventures; the archetypes do not stand as symbols of something else, they are the symbolized. And since the archetype and mythic level are the same, myths are inherited, not invented.

> Everyone inherits the same archetypes, which together comprise what Jung calls the collective unconscious. In every society a few persons invent specific stories to express those archetypes, but myth-makers here are inventing only the manifestations of already mythic material. Odysseus, for example, gets either invented or appropriated to serve as a Greek expression of the hero archetype. Heroism itself is not invented, the way it is for Tyler, Frazer, or Freud. Only actual myths expressing it are.[76]

As with his approach to the origin of myth, Jung set himself apart from others with his understanding of archetypes. For Frazer and Freud, experience was the spark that resulted in the creation of myth. But for Jung, experience provided the occasion for the expression of a pre-existent archetype. "Archetypes *shape* experience rather than . . . *derive* from it. The archetype of the Great Mother does not, as for Freud, result from the magnification of one's own mother but on the contrary expresses itself through her and thereby shapes one's experience of her."[77]

In *Myths to Live By*, Campbell further extols Jung's approach:

> All my life, as a student of mythologies, I have been working with these archetypes, and I can tell you, they *do* exist and are the same all over the world. In the various traditions they are variously represented; as, for instance, in a Buddhist temple, medieval cathedral, Sumerian ziggurat, or Mayan pyramid. The images of divinities will vary in various parts of the world according to the local flora, fauna, geography, racial features, etc.

75. Ibid., 249.
76. Ibid., 250.
77. Ibid., 250–51; italics in original.

the myths and rites will be given different interpretations, different rational applications, different social customs to validate and enforce. And yet the archetypal, essential forms and ideas are the same—often stunningly so. And so what, then, *are* they? What do they represent?

The psychologist who has best dealt with these, best described and best interpreted them, is Carl G. Jung, who terms them "archetypes of the collective consciousness," as pertaining to those structures of the psyche that are not the products of merely individual experience but are common to all mankind. In his view, the basal depth or layer of the psyche is an expression of the instinct system of our species, grounded in the human body, it's nervous system and wonderful brain . . . The repressed personal memories, on the other hand, of the shocks, frustrations, fears, etc., of infancy, to which the Freudian school gives such attention, Jung distinguishes it from the other and calls the "personal unconscious." As the first is biological and common to the species, so the second is biographical, socially determined, and specific to each a separate life. Most of our dreams and daily difficulties will derive, of course, from the latter; but in a schizophrenic plunge one descends to the "collective," and the imagery they experience is largely of the order of the arch types of myth.[78]

Few authors influenced Campbell's view of myth or better enabled him to bring together psychology, psychiatry, religion and myth as Carl Jung.

But nothing here should be construed to imply that Campbell was "Jungian" in his thinking about myth or that he hesitated to disagree with Jung. On the contrary, he denied being Jungian while at the same time expressing his appreciation for Jung's approach,

You know, for some people, "Jungian" is a nasty word, and it has been flung at me by certain reviewers as though to say, "don't bother with Joe Campbell; he's a Jungian." I'm not a Jungian! As far as interpreting myths, Jung gives me the best clues I've got. But I'm much more interested in diffusion and relationships historically than Jung was, so that the Jungians think of me as a kind of questionable person. I don't use those formula words very often in my interpretation of myths, but Jung gives me the background from which to let the myth talk to me.[79]

---

78. Campbell, *Myths To Live By*, 209–10; italics in original.
79. Maher and Briggs, *An Open Life*, 123.

Campbell never hesitated to clarify how and why he disagreed with Jung, saying in one place, "Now, where I am separated from Jung is in my interest in the historical development of mythology—what Bastian [anthropologist Adolf Bastian, 1826–1905] called the folk transformations of the great archetypes which occur in the different provinces of human life."[80]

In comparing and contrasting Campbell's thinking on Jung, Robert Segal identified the similarities and differences:

> For both Campbell and Jung, myth functions above all to link humans to the unconscious. But they differ over the linkage. Campbell, whose knowledge of the unconscious derives from reading myths, has a detached, imperious attitude toward the unconscious. He seeks to *use* myth to enrich human lives. Jung, whose knowledge of the unconscious stems from a terrifying encounter with it, has a far warier and humbler stance. While he, too, seeks enrichment from the unconscious, he also fears the unconscious, which he realizes can overcome those who attempt to control it. Where Campbell can confidently advocate surrender to the unconscious, Jung, trepidatious at the prospect, promotes only a "dialogue" with the unconscious. Where Campbell assumes that the ego will somehow remain in place, Jung does not.[81]

For Campbell, myth was not only necessary, it was sufficient for human fulfillment. He disagreed with those who saw a need for therapy arguing "therapy is only for those without myth."[82] Jung, on the other hand, was far more cautious with myth believing it should be indulged only with therapy saying "Primitives can never be fulfilled because they have no therapy, which is a modern invention."[83]

Campbell's admission that "As far as interpreting myths, Jung gives me the best clues I've got" is perhaps the fairest evaluation of the respect he had for Jung's influence. Jung did not lead him by the hand to any final conclusions, but he did provide the clues necessary for Campbell to come to his own understanding and interpretation of myth. Campbell would agree that if he saw further than others, it was because he too stood on the shoulders of giants such as Carl Jung to whom he had an enormous intellectual indebtedness.

80. Ibid., 51.
81. Segal, *Joseph Campbell*, 261–62; italics in original.
82. Ibid., 260.
83. Ibid.

STATEMENT OF CAMPBELL'S VIEW ON MYTH

To Joseph Campbell myth is indispensable to the human condition, without myth humanity and civilization would self-destruct,

> For not only has it always been the way of multitudes to inter-pret their own symbols literally, but such literally read symbolic forms have always been—and still are, in fact—the supports of their civilizations, the supports of their moral orders, their co-hesion, vitality, and creative powers. With the loss of them there follows uncertainty, and with uncertainty, disequilibrium . . . since life . . . requires life-supporting illusions; and where these have been dispelled, there is nothing secure to hold on to, no moral law, nothing firm. We have seen what has happened, for example, to primitive communities unsettled by the white man's civilization. With their old taboos discredited, they immediately go to pieces, disintegrate, and become sorts of vice and disease.
>
> Today the same thing is happening to us. With our old mythologically founded taboos unsettled by our own modern sciences, there is everywhere in the civilized world a rapidly ris-ing incidence of vice and crime, mental disorders, suicides and dope addictions, shattered homes, impudent children, violence, murder, and despair.[84]

Myth is a necessary human component to human existence. Myth not only serves to hold civilizations together, but it reveals that all peoples are one. In the preface to *The Hero with a Thousand Faces* he says, "My hope is that a comparative elucidation may contribute to the perhaps not-quite-desperate cause of those forces that are working in the present world for unification . . . in the sense of human mutual understanding."[85] So significant is myth's role that they "will identify the individual not with his local group but with the planet."[86]

As argued throughout this book, one cannot speak of a "definition" or "view" of myth in the singular. Instead, the conversation revolves around definitions and views. And such discussions often appear to be circular; one's definition comes from one's view and one's view rises out of one's definition.

Aside from those found in his many books, some of Campbell's most personal insights regarding myth can be gleaned from a series of informal interviews with his friend and radio talk show host, Michael Toms. Begin-ning in 1975, and continuing for the next twelve years, Campbell shared

84. Campbell, *Myths to Live By*, 10–11.
85. Campbell, *The Hero with a Thousand Faces*, viii.
86. Campbell, *The Power of Myth*, 24.

with Toms his understanding of myth and explained its purpose and function. In summing up what he called the "main drift of mythology," Campbell explained:

> The main drift of mythology, if you want to put it into a sentence or two, is that the separateness that is apparent in the phenomenal world is secondary; beyond, and behind, and within, and supporting that world is an unseen experienced unity and identity in us all. And the first level of unity that is recognized is that of the family. And the second level of unity, which is deeper, is of the tribe or the social unit. But beyond that is a common human identity.[87]

It was this common "unity and identity" that tied together everything he read and considered on myth and religion. Irrespective of where one looks, from the most primitive to the most advanced culture, there are myths handed down from one generation to the next with themes matching a corresponding drama in a story from an entirely different time and culture. Such amazing similarities prompted Campbell to ask:

> What are you going to do with the fact that the same motifs appear everywhere? There's a constellation of motifs that are fundamental. How do you explain it? Myths come from the same zone as dreams, so that individual dreams won't be alike. But here we come to a level of what might be called radical dreams—the myths—and they match, they match, they match. The term "collective unconscious," or general unconscious, is used in recognition of the fact that there is a common humanity built into our nervous system out of which our imagination works. The appeal of these constants is very deep.[88]

This universal thread found among all cultures intrigued Campbell. How to explain it? Since no two people are exactly alike and cultures vary greatly in time, geography, education, and technology, how can one understand the metanarratives clearly evident in myth worldwide? This "constellation of motifs" must have a common bond within the human psyche, but what is it?

Campbell believed the bond was in the human imagination. Since all humanity shared the capacity to imagine along with the human experiences of birth, suffering, joy, life, and death, it was the natural result of the collective unconscious for people everywhere to find symbolic ways to describe

---

87. Maher and Briggs, *An Open Life*, 52.
88. Ibid., 122.

and explain such critical human events. In disagreeing with Freud's theory Campbell said,

> Now, the explanation that is often given in Freudian circles of individual experiences being the source of dream biography, and different racial histories being the source of their myth, is inadequate. That won't explain it! It doesn't fit. It may say something about a certain inflection or aspect of this mythology as compared with that one. Why does this group see themselves as the special people, though a group over there doesn't think that way—their deities have to do with the world of nature? What is it that gives those different pitches to the different cultures systems—not special history and biography—but what about the general humanity? You can recognize a human being no matter where you see him. He must have the same kind of basic nervous system, therefore his imagination must work out of a comparable base. What's so damn mystical about all that? That seems to me to be obvious. And that's what the term "collective unconscious" covers.[89]

Campbell's thrice repeated "they match" emphasizes the importance of this observation. The fact that there are commonalities within such divergent cultures can only lead to one simple conclusion: imagination is part of being human, it is a facet of the human consciousness, so it should come as no surprise that people everywhere produce myths that bridge what appears reasonable to what is perceived as divine and inscrutable.

Where do such myths originate and how do they become an integral part of life as evidenced in some religious beliefs? Campbell explains,

> A myth originates from a poetical insight on somebody's part. He has experienced potentials that all of them might have experienced had they been poets.
>
> Now, a ritual is the enactment of a myth: by participating in the rite, you participate in the myth. Myths don't count if they're just hitting your rational faculties—they have to hit the heart. You have to absorb them and adjust to them and make them your life. And in so far as the myth is a revelation of dimensions of your own spiritual potential, you are activating those dimensions yourself and experiencing them.
>
> When you find a poem or a picture that really appeals to you, and awakens you, there is someone who went ahead of you and

---

89. Ibid., 122–23.

> gives you that experience; and it may be life-shaping. A myth is
> a life-shaping image.[90]

So myth comes up from deep within the human psyche and shapes the life of the individual and culture.

From such an understanding of the *origin* of myth Campbell was able to explain the *function* of myth. Myths are not simply stories to entertain children or ways for a culture to pass down beliefs of previous generations, instead; "The first function of a mythology is to waken and maintain in the individual a sense of wonder and participation in the mystery of this finally inscrutable universe."[91] In other words, myth provides a worldview or frame of reference typically thought to be found only in philosophy or religion. But myth has an advantage over both philosophy and religion since it can comfortably envelope both disciplines, as well as tie together the entire human race since, unlike philosophy or religion, all of humanity evidences the same mythical themes. Myth pulls humanity together and moves the human race forward.

> It has always been the prime function of mythology and rite
> to supply the symbols that carry the human spirit forward, in
> counteraction to those other constant human fantasies that tend
> to tie it back. In fact, it may well be that the very high incidence
> of neuroticism among ourselves follows from the decline among
> us of such effective spiritual aid.[92]

As a nexus of life and belief myths serve a timeless purpose. They still offer today what they have always provided to humanity: a way to understand life and a means for coming to terms with the difficult life experiences faced by all people.

> Actually, that's one of the main functions of myth. It's what I call
> the pedagogical: to carry a person through the inevitable stages
> of a lifetime. And these are the same today as they were in the
> paleolithic caves: as a youngster you're dependent on parents
> to teach you what life is, and what your relationship to other
> people has to be, and so forth; then you give up that dependence
> to become a self-responsible authority; and, finally, comes the
> stage of yielding: you realize that the world is in other hands.

---

90. Ibid., 34–35.

91. Ibid., 17.

92. Campbell, *Hero with a Thousand Faces*, 11.

> And the myth tells you what the values are in those stages in
> terms of the possibilities of your particular society.[93]

Myth, then, has depth and breadth. On the one hand, it provides answers,
or at least offers hope and guidance for the deep questions of life. Questions
such as the origin of life, birth, joy, growth, tragedy, and death are asked by
each person old enough to think about them and so myth is common to
all individuals since there will always be a desire for answers to satisfy such
questions. Most people want to understand the "Why?" of life.

On the other hand, myth has a global breadth to it as well. Since such
experiences are faced by people everywhere, myth spans the entire human
race. Wherever there is humanity, by necessity, one finds the human experience and myth. There is no way to separate myth from humanity for it is
as human as thinking and as necessary to the human psyche as knowledge
and hope.

Myth and "Follow Your Bliss"

Of the many insights and quotes, Joseph Campbell is famous for none as
well known as his three-word counsel, "Follow your bliss." Following one's
bliss was advice he first followed himself, then taught to his students at Sarah
Lawrence He referred to it often in his lectures and books, and put it in at
least one book title, *Pathways to Bliss: Mythology and Personal Transformation*.[94] But what did Campbell mean by encouraging people to follow their
bliss? How did he understand bliss and how could such counsel be heeded
by all people everywhere? And what relation did bliss have to Campbell's
thinking about myth and the place of mythology in culture?

To Joseph Campbell, following one's bliss succinctly summed up
one true way to find meaning, joy, and satisfaction in life. He arrived at
this directive from his understanding of human nature and wove the idea
throughout his teachings on myth, religion, and life in general.

In his book *Pathways to Bliss*, Campbell discusses at length how following bliss brings together the physical and the ideal. It is interesting how
Campbell is able to tie bliss in with vocation, myth, religion, wisdom, the
spiritual or transcendent, and a general sense of satisfaction with life. In
other words, "Following your bliss" is Campbell's shorthand for how to attain a sense of self understanding and personal well-being. Campbell would
tell his students at Sarah Lawrence:

93. Maher and Briggs, *An Open Life*, 32.
94. Campbell, *Pathways to Bliss*.

> [F]ollow your bliss. You'll have moments when you will experi-
> ence bliss. And when that goes away, what happens to it? Just
> stay with it, and there's more security in that than in finding out
> where the money is going to come from next year. For years I've
> watched this whole business of young people deciding on their
> careers. There are only two attitudes: one is to follow your bliss;
> and the other is to read the projections as to where the money
> is going to be when you graduate. Well, it changes so fast. This
> year it's computer work; next year it's dentistry, and so on. And
> no matter what the young person decides, by the time he or she
> gets going, it will have changed. If they have found where the
> center f their real bliss is, they can have that. You may not have
> money, but you'll have your bliss.[95]

Following one's bliss needs to guide thinking regarding the daily decisions
of work and career and if the two come into conflict, it is imperative to "follow your bliss" no matter what the cost. This deep sense of joy or well-being
must be allowed to determine life-changing decisions because no decision
is final and circumstances in life are so susceptible to change that only a
sense of personal bliss can be counted on to result in one's best interest being
realized.

But bliss is more than an act of the mind or of reasoning through a
decision. Bliss is much deeper. It is inspirational; it brings to the consciousness powers that lie deep within.

> Your bliss can guide you to that transcendent mystery, because
> bliss is the welling up of the energy of the transcendent wisdom
> within you. So when the bliss cuts off, you know that you've cut
> off the welling up; try to find it again. And that will be your
> Hermes guide, the dog that can follow the invisible trail for you.
> And that's the way it is. One works out one's own myth that way.
>   You can get some clues from earlier traditions. But they have
> to be taken as clues. As many a wise man has said, "You can't
> wear another person's hat." So when people get excited about
> the Orient and began putting on turbans and saris, what they've
> gotten caught in is the folk aspect of the wisdom that they need.
> You've got to find the wisdom, not the clothing of it. Through
> those trappings, the myths of other cultures, you can come to
> a wisdom that you've then got to translate into your own. The
> whole problem is to turn these mythologies into your own.[96]

---

95. Ibid., xxiv.
96. Ibid.

So to follow one's bliss involves tapping into the energy within, but it also involves the myths and religious beliefs handed down, whether they come from one's upbringing or from an entirely different religion or culture. Speaking of his courses at Sarah Lawrence, Campbell says:

> I taught people of practically every religious faith you could think of. Some have a harder time mythologizing than others, but all have been brought up in a myth of some kind. What I've found is that any mythic tradition can be translated into your life, if it's been put into you. And it's a good thing to hang on to the myth that was put in when you are a child, because it is there whether you want it there or not. What you have to do is translate that myth into its eloquence, not just into the literacy. You have to learn to hear its song.[97]

To Campbell, following one's bliss is the way to make the great mythical themes of human history personal; it's how to "turn these mythologies into your own" wisdom. But following one's bliss should not be dismissed as simply a variation of positive thinking or as a bromide of common sense. Following one's bliss is rooted in religious thinking, of which myth is a part, and was foundational for Campbell's theology. As Larsen explains:

> Even in Campbell's very latest years, he would quote the insights of the Hindu saint, so direct and refreshing they seemed to him as comments on the ineffable. It was Ramakrishna to whom a Western theologue came, asking to talk about God. "Do you wish to talk about God with qualities (*sa-guna*) or without qualities (*nir-guna*)?" Ramakrishna asked—a question for an answer, intended to bring the supplicant in a *vajra* flash to the brink of the abyss that lies beyond all human knowing. These insights permeated Campbell's later definitions of "bliss" and informed his ultimate theology: that the moment one began to *talk* about God, one was already in the realm of concepts and categories—a human knowledge, not divine. It was only in the wordless absorption of *nirvikalpa samadhi* that the human could unite with the transcendent Source. In effect, the experience could never be communicated. Yet the deepest portion of the insight, as it came to Ramakrishna, was that the Divine Source permeates all life. Though he accepted no personal guru, this was a credo by which Joseph Campbell found that he could live.[98]

97. Ibid.
98. Larsen and Larsen, *Joseph Campbell*, 283; italics in original.

When asked by Bill Moyers how someone can "tap into that spring of eternal life, that bliss that is right now?" Campbell answered:

> We are having experiences all the time which may on occasion render some sense of this, a little intuition of where your bliss is. Grab it. No one can tell you what it is going to be. You have to learn to recognize your own depth.[99]

Later, in the same interview, Campbell explains the spiritual significance of bliss:

> Now, I came to this idea of bliss because in Sanskrit, which is the spiritual language of the world, there are three terms that represent the brink, the jumping-off place to the ocean of transcendence: *Sat, Chit, Anada.* The word *"Sat"* means being. *"Chit"* means consciousness. *"Anada"* means bliss or rapture. I thought, "I don't know whether my consciousness is proper consciousness or not; but I do know where my rapture is. So let me hang on to rapture, and that will bring me both my consciousness and my being." I think it worked.
>
> MOYERS: Do we ever know the truth? Do we ever find it?
>
> CAMPBELL: Each person can have his own depth, experience, and some conviction of being in touch with his own *sit-chit-ananda,* his own being through consciousness and bliss. The religious people tell us we really won't experience bliss until we die and go to heaven. But I believe in having as much as you can of his experience while you are still alive.
>
> MOYERS: Bliss is now.
>
> CAMPBELL: In heaven you will be having such a marvelous time looking at God that you won't get your own experience at all. That is not the place to have the experience—here is the place to have it.[100]

To follow one's bliss is a way to think and a way to believe, but it was also philosophical; it is the way Campbell found to turn myth into personal wisdom, a timeless means of learning how best to live. Following one's bliss is also psychological; it serves as a way to tap into one's deeper consciousness, of finding "self," and following it is a means of self-discovery. As Larsen said of Campbell's interest and writing about mythology, "Campbell had 'found

---

99. Campbell, *The Power of Myth*, 118.

100. Ibid., 120; italics in original.

his bliss,' the thing he did best."[101] This raises the third point Campbell believed about following one's bliss; it is practical. Following your bliss makes you happy; it is the way to discover what best suits your temperament and personality. Campbell illustrates this point in his conversation with Bill Moyers:

> CAMPBELL: Remember the last line of [Sinclair Lewis's *Babbitt*?] "I have never done the thing that I wanted to in all my life." That is a man who never followed his bliss. Well, I actually heard that line when I was teaching at Sarah Lawrence. Before I was married, I used to eat out in the restaurants of town for my lunch and dinners. Thursday night was the maid's night off in Bronxville, so that many of the families were out in restaurants. One fine evening I was in my favorite restaurant there, and at the next table there was a father, a mother, and a scrawny boy about twelve years old. The father said to the boy, "Drink your tomato juice."
>
> And the boy said, "I don't want to."
>
> Then the father, with a louder voice, said, "Drink your tomato juice."
>
> And the mother said, "Don't make him do what he doesn't want to do."
>
> The father looked at her and said, "He can't go through life doing what he wants to do. If he does only what he wants to do, he'll be dead. Look at me, I've never done a thing I wanted to in all my life."
>
> And I thought, "My God, there's *Babbitt* incarnate!"
>
> That's the man who never followed his bliss. You may have a success in life, and then just think of it—what kind of life was it? What good was it—you've never done the thing you wanted to do in all your life. I always tell my students, go where your body and soul want to go. When you have the feeling, then stay with it, and don't let anyone throw you off.[102]

One could say that following bliss is the feeling one has of personal satisfaction based on what one wants to do. It means not conforming to trends in culture if those trends are contrary to personal joy and satisfaction.

---

101. Larsen and Larsen, *Joseph Campbell,* 324.

102. Campbell, *The Power of Myth,* 117–18.

Not surprisingly, Campbell's counsel was not without its critics, since following bliss can sound like simple hedonism dressed in lofty garb. One problem is evident in his illustration: the role and place of authority in a civilized culture. How can a parent responsibly raise a child if the child is allowed to do whatever he or she wants to do? Campbell answers the criticism in the same interview when Moyers asks, "How can those of us who are parents help our children recognize their bliss?"

> CAMPBELL: You have to know your child and be attentive to the child. You can help. When I taught at Sarah Lawrence, I would have an individual conference with every one of my students at least once a fortnight, for a half hour or so. Now, if you're talking about the things that students ought to be reading, and suddenly you hit on something that the student really responds to, you can see the eyes open and the complexion change. The life possibility has opened there. All you can say to yourself is, "I hope this child hangs on to that." They may or may not, and when they do, they have found life right there in the room with them.[103]

Campbell did not intend following bliss to be interpreted as a *lack* of authority, but rather as *exercising* authority with care and compassion. For instance, in the family a parent was to be attentive to the child's leanings, interests, likes, and dislikes; the parent was to help the child follow those specific interests, reminiscent of the Biblical adage "Train up a child in the way he should go; even when he is old he will not depart from it."[104] Following your bliss was to be done within the confines of authority.

A second criticism of following bliss was the place of personal responsibility. To many who heard his counsel without fully appreciating how he followed bliss in his own experience, Campbell's advice sounded like an excuse for laziness, a lofty way to excuse personal irresponsibility. Campbell refuted such implications throughout his writings and interviews. In their biography, the Larsen's quote Campbell explaining the meaning of what French existentialists called *ennui* and they follow with their own personal observation in an endnote:

> When skies get dull with no prospect of clearing, run away, change your hometown—your name—your job—change anything. No misfortune can be worse than the misfortune of resting permanently static. Take a chance—if you lose you are scarcely worse-off than before—if you win you have at least experienced & a new thrill or two gained. My own plan is to

103. Ibid., 118.

104. Prov 22:6.

study psychology so that I may someday be a great teacher. I shall write & teach & do anything that will assist me on my way and win me money. I shall save my money. Then—if my life begins to get tedious I shall pack off to the Orient or to the South seas to write & study & teach there. Someday I shall have gained experience & prestige enough to do as I please—then I think I shall write & teach some more.[105]

Although critics would say that Campbell's mantra was little more than hedonism, it was actually the opposite. He was saying that the responsibility for living a happy and successful life rested squarely on the individual. As anyone who knew Campbell, or studied his life knows, he worked very hard to attain the kind of life he desired. No one should construe anything Campbell said about "Follow your bliss" as implying he endorsed rebellion to authority or promoted hedonism.

In counseling students, Campbell was careful to clarify that following one's bliss could easily involve years of hard work and disappointment. Bliss wasn't what one accomplished so much as how one went about it.

When I taught at a boys' prep school, I used to talk to the boys who were trying to make up their minds as to what their careers were going to be. A boy would come to me and ask, "Do you think I can do this? Do you think I can do that? Do you think I can be a writer?"

"Oh," I would say, "I don't know. Can you endure ten years of disappointment with nobody responding to you, or are you thinking that you are going to write a bestseller the first crack? If you have the guts to stay with the thing you really want, no matter what happens, well, go ahead."

Then Dad would come along and say, "No, you ought to study law because there is more money in that, you know." Now, that is the rim of the wheel, not the hub, not following your bliss. Are you going to think of fortune, or are you going to think of your bliss?[106]

Bliss is not simply a state of delight or happiness. It requires answering hard questions and doing the difficult tasks to accomplish ones goals.

One critical area Campbell apparently had difficulty explaining was the "spiritual" or religious aspect of bliss. In two separate interviews Campbell reflects on this aspect of following one's bliss and, in so doing, he unintentionally contradicts himself as he attempts to explain the positive

105. Larsen and Larsen, *Joseph Campbell*, 66–67.
106. Campbell, *The Power of Myth*, 119.

benefits without resorting to the intervention of a divine being. Responding to a question by Michael Toms, Campbell says,

> If you have the guts to follow the risk, however, life opens, opens, opens up all along the line. I'm not superstitious, but I do believe in spiritual magic, you might say. I feel that if one follows what I call one's "bliss"—the thing that really gets you deep in the gut and that you feel is your life—doors will open up. They do! They have in my life and they have in many lives that I know of.[107]

His carefully nuanced "I'm not superstitious, but I do believe in spiritual magic" makes Campbell appear to be conflicted in articulating the phenomena. The line between superstition and spiritual magic is at best, blurry and at worst, non-existent.

But in an interview with Bill Moyers Campbell is asked, "Do you ever have that sense when you are following your bliss, as I have at moments, of being helped by hidden hands?" he responds,

> All the time. It is miraculous. I even have a superstition that has grown on me as a result of the invisible hands coming all the time—namely, that if you do follow your bliss you put yourself on a kind of track that has been there all the while, waiting for you, and the life that you ought to be living is the one you are living. When you can see that, you begin to meet people who are in the field of your bliss, and they open the doors to you. I say, follow your bliss and don't be afraid, and doors will open where you didn't know they were going to be.[108]

It's hard to know what to make of Campbell's understanding of superstition. On the one hand, he denies being superstitious, yet he admits to having a superstition. He notes that following your bliss is simply a way to discover what you enjoy in life as a result of psychology, personality, temperament, and culture, but then he refers to following one's bliss as a "spiritual magic." It is "miraculous," and involves "invisible hands" that help one find the way. You "put yourself on a kind of track" but the track "has been there all the while."

It's not hard to see how, as in the title of his book, the *Pathways to Bliss* were synonymous in Campbell's thinking with *Mythology and Personal Transformation*. Campbell implies that following one's bliss has a spiritual or religious component to it. It is a way for an individual to live in harmony with all that goes on around him. But by not tying it to any single religious tradition or doctrine it is adaptable to people of any religion and to those

107. Maher and Briggs, *An Open Life*, 24.
108. Campbell, *The Power of Myth*, 120.

with no religion. Following your bliss is a universal principle that brings together philosophy and psychology while providing a religious or spiritual component that speaks to the human need for something beyond the natural. When Moyers asks if "all men at all times felt some sense of exclusion from an ultimate reality, from bliss, from delight, from perfection, from God?" Campbell responds,

> Yes, but then you also have moments of ecstasy. The difference between everyday living and living in those moments of ecstasy is the difference between being outside and inside the Garden. You go past fear and desire, past the pair of opposites.[109]

And when asked "How do I slay that dragon in me? What's the journey each of us has to make, what you call 'the soul's high adventure'?" Campbell answers, "My general formula for my students is 'Follow your bliss.' Find where it is, and don't be afraid to follow it."[110] For Campbell "following your bliss" is a way of life.

Campbell on Myth and History

The student who studies myth is immediately faced with questions regarding facts, fiction, and history. History, as defined by the *Oxford English Dictionary* is

> A written narrative constituting a continuous chronological record of important or public events (esp. in a particular place) or of a particular trend, institution, or person's life. Common in the titles of books. Strictly speaking, a history is a work in which each movement, action, or chain of events is dealt with as a whole and pursued to its natural termination or to a convenient stopping place, as distinct from annals, in which events are simply recorded in divisions of a year or other limited period, or a chronicle, in which events are presented as a straightforward continuous narrative.[111]

So history is typically understood as the collection and presentation of past events.

How does Joseph Campbell resolve questions of myth and history? Does he understand myth as historically true or must it be fictional? Many myths typically contain places and events that can be historically verified

109. Ibid., 107.
110. Ibid., 148.
111. *Oxford English Dictionary*, s.v. "history."

even if certain people and events portrayed are supernatural or divine; if a story is verifiable and factual does Campbell still regard it as myth or does he categorized it as history?

Campbell's approach to myth is as pragmatic as it is philosophical. In other words, it's the personal meaning one discovers or how one applies myth to life that is paramount, not the historicity of the myth. As long as one can find meaning in a myth, its purpose has been realized.

In an interview with Michael Toms, Campbell and Toms carry on a lengthy exchange regarding the vital role of ritual in civilization. They talk not only about the similarities in rituals from one culture to another, but also about the increasing decline of ritual in the West. Toms comments, "It was through ritual that societies expressed their feelings, and we don't have many rituals anymore" to which Campbell, illustrating with the crucifixion of Jesus Christ, responds with an answer that gives insight into his approach of history and myth.

> And so, understanding the Crucifixion in terms of its mytho-
> logical or spiritual sense opens the image. Then it doesn't matter
> whether Christ lived or not. Actually there is no doubt that Jesus
> lived, that he was crucified, that he died and was buried. But
> it is a little more questionable as to whether he rose again and
> ascended to heaven. That doesn't matter; that's the mythological
> implication of giving yourself; he who loves his life shall find it.
> And this is what we call the creative act—not hanging on, but
> yielding to the new creative moment.[112]

He has no doubt that Jesus of Nazareth lived, was crucified, died and was buried, but that is not the critical point. If Jesus ever existed, whether "he lived or not," is not important or, as Campbell remarks, "it doesn't matter." What matters is what an individual *does* with the story of Jesus' life, death, and (purported) resurrection. The significance is in the application of the myth, how the myth pertains to life, the lessons one learns for today, and how one applies these lessons in the present context.

This approach resolves two enormous difficulties. First, on a practical level, it makes irrelevant the question of historicity, and second, it points to the abiding need for myth. As long as one can derive meaning from or impart meaning to a myth, then it is not important whether the people, places, or events ever existed. None of this is to say such questions don't have a place or should not be asked, it's just that, regardless of the answer, the myth will remain valid and useful; myth needs no historical verification.

---

112. Maher and Briggs, *An Open Life*, 68–69.

As one reads Campbell's books and interviews, it becomes evident that his interpretation of the meaning of myth is essential in his approach. While interesting, the history and origins of myths, along with the telling of myths, are not Campbell's main focus even though he is well known as an authority in both fields. In addressing the question "What accounts for Campbell's popularity?," Segal pinpoints Campbell's greatest strength as his interest in the ahistorical and symbolic meaning of myth. He writes:

> Many fans laud Campbell as above all a masterly storyteller. He does not simply know all the world's myths but also relishes reciting them. Yet in his writings he tells surprisingly few myths, at least whole ones. Instead, he cites portions of myths. In *Hero* Campbell presents barely one complete myth. In other works he plainly ignores the plot of myths and focuses instead on either the beliefs underlying the plot or else specific archetypes in the plot. The fact that myths for Campbell can be creeds and even rituals as well as stories underscores the limited role storytelling plays. Surely, then, Campbell's popularity does not stem primarily from his undeniable knack for telling tales.
>
> In fact, Campbell himself would doubtless have been miffed if it had. For he sought not only to tell myths but even more to analyze them. He analyzes the origin, function, and meaning of myth. True, in *Hero* he states modestly that he is seeking only to *establish* a heroic pattern. But *analyze* that pattern he proceeds to do. In *The Mythic Image* he does boldly reject interpretation as an impediment to the unmediated experience of myth, but in all his other works he conspicuously deciphers, not just imbibes, myth. He is a *theorist* of myth.
>
> Yet Campbell's popularity likely does not rest on his analysis of the *origin* and *function* of myth. In some works, including *Hero*, he discusses the origin and function only briefly. In other books he gives varied explanations.
>
> By contrast, Campbell's interpretation of the meaning of myth is unchanging, and it is that interpretation which no doubt captivates Campbell's devotees. From first work to last the true meaning of myth is ahistorical rather than historical and symbolic rather than literal. The symbolic meaning is simultaneously psychological and metaphysical. Psychologically and metaphysically alike, the meaning of myth is mystical: myth preaches the oneness of at once consciousness with unconsciousness and the everyday world with the strange, new one.[113]

---

113. Segal, *Joseph Campbell*, 264–65; italics in original.

By concentrating on the psychological and metaphysical aspects of myth, Campbell was able to arrive at a mystical meaning that, as Segal said, "preaches the oneness of at once consciousness with unconsciousness and the everyday world with the strange, new one," an approach that, in Campbell's thinking, brings together the best of psychology and religion, the material and immaterial. In so doing, he sidesteps questions of historicity and fiction since the purpose of myth is not dependent on such answers. None of this is to say myth is completely unaffected by such questions, particularly in a modern, scientific age. It is only to say that to Joseph Campbell such questions distract from the function of myth.

Campbell on Myth and Christianity

As in the case of myth, there are as many definitions of Christianity as there are people to define it. As Huston Smith observes: "Of all the great religions Christianity is the most widespread and has the largest number of adherents . . . Nearly two thousand years of history have brought an astonishing diversity to this religion."[114] In the face of such complexity, attempting definitions is futile. Campbell's writings and interviews will explain his understanding of Christianity and its relation to myth.

Campbell's fault line regarding Christianity is the supernatural and miraculous. He grants that aspects of the Christian faith, certain people, places, and events, are historical, but contends the supernatural aspects did not happen since it was not possible for them to happen. From a myth-perspective this does not really matter for Campbell. This scientific approach to the faith put Campbell at odds not only with his own traditional Catholicism but with anyone, such as C. S. Lewis, who finds it reasonable to grant that a divine creator can interrupt his own natural laws.

Instead of attacking miraculous events, Campbell suggests such stories be understood in a mythical way that allows one to find relevant, personal meaning. For instance, when asked about the scarcity of ritual in Western society he illustrated by alluding to attending Mass in the Roman Catholic Church. He maintains that *participating* in the Mass is the most important aspect, more important in fact than whether Jesus Christ rose physically from the dead, a historical act assumed in the symbolism of the Mass. What is critical is not the historicity of the account, but the mythical implications one derives from participating in a religious act. It is in participating that one finds meaning; it is the function of religious ceremony that allows the

114. Smith, *The World's Religions*, 317.

participant to enter into the deeper meaning of the myth, what Campbell calls "a mythologically grounded ritual." He explains:

> It's astonishing how little ritual we have in our life—even the rituals of courtesy have gone. But the function of a ritual—a mythologically grounded ritual—is to engage you in the experience of the myth. A ritual is the enactment of a myth—either in a very literal way, or in an extremely abstract way. The ritual of the sacrifice of the Mass in the Roman Catholic Church is the re-enactment of the Crucifixion. So you're participating in the sense of the Crucifixion. And that sense of the Crucifixion is twofold. One is that the divine transcendent has come into the world and has accepted the crucifixion of life; the other is that the individual has yielded his individual self to the grace of a transpersonal realization. The Cross is the threshold of the passage of eternity into time and of time into eternity; and in participating in this, you are giving yourself to the Christ—the Christ in you, namely the knower of the father.[115]

This enactment, engagement, and experiencing of ritual is the *telos* of myth. The moment a person enters into the meaning of the myth, once the myth is practiced and realized, it can be fully appreciated on a personal level. And so as seen earlier, for Campbell, approaching Christian events such as the Mass or Easter with a mythological understanding

> opens the image. Then it doesn't matter whether Christ lived or not. Actually there is no doubt that Jesus lived, that he was crucified, that he died and was buried. But it is a little more questionable as to whether he rose again and ascended to heaven. That doesn't matter; that's the mythological implication of giving yourself; he who loves his life shall find it.[116]

Campbell's conclusion is significant; what is important is the mythological implication one brings to the event, not whether the event ever took place. Even granting that Jesus lived and died is not as important as participating in the act and importing personal meaning into it and receiving meaning from it.

Campbell was not neutral about how one should understand the Bible or the claims of the Christian faith nor did he have much respect for the traditional approach. He believes that people who take the miraculous elements of the Bible in a literal, historical way are putting themselves at a great

115. Maher and Briggs, *An Open Life*, 68–69.
116. Ibid.

disadvantage by denying scientific and historical research. And worse, they are preventing themselves from finding the intended deeper meaning of the texts. Looking only at what the text says and interpreting it at face value robs the story of its intended purpose of speaking to the reader with relevant meaning for today.

In a radio interview, Campbell was asked about finding a center to one's life, of something that really matters. When asked, "So it's like coming in touch with the deeper part of life and being willing to let go," he responds, "And if you understand the spiritual aspect of your religious tradition, it will encourage you to do that. But if you interpret it in terms of hard fact, it's going to hinder you."[117] When asked about the multitude of people who interpret the Bible literally as "hard fact" Campbell responds,

> Well, literal interpretation of the Bible faces the problem of scientific and historical research. We know that there was no Garden of Eden; we know that there was no Universal Flood. So we have to ask, what is the spiritual meaning of the Garden of Eden? What is a spiritual meaning of the Flood? Interpreting biblical texts literally reduces their value; it turns them into newspaper reports. So there was a flood thousands of years ago. So what? But if you can understand what the Flood means in terms of a reference to spiritual circumstances—the coming of chaos, the loss of balance, the end of an age, the end of a psychological posture—then it begins to talk to you again.[118]

Campbell's response to the historical narrative is that it "doesn't matter" and "so what?" What is important is finding a spiritual meaning because to do otherwise is to miss the significance of the story and of ritual and religion. Some people may speculate that such questions cannot stand against the counter-narrative of modern science but to Campbell science is a separate discipline not intended to provide spiritual answers.

Not only is it detrimental to take miraculous events literally, but understanding them spiritually is the only way of preventing religion from leading one away from its true intent. When asked about his experiences with people from established religions and his attempts to have them adopt a symbolic hermeneutic, Campbell answered:

> I taught a course at Sarah Lawrence College on comparative mythology for thirty-eight years. I taught young people of every available creed. More than fifty percent of my students from the New York area were Jewish; many were Christians—Protestant,

117. Ibid., 67.
118. Ibid., 67–68.

Catholic; there were Mormons and Zoroastrians and Buddhists. There wasn't much of a problem with the Buddhists, but all the others were somewhat stuck in their provincial traditions.

It was the simplest thing; all I did was to point out the parallels and identities all over the place. You see, when there is a motif—such as that of the virgin birth—which occurs in American Indian mythologies, in Greek mythology, and so on, it becomes obvious that the virgin birth could not have referred to a historical event. It's a spiritual event that's referred to—even in the Christian tradition. One after another, these motives became spiritualized instead of historicized. And the interesting thing is that instead of the person losing her religion, she gained it. It became a religion instead of a misleading theory.[119]

Myth not only helps one to understand religion, myth is what makes it religion. When someone is able to see beyond their provincial tradition to the universal principle, the "spiritual event" underlying all beliefs, one finds the true sense of religion.

Campbell's understanding of myth and Christianity differs little from his understanding of myth and other religions. He maintains that modern scholarship and science have flattened all religions so they all say the same thing in their own language and symbols. This means all the world's religions are variations of myth. The religious question is one of focus; will individuals focus on the unique characteristics of their religion or on the similarities their belief system has with all religions?

Modern scholarship, systematically comparing the myths and rites of mankind, has found just about everywhere legends of virgins giving birth to heroes who die and are resurrected. India is chock-full of such tales, and its towering temples, very like the Aztec ones, represent again our many-storied cosmic mountain, bearing Paradise on its summit and with horrible hells beneath. The Buddhists and the Jains have similar ideas. And looking backward into the pre-Christian past, we discovered in Egypt the mythology of the slain and resurrected Osiris; in Mesopotamia, Tammuz; in Syria, Adonis; and in Greece, Dionysos: all of which furnished models to the early Christians for their representations of Christ.[120]

Religious concepts have always been deep within the human imagination; the only difference has been the symbols. Humans everywhere have the

119. Ibid., 82.
120. Campbell, *Myths to Live By,* 9–10.

same life experiences, where they differ is in how they express them. If individuals will look beyond the symbols, while still respecting them, they will find the common ground they have with all humanity.

Problems arise only when people make their religious distinctive central and understand the symbolic literally, an unfortunate habit of people everywhere:

> Now the peoples of all the great civilizations everywhere have been prone to interpret their own symbolic figures literally, and so to regard themselves as favorite in a special way, in direct contact with the Absolute. Even the polytheistic Greeks and Romans, Hindus and Chinese, all of whom were able to view the gods and customs of others sympathetically, thought of their own as supreme or, at the very least, superior; and among the monotheistic Jews, Christians, and Mohammedans, of course, the gods of others are regarded as no gods at all, but devils, and their worshipers as godless. Mecca, Rome, Jerusalem, and (less emphatically) Benares and Peking have been for centuries, therefore, each in its own way, the navel of the universe, connected directly—as by a hot line—with the Kingdom of Light or of God.[121]

This interpreting of the symbolic literally, along with believing in a superiority of one belief over another, is, to Campbell, the fatal flaw not only of Christianity but of all major religions. And not only is it erroneous and misleading, but it leads to the dangerous assumption that one has a "hot line with the Kingdom of Light or of God." Campbell writes:

> However, today such claims can no longer be taken seriously by anyone with even a kindergarten education. And in this there is serious danger. For not only has it always been the way of multitudes to interpret their own symbols literally, but such literally read symbolic forms have always been—and still are, in fact—the supports of their civilizations, the supports of their moral orders, their cohesion, vitality, and creative powers. With the loss of them there follows uncertainty, and with uncertainty, disequilibrium, since life, as both Nietzsche and Ibsen knew, requires life-supporting illusions; and where these have been dispelled, there is nothing secure to hold on to, no moral law, nothing firm. We have seen what has happened, for example, to primitive communities unsettled by the white man's civilization.

---

121. Ibid., 3, 9–10.

> With their old taboos discredited, they immediately go to pieces, disintegrate, and become resorts of vice and disease.[122]

So the importance of myth is clear. Myth is able to do what religion has failed to do and what monotheistic religions such as Judaism, Christianity, and Islam cannot do. It provides humanity answers to life's great questions; answers that are timeless since they are handed down from generation to generation, but answers that can adapt comfortably to each culture. Myth is the meta-narrative of religion, bringing together the best qualities of religion without the unique convictions that set individuals and cultures apart. Convictions which while necessary, are problematic.

In one interview, Campbell takes time to carefully explain the historical commonality of all religions and then explains the "accident" made by Christianity's emphasis on Jesus Christ being the one true savior for all humanity.

> The myth of the great savior, for example, represents the culmination or fulfillment of human potentiality. In the Hindu and Buddhist systems, the point is made that this potential is within all of us. And we are all to become fulfilled in that sense. In the Christian system, however, the accident was put on one's savior.
>
> Then comes the question of why in the West there is only one incarnation of the potential. It's a complicated historical question concerning the first four centuries A.D. in the world of Byzantium. What finally happened was that Theodosius I (378–395, approximately) proclaimed Christianity to be the only religion permitted within the Roman Empire, and only the Augustinian interpretation of the doctrines was accepted. So you have a system set up principally by a small group of theologians, and this becomes enforced to the advantage of the institution. The individual is taught to find his salvation through the medium of the institution. And there is a whole interpretation of the life of the Savior, which gives authority to this institution.[123]

Prior to the Roman Empire and Augustinian influence, a belief in the potential within each individual was universal and from it sprang the myth of a great savior. But religious rulers within the Roman Empire took this universal truth captive and relegated it to an exclusively Christian doctrine found only in the Church. But as Campbell points out, in spite of the Church's insistence that Jesus Christ alone is savior of the world,

---

122. Ibid., 9–10.
123. Maher and Briggs, *An Open Life*, 60.

> The interesting thing is that when you read the life of the sav-
> iors—Jain saviors, Buddhist saviors, Hindu saviors, the Christ—
> the same motives are there, time and time and time again.
>
> Turn to the wonderful Greek mystery religions, and again
> there are virgin births, deaths and resurrection. And the savior's
> death and resurrection becomes a model for the casting off of
> the old Adam in the un-shelling of the new. These are great,
> great themes.[124]

These ideas are universal because they are spiritual. They spring up from within the human heart. There is nothing exclusively Christian about the human condition. People everywhere have the same experiences irrespective of time, language, culture, or location. But in Campbell's thinking the Christian tradition went wrong when it sought to harness the power of myth and to make it subservient to the Church.

> In our Christian tradition, however, they have been carried in
> such a way that in order to get the grace, you might say, one
> has to approach the theme through the doctrines and the sacra-
> ments of the Church—that's the important thing. Man is born
> in Original Sin; the only salvation is through the sacraments of
> the Church. Now, that's fixing it down pretty fast. I find this has
> dislocated many young people. In my own teaching career I saw
> that when students found the analogues of their Christian or
> Jewish beliefs and other traditions, it actually reinforced their
> Christian and Jewish symbols, because now they saw how they
> had psychological value to them.[125]

So the Christian tradition went astray when it shifted the focus from the universal divinity inherent in each human, as held in Hindu systems, to the necessity of having a relationship with the person of Jesus Christ as one's personal savior from sin. Further complicating the issue are millenniums of church history, authority, and tradition. Campbell's solution to this Christian exclusivity is myth since myth allows for the great themes of Christianity such as the virgin birth, death, and resurrection of Jesus to thrive, while giving equal respect to the views of other religions and the non-religious. Christ is "the way, and the truth, and the life"[126] for the Christian but equally good ways are available for others.

Campbell's relationship with Christianity was conditioned by his childhood exposure to the beliefs of Native Americans and his upbringing

124. Ibid., 60–61.
125. Ibid.
126. John 14:6.

in Roman Catholicism. His earliest years of learning were similar to those of any child raised in the beliefs of his parents. But as he matured he questioned, criticized, and to a large degree abandoned the faith of his family and youth. But as he began to study myth, he was able to appreciate the benefits of the Christian faith, along with all faiths, while at the same time discovering where it, and other historically rooted religions such as Judaism, went wrong.

Throughout his long career of teaching and writing, Joseph Campbell endeavored to communicate clearly his understanding of myth. From the religious influences of his boyhood, to his study of scholars such as Sir James Frazer, Sigmund Freud, and Carl Jung, to his almost forty years of teaching at Sarah Lawrence College, Campbell was convinced that a misunderstanding of myth and religion was detrimental to the human condition. By taking the mythical and symbolic elements of religion, especially Judaism and Christianity, literally, adherents of such faiths promote an exclusivistic approach to God. To counter this negative approach and as a way to promote a better understanding among people Campbell advocated an inclusive approach by an appeal to myth.

He understood that to be human meant to have myths. As far back as one can study, and irrespective of the culture into which one looks, myth exists. But not only is myth universal, the themes and symbols of myth are also common. Campbell believed that a greater understanding of these themes could go a long way to bringing about a greater appreciation of the human condition and what all people have in common.

One of the biggest obstacles to achieving this goal is religion. Because of the corrupting influence of pride and the destructive force of authority, religion has sought to lay claim to the power of myth, resulting in numerous religions, each claiming to possess the truth for all of humanity. Campbell believed that once people could see through their religion and discern the deeper metanarratives running through all religions, the result would be a greater appreciation for the similarities and less of an emphasis on the differences.

Campbell's views on myth and religion are not without critics.[127] Adherents of some religions, such as Judaism and Christianity, have concerns about his approach to Bible interpretation and how he distinguishes the symbolic from the literal. But in spite of these differences, or perhaps because of these differences, Joseph Campbell is considered one of the greatest mythologists of all time.

127. Segal, *Theorizing About Myth*, 138–41, discusses seven criticisms of Joseph Campbell's work on myth including "A final weakness is Campbell's pitting of myth against religion."

5

Christianity as History,
Mystery, and Myth

T HE PURPOSE OF THIS chapter is to address how Campbell and Lewis understood Christianity as history, mystery, and myth. Both men agreed
that the Bible recorded some history, that Christianity possessed mystery,
that myth was a necessary component for a relevant Christian faith, and that
myth could be used as a hermeneutical tool for interpreting the Bible. Both
men were raised in religious homes; Campbell grew up in the tradition of
Roman Catholicism and Lewis in the Church of Ireland. Both men left the
faith tradition of their upbringing at about the same age, and both spoke
often of the influence of their childhood exposure to religion and of the
place of myth in the Christian faith.

But in spite of such areas of agreement the men differed dramatically on the ultimate importance of myth, history, and the exclusive salvific
claims of Christianity. While C. S. Lewis viewed myth entering and becoming history Joseph Campbell kept myth and history separate and advocated
an inclusive approach to matters of faith and religion.

COMPARATIVE VIEWS OF HISTORY

Irrespective of how one defines specific terms, if one accepts that Christianity regards the Bible as its foundational document, the roles played by
history, mystery, and myth must be understood and appreciated. While
Christianity has traditionally been understood as a historical faith consist-
ing of great and timeless mysteries, the role of myth within Christianity

remains controversial. Former professor of New Testament Literature at the University of Bonn, Erich Dinkler, observes concerning Christianity's historicity:

> There is no disputing the historical roots of Christianity. The question has often been discussed whether Jesus of Nazareth is a historical person at all or simply a mythical figure. Today there is agreement that we have Christian and non-Christian sources enough to reject the doubts of Jesus' historicity.[1]

As will be seen, neither Joseph Campbell or C. S. Lewis had any doubts concerning the historicity of Jesus of Nazareth nor much of what comprises the biblical record and Christian faith. They did, however, have differences of interpretation and in their understanding of history and myth as it pertained to Christianity.

No one denies that biblical locations such as Mount Moriah, the Jordan River, Jerusalem, and Bethlehem exist. These locations have been visited and excavated for millennia. Each year at Christmas and Easter, thousands of Christians converge at the birthplace and tomb of Jesus Christ. Granted, these sites are traditional and their exact locations are debated, but the traditions are ancient and credible and the debates are over the location of the historic events and not the historicity of them. Neither Campbell or Lewis deny Jesus was born and died.

Ancient holy days and festivals mentioned throughout the Old and New Testaments, such as Purim and Passover, have also existed for millenniums and are still practiced. Each year Jews celebrate Purim (Persian for "lot") in remembrance of their deliverance from near annihilation as recorded in the Old Testament book of Esther. And for 2,000 years Christians around the world have regularly celebrated Eucharist or Communion, a service rooted in Christ's celebration of his final Jewish Passover meal just prior to his arrest and crucifixion, a service later explained and applied to the church by the apostle Paul.[2]

None of these aspects of the faith are challenged or questioned by either Campbell or Lewis. Author and New Testament scholar Ben Witherington III, encourages Bible scholars to pay close attention to the history uncovered by archaeology because:

---

1. Dinkler, *The Interpreter's Dictionary of the Bible*, 488. For discussions on the current state of studies on Jesus and historicity, see for example Bock, *Studying the Historical Jesus: A Guide to Sources and Methods*, and *Jesus According to Scripture: Restoring the Portrait from the Gospels.*

2. 1 Cor 11:17–34.

> [H]istory matters! Judaism and Christianity are historical reli-
> gions, grounded in specific cultures, with specific histories at
> specific points in time. If Christianity were merely some sort of
> spiritual gumbo for the soul, some sort of philosophy of life, his-
> tory might not matter. But that is not Christianity. At the heart
> of Christianity is the life, death, and resurrection of a historical
> person named Jesus, and the more one knows about his histori-
> cal context, the better one can know the man in various regards.
> History matters, and its subset—archaeology—matters as well.[3]

Christians traditionally have argued that faith and history are not threats
to each other, contending that the events of the Bible, even supernatural
events, take place in time and space and, though faith is required to *believe*
they happened, faith does not affect the veracity of their happening. The
significance of the historical question is summed up this way by historian
Eric Miller:

> If Jesus Christ did indeed rise from the dead on the third day,
> and if the heavens do declare the glory of God, and if someday
> we will beat our swords into plowshares, then we must summon
> the intellectual integrity, rhetorical vision, and literary verve to
> render such realities through narratives that seek to unveil this
> world — this real world, with its real past.[4]

Joseph Campbell and C. S. Lewis came to different conclusions about the role
of history regarding the biblical record, but their differences were matters
of degree and not antithetical; there was agreement as well as disagreement.
Both men maintained that the Bible records human *history* and describes
historical events of people living at a different time in a different place, but
both men also argue that myth is necessary for correctly understanding the
biblical record.

For Lewis, the incarnation and birth of Jesus Christ was a true myth
that was also a historical fact. Such an idea at first seems irreconcilable since
myth is usually not understood as events occurring in space and time. As
long as a story remains a myth it cannot be a fact; once it is determined to
be fact it is no longer myth. How Lewis was able to square this apparently
irreconcilable dilemma and how he reconciled the universal allure of myth
with the historical convictions he held concerning the gospels will be explored in this chapter.

For Joseph Campbell, although Christianity is replete with historical
events of people and events, it is an overall mythological understanding

---

3. Witherington, *Is There A Doctor In The House?*, 56.

4. Miller, "So What Is the Historian's Vocation?," 22.

that gives Christianity its power and makes it a faith that remains relevant to any age and people. According to Campbell, a historical reading of the Bible, especially of the miraculous elements and supernatural appearances of God, angels, or demons, works against the true message and purpose of the Christian faith. For the Bible to be relevant, and for the Christian faith to accomplish its original purpose and remain viable in a technological age, it is necessary to understand Christianity's mythological nature. This chapter will explain how Campbell was able to maintain a balance between the mystical, the historical, and the mythical.

CHRISTIANITY AS HISTORY: JOSEPH CAMPBELL

In response to an interviewer's observation that, "It was through the ritual that societies expressed their feelings, and we don't have many rituals anymore" Joseph Campbell answered that the ritual of the Mass in Roman Catholicism is a re-enactment of the crucifixion of Jesus Christ and the crucifixion needs to be understood in two ways. First, that divine transcendence has entered the world and accepted crucifixion. Second, the mass has to be understood on a personal level as an individual yielding of self to "the grace of a transpersonal realization."[5] Following this explanation Campbell admits, "Actually there is no doubt that Jesus lived, that he was crucified, that he died and was buried."[6]

The historical roots of the Jewish and Christian faith were not Campbell's primary concern. The possibility of a reader of the Bible not recognizing the mythical element of the Scriptures is what troubled him. He was concerned by people taking what the Bible said, including the supernatural and miraculous elements, literally, as events that happened in space and time. He believed this literal approach was detrimental to a healthy and vibrant Christian faith and it worked against the purpose of the faith. This practice of taking the symbolic literally is what Campbell often cited as his biggest criticism of traditional Christianity and it was the reason he gave for ultimately parting ways with Christianity generally and the Roman Catholic Church specifically. He stated:

> I was born and grew up a Catholic, and I was a very devoted Catholic. My beliefs, however, fell apart because the Church read and then presented its symbols in concrete terms. For a long time I had a terrible resentment against the Church and

5. Maher and Briggs, *An Open Life,* 69.
6. Ibid.

I couldn't even think of going into a Catholic Church. Then through my own study of mythology and related subjects, I began to understand what had really happened—that is, that, as it had to me, organized religion must present itself in one way to children and in another to adults. What I rejected was the literal, concrete, historical forms that were appropriate when I was young. After I realized that, I grasped better what the message was. One can do that. It is inevitable that children should be taught in purely concrete terms. But then the child grows up and realizes who Santa Claus is. He is really Daddy. So, too, we must grow in the same way in learning about God, and the institutional churches must grow in presenting the message of the symbols to adults.[7]

Campbell saw myth as the means by which a person could transition from a naïve childhood faith to an adult belief without having to give up any of the signs, symbols, meaning, and stories.

Critical to understanding Campbell's view of history in Christianity is the realization that the historicity of biblical events is not vital to him. Whether the people or events ever happened was secondary; what is important is what the reader does with the narrative.

After saying he had no doubt that Jesus lived, was crucified, died and was buried, as noted earlier Campbell also says,

But it is a little more questionable as to whether he rose again and ascended to heaven. That doesn't matter; that's the mythical implication of giving yourself; he who loses his life shall find it. And this is what we call the creative act—not hanging on, but yielding to the new creative moment.[8]

Campbell's observation that it "doesn't matter" whether Christ was resurrected and ascended to heaven is illuminating. Into an otherwise seamless Gospel narrative Campbell hesitates when what he considered historical or scientific became supernatural and miraculous.

Campbell argued that the emphasis should not be put on the historicity of the biblical events, but on the end result of the biblical narrative. What the story says to the reader, not its historical veracity. And, since a historical Jesus who lived and died does not involve the supernatural, as would a resurrection and ascension, Campbell is comfortable with a literal Jesus but doubts the resurrection and ascension; so he posits a mythical understanding of the latter events. But the question then becomes, "How

7. Campbell, *Thou Art That*, 59.
8. Maher and Briggs, *An Open Life*, 69.

one can distinguish the historicity of a physical Jesus living, being crucified, and dying, from a physical Christ rising from the grave and ascending to heaven?"

Campbell's approach presents the dilemma of the age-old question of whether the world is self-explanatory or if it is necessary for revelation from outside the present world, outside of human history, to explain it. Is a strictly historical, scientific worldview adequate to understand the universe humanity inhabits? Is it a matter of operation by what is often referred to as natural law, dependent on a divine source, or something else?

Campbell's challenge is how to make sense of the supernatural elements that comprise much of the Christian faith since such elements read as part of the historical record. The same historical Jesus who lived and died is, according to the Scripture, the same one who physically rose and ascends to heaven. But here Campbell goes only as far as a natural explanation will take him. Since he dismisses supernatural intervention, miracles as factual events are ruled out and what cannot be explained according to natural history must be relegated to either make-believe or magic, or elevated to the status of myth. He either dismisses such events on scientific grounds, or chooses to mythologize them and understand them as referring to mythological truths rather than actual events. As he explains the role of modern science,

> We can understand the problem; for we are now facing it ourselves, twenty-six hundred years later, in our own mythological inheritance of the Bible and ecclesiastical dogma. The completely unforeseen and still unpredictable findings of modern science have blasted forever the geocentric universe, where a Joshua could have caused the sun to stand at Gibeon and the moon in the valley of Ajalon, while the Creator assisted him in the slaughter of his enemies by tossing down great stones upon them from a heaven just above the clouds (Joshua 10: 12-13)—to which, twelve hundred years later, Jesus and his Virgin mother would magically ascend.[9]

In his view, science has "blasted forever" the supernatural as a way of explaining miraculous elements of the Bible. This is not only true of miraculous events in the Old Testament such as the Israelites passing through the Red Sea in the book of Exodus, or the sun standing still in Joshua, but it "blasts away" similar ideas in New Testament record as well. Concerning the supernatural events surrounding Christ's virgin birth, Campbell says, "The

---

9. Campbell, *The Mythical Dimension*, 18.

'star' at Christ's birth was real, the other events were not."[10] Regarding Jesus's ascension, Campbell says, "Jesus could not literally have gone to Heaven because there is no geographical place to go."[11]

In addressing doctrines pertinent to the Roman Catholic faith of his youth, Campbell took the same critical approach toward the supernatural. In a telephone interview dated October 1990 with Stephen and Robin Larsen, Edward Rivinus, a Foreign Service officer during 1957–1959 who hosted Campbell in his home when Campbell taught, recalled:

> We had become pretty good friends, and Joe came down once and stayed with us while he was talking at St. John's College in Annapolis. I went along to the lecture. Now, St. John's likes to be pretty avant-garde, but Joe shocked them all by talking about the difficulties of reconciling basic mythologies of Christianity, and particularly Catholicism, with some of the findings of science. And I remember the image that almost finished them off was that if the Virgin Mary (during her miraculous Assumption) had left the surface of the earth at the speed of light—the fastest speed known in this universe for a material body to move—on the feast of the Assumption, she would still be in our galaxy.[12]

As with Jesus Christ, Campbell does not deny the historical existence of a woman named Mary who gave birth to a son, Jesus, in Bethlehem. But as with Jesus's physical resurrection and ascension, Campbell denies a miraculous Assumption of Mary because it does not comport with a scientific worldview.

An interesting quotation of Scripture gives insight into Campbell's thinking concerning divine revelation as an explanation for human events. Matthew's gospel records a conversation between Jesus and the Apostle Peter regarding the full identity of Jesus. After Jesus asks Peter who people say he is, Peter repeats what he heard, "Some say John the Baptist, others say Elijah, and others Jeremiah or one of the prophets." When Jesus then presses Peter for his own conclusion, he confesses, "You are the Christ, the Son of the living God" and Jesus explains this identification as the result of divine revelation. Matthew records the conversation:

> And Jesus answered him, "Blessed are you, Simon Bar-Jonah! For flesh and blood has not revealed this to you, but my Father who is in heaven. And I tell you, you are Peter, and on this rock I will build my church, and the gates of hell shall not prevail

10. Campbell, *Thou Art That*, 61.

11. Ibid., 48.

12. Larsen and Larsen, *Joseph Campbell*, 429.

against it. I will give you the keys of the kingdom of heaven, and whatever you bind on earth shall be bound in heaven, and whatever you loose on earth shall be loosed in heaven."[13]

While some may question whether Jesus actually made this statement, and people differ over its implications, if taken at face value Jesus is attributing Peter's correct identification to something other than human insight or intuition. Jesus is saying this identification was revealed to Peter by God, his Father, who is in heaven. But Campbell takes this affirmation of revelation and rewords it so Christ is commending Peter for having a certain ignorance regarding spiritual truth. As he rewords the passage in *Thou Art That,* "Remember that he said to St. Peter, 'St. Peter, you do not understand spiritual things, I will make you the head of my church.'"[14] This presupposition against divine revelation necessitates that Campbell reword passages and events in order to explain them in a way that fits his scientific worldview.

For Campbell the history of science ran parallel to, and slowly eroded, religious belief. "For it is simply an inconvertible fact that, with the rise of modern science, the entire cosmological structure of the Bible and the Church has been destroyed and not the cosmological only but the historical as well."[15] Modern science has provided a way for readers of the Bible to separate fact from fiction and this advantage needs to be utilized by the devout so they can exercise a strong, vibrant, and intelligent faith in a technological society instead of maintaining a divisive and dying belief, or worse, trying to find a hopeless compromise that misunderstands myth and denies science. He writes:

> The Protestant theologian Rudolf Bultmann, who has been suggesting, meanwhile, what he calls a "demythologization," or rationalization, of the Christian religion, has found it necessary to hold—if there is to be any specifically "Christian" religion at all—to the Resurrection of Jesus from the grave, not as a mythic image, but as a fact—which is, of course, what has been the problem here, all along: the concretization of myth. Compare the so-called Second Letter of Peter (which is actually not of Peter but of some later hand): "For we did not follow cleverly devised myths when we made known to you the power and coming of our Lord Jesus Christ, but we were eye-witnesses of his majesty" (II Peter 1:16).

---

13. Matt 16:17–19.
14. Campbell, *Thou Art That*, 75.
15. Campbell, *The Flight of the Wild Gander*, 225.

One can only suggest to these stubborn gentlemen that if, instead of insisting that their own mythology is history, they would work the other way and dehistoricize their mythology, they might recover contact with the spiritual possibilities of this century and salvage from what must otherwise be inevitable discard whatever may still be of truth to life in their religion.[16]

For Campbell, the problem has been the Church trying to hold on to a literal and historical reading of all the Bible, including the miraculous, when the solution is to use the scientific method to identify what is natural from what is clearly symbolic. But since its inception, the Church has hurt itself by resisting such accommodation. He states:

The gradual, irresistible, steady development of this new realization of the wonder of the world and of man's place and possibilities within it, against every instrument of resistance of the Church—resistance even to the present hour—has been, and continues to be, the fruit of the labors of a remarkably small number of men with of the wit and courage to oppose authority with accurate observation.[17]

Campbell includes among the earliest of this "small number of men" Adelard of Bath (c. 1080—c. 1152) and identifies two moments of climax as the publication of Copernicus' *De revolutionibus oebium coelestium* (1543) and Darwin's *Origin of Species* (1859). What these few men did to change worldviews and the understanding of religious belief cannot be overstated. As Campbell observes:

For in the broadest view of the history of mankind, it can be said without exaggeration that, with the rise of the modern scientific method of research in the sixteenth and seventeenth centuries, and development in the eighteenth, nineteenth, and twentieth of the power-driven machine, the human race was brought across a culture threshold of no less magnitude and import than that of the invention of agriculture in the ninth or eighth millennium B.C. and the rise of the earliest cities and city states in the fourth.[18]

But, according to Campbell, these shifts in thinking have been resisted by a Church that fears for its own welfare, for if the Church which has existed

---

16. Ibid., 224–25.

17. Ibid., 225.

18. Ibid., 225–26; italics in original.

for 2,000 years was to admit what is obvious to everyone else, that what it maintained as history was myth, it would cease to exist.

But to Campbell such an ending of the traditional church would be liberating, enabling the church to be in modern society what it originally was in more primitive cultures. Though such an evolution of religion is a natural process, one that takes place all the time in every area of life including the religious, Christianity has remained one of the few faiths to resist this inevitable process. He writes:

> Furthermore, just as the mythologies and rituals of the primitive hunting and root-gathering tribes of the earlier million-or-so years of human life had to give place to those that arose of the high bronze and iron age civilizations, so also, now, must those of our outdated bronze and iron age heritages give place to forms not yet imagined. And that they are already giving place surely is clear. For, firstly, in so far as the Waste Land condition recognized by the poets of the Middle Ages persists within the Christian fold—where the sense of the sacred is still officially dissociated from this earth and its life (*mythic dissociation*) and the possibility of establishing a *relationship* with ultimate ends is still supposed to be achievable only through participation in the faith and rites of Christ's Church (*social identification*)—the situation has worsened, not improved, since, for many, not only is the earth (as taught) mere dust, but the claims of the church and its book to supernatural authorship has been destroyed absolutely and forever.[19]

Campbell argues that, from its inception, the Church has been opposed to accepting the discoveries and changes that go on around it, discoveries that ironically its very members accept in other areas of their lives. If such openness and acceptance could move from the congregational level to those in authority, the Church could once again undergo a much-needed reformation.[20]

In spite of his pessimism, Campbell remained hopeful that the Church would someday be able to distinguish between the historical and symbolic. But such a shift in thinking would need to come from outside the organized Church, from among individuals who, alone or in small groups, would be humble enough to know their place in the universe but courageous enough

---

19. Campbell, *The Flight of the Wild Gander*, 226; italics in original.

20. It is worth nothing that, post-Campbell, a school of thought has flourished arguing Christianity supports rather than opposes science and that by giving it a foundation and platform Christianity has allowed science to flourish in the West. See Hannon, *The Genesis of Science.*

to venture outside Church walls and dogma to make sense of the wonder of life. He writes:

> "Man is condemned," as Sartre says, "to be free." However, not all, even today, are of that supine sort that must have their life values given them, cried at them from the pulpits and other mass media of the day. For there is, in fact, in quiet places, a great deal of deep spiritual quest and finding now in progress in this world, outside the sanctified social centers, beyond their purview and control: in small groups, here and there, and more often, more typically (as anyone who looks about may learn), by ones and twos, there entering the forest at those points which they themselves have chosen, where they see it to be most dark, and there is no beaten way or path.[21]

So religion has a future but it lies outside of the organized church.

CHRISTIANITY AS HISTORY: C. S. LEWIS

C. S. Lewis was an unapologetic supernaturalist concerning Christianity and history. As he explained it, "[W]e admit that history . . . is a story written by the finger of God."[22] Lewis had no reservations that a divine being was overseeing all human history, and as such, his views stand in stark opposition to Campbell's.

History, and Christianity as history, were topics Lewis spent much time considering and explaining. In an October 1950 article entitled "Historicism," he expounds on the many ways history can be understood and suggests six approaches:

> We must remind ourselves that the word *History* has several senses. It may mean the total content of time: past, present, and future. It may mean the content of the past only, but still the total content of the past, the past as it really was in all its teeming riches. Thirdly, it may mean so much of the past as it is discoverable from surviving evidence. Fourthly, it may mean so much as has been actually discovered by historians working, so to speak, 'at the face,' the pioneer historians never heard of by the public who make the actual discoveries. Fifthly, it may mean that portion, and that version, of the matter so discovered which has been worked up by great historical writers. (This is perhaps the most popular sense: *history* usually means what you read

---

21. Campbell, *The Flight of the Wild Gander*, 226.

22. Lewis, "Historicism," in *Christian Reflections*, 105.

when you are reading Gibbon or Mommsen, or the Master of Trinity.) Sixthly, it may mean that vague, composite picture of the past which floats, rather hazily, in the mind of the ordinary educated man.[23]

It was in the first sense, the total content of past, present, and future that Lewis defined history as a story written by the finger of God.

In this essay, Lewis expresses concern with people who confuse the first definition (the total content of time) with the sixth (the vague composite picture of the past) and conclude they can discover the meaning of historical events within the historical process. "What I mean by a Historicist is a man who asks me to accept his account of the inner meaning of history on the grounds of his learning and genius,"[24] an idea Lewis considered an illusion claiming that "Historicists are, at the very best, wasting their time."[25] Although Historicism is not the concern of this book, Lewis's criticism of it sheds light on his understanding of history. And while Lewis had no concern with someone who claimed to know the meaning of history based on a vision or outside revelation (a different topic entirely), he found the notion that someone had the omniscience to explain the express purpose of an event based on nothing more than observation and human understanding indefensible. So an acceptance of studying history based on outside revelation is critical to his view of Christianity and history.

Any disagreement between Campbell and Lewis regarding Christianity and history centers on the supernatural or miraculous. As seen earlier, Campbell explained the miraculous in terms of myth. Miracle stories are fine for children whose "make believe" world of imagination does not question angelic appearances or resurrections from the dead. But as children mature, another and more scientific approach is necessary to explain the supernatural. Children understand concepts best in concrete terms and so the Bible stories must be explained to children in literal, historical terms, but as they mature, it is critical to have the child transition from the literal to the symbolic. As Campbell admits, it was this lack of a transition, later remedied by the discovery of myth, that shipwrecked his Roman Catholic faith. As observed earlier he admits "My beliefs, however, fell apart because the Church read and then presented its symbols in concrete terms."[26] If someone had explained to a young Joseph Campbell that Santa Claus was

---

23. Ibid.; italics in original.

24. Ibid., 100.

25. Ibid., 101.

26. Campbell, *Thou Art That*, 59.

Daddy and physical resurrection meant a new beginning, he might have remained a devout Roman Catholic.

Lewis approached the intervention of the supernatural in history in very different terms. To believe in the miraculous was not a matter of maturity or intelligence; it was a matter of presuppositions. One could accept the miraculous in history by simply being open-minded and not prejudiced against them in advance. Lewis writes in an essay entitled "Miracles" of the nature of miracles:

> The experience of a miracle in fact requires two conditions. First we must believe in a normal stability of nature, which means we must recognize that the data offered by our senses recur in regular patterns. Secondly, we must believe in some reality beyond nature. When both beliefs are held, and not till then, we can approach with an open mind the various reports which claims that this super- or extra-natural reality has sometimes invaded and disturbed the sensuous content of space and time which makes our 'natural' world. The belief in such a supernatural reality itself can neither be proved nor disproved by experience. The arguments for its existence are metaphysical, and to me conclusive. They turn on the fact that even to think and act in the natural world we have to assume something beyond it and even assume that we partly belong to that something. In order to think we must claim for our own reasoning a validity which is not credible if our own thought is merely a function of our brain, and our brains a by-product of irrational physical processes. In order to act, above the level of mere impulse, we must claim a similar validity for our judgments of good and evil.[27]

Lewis did not find it difficult to believe an outside being could interrupt the normal routine of life if such a being first created the routines. One simply had to leave room for the possibility and, in fact, to his way of thinking, one *has* to leave room for the possibility simply because it "can neither be proved or disproved by experience."

But if anyone should object by saying such a subjective approach demands scientific evidence to "prove" the supernatural, Lewis responds that such evidence is everywhere for anyone willing to see it, because it is throughout human history and appears all the time. He argues:

> If we frankly accept this position and then turned to the evidence, we find, of course, that accounts of the supernatural meets us on every side. History is full of them—often in the same documents

27. Lewis, "Miracles," in *God in the Dock*, 27.

which we accept wherever they do not report miracles. Respectable missionaries report them not infrequently. The whole Church of Rome claims their continued occurrence. Intimate conversation elicits from almost every acquaintance at least one episode in his life which is what we would call 'queer' or 'rum.' No doubt most stories of miracles are unreliable; but then, as anyone can see by reading the papers, so are most stories of all events. Each story must be taken on its merits: what one must not do is to rule out the supernatural as the one impossible explanation. Thus you may disbelieve in the Mons Angels because you cannot find a sufficient number of sensible people who say they saw them. But if you found a sufficient number, it would, in my view, be unreasonable to explain this by collective hallucination. For we know enough of psychology to know that spontaneous unanimity in hallucination is very improbable, and we do not know enough of the supernatural to know that a manifestation of angels is equally improbable. The supernatural theory is the less improbable of the two. When the Old Testament says that Sennacherib's invasion was stopped by angels, and Herodotus says it was stopped by a lot of mice who came and ate up all the bow strings of his army, an open-minded man will be on the side of the angels. Unless you start by begging the question, there is nothing intrinsically unlikely in the existence of angels nor any action ascribed to them. But mice just don't do these things.[28]

Lewis's observation that "History is full of [miracles]—often in the same documents which we accept wherever they do not report miracles" is critical when considering Christianity in history since the Bible narrates such unusual events as part of normal everyday occurrences. Lewis could refer to the Apostle Paul's argument that Christ in his resurrected body "appeared to more than five hundred brothers at one time, most of whom are still alive"[29] as an example of such historical evidence for the miracle. Such an invitation is in keeping with the normal process of verifying an event.

A common approach to explaining away the appearance of miracles is the people living in the days of Christ and the early church were primitive compared to those in a technological age. Such people simply could

---

28. Ibid., 27–28. On August 22–23, 1914, the first major engagement of the British Expeditionary Force in WWI occurred at the Battle of Mons, Belgium, where German forces were pushed back by a smaller number of British soldiers. Though the British suffered heavy causalities and were forced to retreat the next day, this victory led to a popular legend that angels had protected the British troops.

29. 1 Cor 15:6.

not understand how the laws of nature worked, so when they came upon something unusual that they could not explain they resorted to supernatural intervention. But Lewis found this a less credible explanation than the miraculous and, in his words, it was nonsense. He writes:

> It is said that our ancestors, taking the supernatural for granted and greedy of wonders, read the miraculous into events that were really not miracles. And in a sense I grant it. That is to say, I think that just as our preconceptions would prevent us from apprehending miracles if they really occurred, so their preconceptions would lead them to imagine miracles even if they did not occur. In the same way, the doting man will think his wife faithful when she is not and the suspicious man will not think her faithful when she is: the question of her actual fidelity remains, meanwhile, to be settled, if at all, on other grounds. But there is one thing often said about our ancestors which we must *not* say. We must not say 'They believed in miracles because they did not know the Laws of Nature.' This is nonsense. When St. Joseph discovered that his bride was pregnant, he was 'minded to put her away.' He knew enough biology for that. Otherwise, of course he would not have regarded pregnancy as a proof of infidelity. When he accepted the Christian explanation, he regarded it as a miracle precisely because he knew enough of the Laws of Nature to know that this was a suspension of them. When the disciples saw Christ walking on the water they were frightened: they would not have been frightened unless they had known the laws of Nature and known that this was an exception. If a man had no conception of a regular water in Nature, then of course he could not notice departures from that order: just as a dunce who does not understand the normal metre of a poem is also unconscious of the poet's variations from it. Nothing is wonderful except the abnormal and nothing is abnormal until we have grasped the norm. Complete ignorance of the laws of Nature would preclude the perception of the miraculous just as rigidly as complete disbelief in the supernatural precludes it, perhaps even more so. For while the materialist would have at least to explain miracles away, the man wholly ignorant of Nature would simply not notice them.[30]

Lewis found it not only reasonable to see miracles occurring in history, but such an approach was the only way to have all the evidence hang together; otherwise one had to determine what is history and what is not based on

---

30. Lewis, "Miracles," in *God in the Dock*, 26–27.

a criteria of human intellect fraught with even more difficulties than the miraculous.

Another argument Lewis makes regarding Christianity and history is that, since all history is superintended by God (while allowing for human action and freedom of the will), miraculous events are simply the occasional physical manifestations of a deity who continually operates the "normal" working of the universe. If someone is open to the possibility of a deity, then miracles come as no surprise; they happen all the time. Lewis writes:

> There is an activity of God displayed throughout creation, a wholesale activity let us say which men refuse to recognize. The miracles done by God incarnate, living as a man in Palestine, performed the very same things as this wholesale activity, but at a different speed and a smaller scale. One of their chief purposes is that men, having seen a thing done by personal power on the small scale, may recognize, when they see the same thing done on a larger scale, that the power behind it is also a personal—is indeed the very same person who lived among us two thousand years ago. The miracles in fact are a retelling in small letters of the very same story which is written across the whole world in letters too large for some of us to see. Of that larger script part is already visible, part is still unsolved. In other words, some of the miracles do locally what God has already done universally: others do locally what He has not yet done, but will do. In that sense, and from our human point of view, some are reminders and others prophecies.[31]

In other words, if one is willing to accept the existence of a deity outside of the material universe, then accepting anything that deity does is not only logical but reasonable. But as Lewis argues, denying such an existence is not a matter of evidence or intelligence, it's a deliberate and willful refusal to believe in it or to attribute the activities of the deity to some other cause. He argues:

> God creates the vine and teaches it to draw up water by its roots and, with the aid of the sun, to turn that water into a juice which will ferment and take on certain qualities. Thus every year, from Noah's time till ours, God turns water into wine. That, men fail to see. Either like the pagans they refer the process to some finite spirit, Bacchus or Dionysus: or else, like the moderns, they attribute real and ultimate causality to the chemical and other material phenomena which are all that our senses can discover

31. Ibid., 29.

in it. But when Christ at Cana makes water into wine, the mask is off. The miracle has only half its effect if it only convinces us that Christ is God: it will have its full effect if whenever we see a vineyard or drink a glass of wine we remember that here works He who sat the wedding party in Cana. Every year God makes a little corn into much corn: the seed is sown and there is an increase, and men, according to the fashion of their age, say 'It is Ceres, it is Adonis, it is the Corn King,' or else 'It is the laws of Nature.' The close-up, the translation, of this annual wonder is the feeding of the five thousand. Bread is not made there of nothing. Bread is not made of stones, as the Devil once suggested to Our Lord in vain. A little bread is made into much bread.[32]

The miraculous is not unbelievable to someone who knows the being behind the miracle. There is a family resemblance, or "style," evident in how miracles are performed. As Lewis observes:

The Son will do nothing but what he sees the Father do. There is, so to speak, a family *style*. The miracles of healing fall into the same pattern. This is sometimes obscured for us by the somewhat magical view we tend to take of ordinary medicine. The doctors themselves do not take this view. The magic is not in the medicine but in the patient's body. What the doctor does is to stimulate Nature's functions in the body, or to remove hindrances. In a sense though we speak for convenience of healing a cut, every cut heals itself; no dressing will make skin grow over a cut on a corpse. That same mysterious energy which we called gravitational when it steers the planets and biochemical when it heals a body is the efficient cause of all recoveries, and if God exists, that energy, directly or indirectly, is His. All who are cured are cured by Him, the healer within. But once He did it visibly, a Man meeting a man. Where He does not work within in this mode, the organism dies. Hence Christ's one miracle of destruction is also in harmony with God's wholesale activity. His bodily hand held out in symbolic wrath blasted a single fig tree; but no tree died that year in Palestine, or any year, or in any land, or even ever will, save because He has done something, or (more likely) ceased to do something, to it.[33]

Perceived miracles in human history must be explained as something other than supernatural only if one assumes nothing supernatural exists and to

---

32. Ibid., 29–30.

33. Ibid., 30; italics in original.

this Lewis would ask, "How can one know?" But if one begins by granting the possibility of a known, though not fully understood, supernatural realm, then miracles come as no surprise.

Lewis believed the biblical record of Christianity took place in history and that nothing that happened in the world of the Bible took place outside of human history. The single loaf of bread used to feed more than five thousand people and recorded in four different gospel accounts[34] was an actual loaf of bread, as real as the people it fed and the hillside on which they sat. There was no illusion or sleight of hand, nor were the thousands of eyewitnesses confused or mislead concerning what they experienced. Lewis does not deny that one cannot feed over five-thousand people from a single loaf of bread, but he would contend that the unusual element in the event wasn't in the people's perception, it was in the person distributing the bread. His nature made what he did remarkable only to those who did not identify who he was.

While Lewis did not agree that all narratives in the Bible were historical,[35] he understood the separation often made between history and the miraculous as a relatively new phenomenon that could be attributed to the influence of the Renaissance and later to the scientific revolution. He cited two reasons why it was, in his words, "modern people" who were skeptical of the miraculous.

> In the first place, modern people have an almost aesthetic dislike of miracles. Admitting that God can, they doubt if He would. To violate the laws He Himself has imposed on his creation seems to them arbitrary, clumsy, a theatrical device only fit to impress savages—a solecism against the grammar of the universe. In the second place, many people confuse the laws of nature with the laws of thought and imagine that their reversal or suspension would be a contradiction in terms—as if the resurrection of the dead were the same sort of thing as two and two making five.[36]

The problem wasn't a matter of the evidence or intellect. It was a matter of the heart or will. One could believe if one chose to.

In closing, C. S. Lewis was not interested in proving or even defending a Christian faith in which supernatural events took place in history; he was convinced they did take place. Rather, his concern was with those

34. Matt 14:21; Mark 6:44; Luke 9:14; John 6:10.

35. "The universally admitted unhistoricity (I do not say, of course, of falsity) of at least some narratives in Scripture (the parables), which may well extend also to Jonah and Job" (Hooper, *The Collected Letters of C. S. Lewis*, 3:1045).

36. Lewis, "Miracles," in *God in the Dock*, 27–28.

who disagreed and tried to explain away such events, for he felt they were the ones who lacked good explanations for what seemed to him reasonable. "History is full of [miracles]—often in the same documents which we accept wherever they do not report miracles."[37]

Lewis was not naïve; he realized one could not be argued into believing what one concluded could not be true. No matter how much evidence or how convincing and logical the arguments, people who refuse to simply believe the record will seek to explain the miraculous in ways that comport with a natural, materialistic universe. In his essay "Miracles," Lewis opens with an illustration of one such person:

> I have known only one person in my life who claimed to have seen a ghost. It was a woman; and the interesting thing is that she disbelieved in the immortality of the soul before seeing the ghost and still disbelieves after having seen it. She thinks it was a hallucination. In other words, seeing is not believing. This is the first thing to get clear in talking about miracles. Whatever experiences we may have, we shall not regard them as miraculous if we already hold a philosophy which excludes the supernatural. Any event which is claimed as a miracle is, in the last resort, an experience received from the senses; and the senses are not infallible. We can always say we have been the victims of an illusion; if we disbelieve in the supernatural this is what we always shall say. Hence, whether miracles have really ceased or not, they would certainly appear to cease in Western Europe as materialism became the popular creed. For let us make no mistake. If the end of the world appeared in all the literal trappings of the Apocalypse, if the modern materialist saw with his own eyes the heavens rolled up and the great white throne appearing, if he had the sensation of being himself hurled into the Lake of Fire, he would continue forever, in that lake itself, to regard his experience as an illusion and to find the explanation of it in psycho-analysis, or cerebral pathology. Experience by itself proves nothing. If a man doubts whether he is dreaming or waking, no experiment can solve his doubt, since every experiment may itself be part of the dream. Experience proves this, or that, or nothing, according to the preconceptions we bring to it.[38]

C. S. Lewis believed one could not separate Christianity from history any more than one could separate any human event from history, for Christian history was human history.

37. Ibid., 27.
38. Ibid., 25–26.

Comparative Views of Mystery

As with most of the world's great religions, Christianity consists of both the natural and supernatural and when these two combine they result in mystery. Without supernatural mysteries there would be no Christianity as traditionally understood. Mysteries of the Christian faith are many and include such things as the doctrine of the trinity, the incarnation, the power of prayer, eternal existence after death, and the spiritual realm of demons and angels. Irrespective of how much one believes such things exist or not, the Bible assumes their existence in a supernatural realm and manifested in the natural world.

To practice a religion one must deal with its mysteries and the role they play in the believer's life and belief system, understand what they mean, and be able to explain them to someone who does not adhere to the same beliefs. In response to this need, religions typically offer an explanation for their specific mysteries. For instance, in the *Catechism of the Catholic Church* one reads,

> Liturgical catechesis aims to initiate people into the mystery of Christ (It is "mystagogy.") by proceeding from the visible to the invisible, from the sign to the thing signified, from the "sacra-ments" to the "mysteries." Such catechesis is to be presented by local and regional catechisms. This Catechism, which aims to serve the whole Church in all the diversity of her rites and cultures, will present what is fundamental and common to the whole Church in the liturgy as mystery and as celebration . . . and then the seven sacraments and the sacramentals.[39]

The Roman Catholic Church makes no apologies for the mysteries of the Christian faith, instead it assumes them and provides the initiate with an in-troduction to them in a way that maintains the tension of cultural diversity with the need for unity within the religion as a whole. It is hard to imagine Roman Catholicism without mystery and a means to explain it.

The etymology of "mystery" traces its meaning to the classical Latin *mystērium*, or secret. In post-classical Latin, the word also refers to mys-tical religious truths. By the second century the church father Tertullian used the term in relation to Christian rites and by the fourth century it was used for the elements in the Eucharist. The ancient Greek term, μυστήριον, meaning mystery or secret, was extended to cover secret rites and the imple-ments used in such rites. In Hellenistic Greek, the word stood for the secrets

---

39. *Catechism of the Catholic Church*, 279.

revealed by God or mystical truths, Christian rites, and a sacrament. The root of the Greek word, μύειν, means to close (the lips or eyes).[40]

If one simply dismisses religion, there is no need to explain the mystical; it is nothing more than an idea, a mistaken notion, or something made up to make one feel good or empowered by being able to explain what others cannot understand. But if one takes religion seriously, then mystery must have meaning. If mystery is thought to be a necessary part of human existence, it has to have a purpose.

One common approach to explaining the supernatural events surrounding the center of Christianity, the life of Jesus Christ, is evident in the opinion of New Testament scholar Erich Dinkler. After declaring "There is no disputing the historical roots of Christianity . . . Today there is agreement that we have Christian and non-Christian sources enough to reject the doubts of Jesus' historicity," Dinkler goes on to observe, "On the other hand, nonhistorical features were added to his life, so that an increasing tendency can be seen to emphasize the supernatural and miraculous aspects."[41] According to Dinkler, Jesus of Nazareth was a historical person who was portrayed as someone who performed miraculous, "nonhistorical," events that no mortal could do, including rising from the dead after three days in the grave. How can such events be explained? Dinkler concludes they were "added to his life" by the gospel authors. Such an approach allows a belief in the clear historical evidence for the person of Jesus Christ while explaining the seamless narrative that has this same historical Jesus performing acts that are mysterious, unexplainable, and impossible from a scientific perspective. But opinions such as Dinkler's are only conclusions; they tell *how* the details got into the story, but they do not explain *why* such features were added to the story. It was explaining these supernatural events that challenged Campbell and Lewis. Both men acknowledged the historicity of Jesus Christ and both men admitted that miraculous events were attributed to him. But the men differed on why the stories were in the gospels. Campbell, like Dinkler, understood such events as added to the life of Jesus while to Lewis such events were simply part of his human existence.

What did Joseph Campbell and C. S. Lewis think of the mystery of Christianity as presented in its narrative and doctrine as recorded in the biblical record? Both men were raised in a Christian home and were familiar with the inscrutability of mystery that faces every believer concerning the supernatural. For a period of time each man abandoned the faith and became critical of its mysteries and later came to have a newfound

---

40. *Oxford English Dictionary*, s.v. "mystery."

41. Dinkler, "Myth in the NT," in *Interpreter's Dictionary of the Bible,* 488.

appreciation for its teachings. How did they explain what they once found so unbelievable?

For thousands of years, learned men and women have believed in things that cannot be explained by the normal laws of nature. A sea opens up to let people pass through,[42] fire comes down from heaven to burn up enemy soldiers,[43] an angelic being suddenly appears to communicate a message then vanishes,[44] a dead child is raised to life and returned to his parents,[45] a demon carries on a conversation through a possessed individual and then is cast out,[46] and a fig tree withers in a moment in response to nothing more than a command to do so.[47] And what is more remarkable is that each of these events is recorded as witnessed by dozens of people as if they actually happened, and not as hyperbole or inserted later to teach some lesson. Both Campbell and Lewis were aware of these challenges, but their explanations differed greatly.

Christianity as Mystery: Joseph Campbell

In his book *Joseph Campbell: An Introduction*, Robert Segal discusses Campbell's knowledge of Jungian and Freudian psychology and concludes that Campbell ". . . is a mystic. His interpretation remains psychological, and his brand of psychology is far more Jungian than Freudian, but it is finally not Jungian."[48] Campbell's lifelong study of psychology, religion, myth, and human history caused him to realize that mysteries abound and even the most learned individual has to be comfortable with elements of life that cannot be explained by science, natural laws, and materialism.

In one of his more extensive treatments of myth and religion, *Thou Art That: Transforming Religious Metaphor*, Campbell explains the four functions of myth and he begins and ends with the importance of mystery, an overwhelming mystery.

> I view traditional mythologies as serving four functions. The first function is that of reconciling consciousness to the preconditions of its own existence—that is, of aligning waking

42. Exod 14.
43. 2 Kgs 1.
44. Luke 1.
45. Luke 8:49–56.
46. Matt 9:31–35.
47. Matt 21:17–19.
48. Segal, *Joseph Campbell*, 58.

consciousness to the *mysterium tremendum* of this universe, *as it is . . .*

The second function of a traditional mythology is interpretive, to present a consistent image of the order of the cosmos . . .

The third function of a traditional mythology is to validate and support a specific moral order, the order of the society of which that mythology arose. All mythologies come to us in the field of a certain specific culture and must speak to us through the language and symbols of that culture. In traditional mythologies, the notion is really that the moral order is organically related to or somehow of a piece with the cosmic order . . .

The fourth function of traditional mythology is to carry the individual through the various stages and crises of life—that is, to help persons grasp the unfolding of life with integrity. This wholeness means that individuals will experience significant events, from birth through midlife to death, as in accord with, first, themselves, and, secondly, with their culture, as well as, thirdly, the universe, and, lastly, with that *mysterium tremendum* beyond themselves in all things.[49]

Campbell never professed he could explain all aspects of myth or the part mystery plays in religion in general or in Christianity in particular. To do so would be self-defeating for the mysteries of faith have their own function and power. In fact what makes myth a necessary part of any belief system, including Christianity, is that it serves to connect mystery with individual consciousness. This is myth's primary function. He writes:

Myth has many functions. The first we might term mystical, in that myth makes a connection between our waking consciousness and the whole mystery of the universe. That is its cosmological function. It allows us to see ourselves in relationship to nature, as when we speak of Father Sky and Mother Earth. There is also a sociological function for myth, in that it supports and validates a certain social and moral order for us. The story of the ten commandments given to Moses by God at Mount Sinai is example of this. Lastly, myth has a psychological function, in that it offers us a way of passing through, and dealing with, the various stages from birth to death.[50]

This awareness or consciousness of existence and of our proper place in the universe is a question, perhaps *the* question, humanity has sought to answer. And while the answer remains elusive—one might call it a

49. Campbell, *Thou Art That*, 2–4; italics in original.

50. Ibid., 103.

mystery—religions offer answers and myth is the means by which people can understand and articulate those answers. "This I would regard as the essentially religious function of mythology—that is, the mystical function, which represents the discovery and recognition of the dimension of the mystery of being."[51]

As he studied, Campbell came to realize aspects of certain myths throughout the world's religions that often conflicted with others. This resulted in a need for the specifics of religion to be in subjection to universality of myth and for people to have a greater exposure to the myths outside of their own religious context as a way of better understanding personal identity and the transcending mystery of belief. In an essay entitled "Comparative Mythology as an Introduction to Cross-Cultural Studies," he illustrates one such conflict and describes how he resolves it:

> In the Orient, the gods do not stand as ultimate terms, ultimate ends, substantial beings, to be sought and regarded in and for themselves. They are more like metaphors, to serve as guides, pointing beyond themselves and leading one to an experience of one's own identity with a mystery that transcends them. I have found that the approach through Freud and Jung greatly helps to make this point clear to students brought up in the mythology of Yahweh—a jealous god, who would hold men to himself and turned mankind away from the Tree of Immortality, instead of leading us to it. Such a guide in the Orient would be regarded as a deluding idol. In fact, heaven itself and our desire for its joys are regarded there as the last barrier, the last obstacle to release, to be transcended. And to escort my students beyond heaven and hell, I take them first to India and then China and Japan.[52]

Campbell contends there is a transcendent mystery that the believer can experience which will enable him or her to find an identity in the cosmos. But in this case the gods of the Orient conflict with the god of Judaism, Yahweh. The gods of the Orient are little more than guides while the god of Israel is an end in himself. To circumvent this dilemma of competing deities and to experience the "transcendent mystery," Campbell integrates the work of Freud and Jung and advocates a comparison of religions. This results not only in a greater understanding and tolerance of different religions; but enabling the individual to achieve his full potential and recognize his proper place in the universe and the kind of life he should live.

---

51. Ibid., 3.
52. Campbell, *The Mythic Dimension*, 6.

According to Campbell, one of the greatest mysteries of religion is the mystery of self. Human beings are the most wonderful and complicated creatures on earth and, as beings with the capacity to believe in a transcendent "other," myth and religion are essentially one and the same; that is, myth has a religious function to serve and that function is to . . .

> awaken and maintain in the person an experience of awe, humility, and respect in recognition of that ultimate mystery that transcends every name and form, "from which," as we read in the Upanisads [sic], "words turn back." In recent decades, theology has often concentrated on a literary exercise in the explanation of archaic texts that are made up of historically conditioned, ambiguous names, incidence, sayings, and actions, all of which are attributed to "the ineffable." Faith, we might say, in old-fashioned Scripture or faith in the latest science belongs equally at this time to those alone who as yet have no idea of how mysterious, really, is the mystery of themselves.[53]

This mystery of self is what religion and myth can help identify, and for those with no religion myth can still serve that purpose since it ties all humanity together with common questions, quests, and goals. In fact, Campbell argues that the religious may be at a disadvantage in understanding such mysteries precisely because they think they can comprehend them and so end up robbing the experience of its mystery. Religion can get in the way of experiencing mystery;

> There can be no real progress in understanding how myths function until we understand and allow metaphoric symbols to address, in their own unmodified way, the inner levels of our consciousness. The continuing confusion about the nature and function of metaphor is one of the major obstacles—often placed in our path by organized religions that focus shortsightedly on concrete times and places—to our capacity to experience mystery.[54]

These obstacles posed by organized religion present some of the greatest threats to understanding myth and the mysteries of life since they attempt to explain what is better left unexplained. Mystery is to be experienced, not necessarily understood. Campbell explains:

> The question sometimes arises as to whether the experience of mystery and transcendence is more available to those who

---

53. Campbell, *Thou Art That*, 13.
54. Ibid., 8.

have undergone some kind of religious and spiritual training, for whom, as I have said, it has all been named completely. It may be less available to them precisely because they have got it all named in the book. One way to deprive yourself of an experience is indeed to expect it. Another is to have a name for it before you have the experience. Carl Jung said that one of the functions of religion is to protect us against the religious experience. That is because in formal religion, it is all concretized and formulated. But, by its nature, such an experience is one that only you can have. As soon as you classify it with anybody else's, it loses its character. A preconceived set of concepts catches the experience, cutting it short so that it does not come directly to us. Ornate and detailed religions protect us against an exploding mystical experience that would be too much for us.[55]

Mystery, by its nature, must be unknowable, unexplainable, and only experienced or it no longer remains a mystery. This definition gives Eastern religions a certain affinity to mystery since, unlike Christianity, they do not emphasize or insist on historically experienced events.

But the challenge with Christianity is its contention that there are not only mysteries in a metaphysical, spiritual, or allegorical sense, but that the creator of all matter is a being in whom "we live and move and have our being"[56] and this being was incarnated and manifested the supernatural in the natural world of time and space. For Campbell this poses a problem,

> Jesus dies, is resurrected, and goes to Heaven. This metaphor expresses something religiously mysterious. Jesus could not literally have gone to Heaven because there is no geographical place to go. Elijah went up into the heavens in a chariot, we are told, but we are not to take this statement as a description of the literal journey.[57]

Since Campbell claims such a physical ascension to a literal heaven impossible, he interprets the record of this event as expressing "something religiously mysterious" and relegates it to metaphor and, in doing so, sets up a paradigm of two kinds of people:

> These are spiritual events described in metaphor. There seem to be only two kinds of people: Those who think that metaphors are facts, and those who know that they are not facts. Those who know they are not facts are what we call "atheists," and those

55. Ibid., 14.
56. Acts 17:28.
57. Campbell, *Thou Art That*, 48.

who think they are facts are "religious." Which will really get
the message?[58]

One is either an atheist or religious advocate based on how one explains
mysteries that defy natural laws. Campbell's use of the more subjunctive
"think" to describe those who understand metaphors as facts versus the
word "know" for those who understand metaphors are not facts makes
his assumptions clear. But Campbell was not comfortable with this either/
or dilemma, finding it too rigid and condemnatory as well as thinking it
unnecessary, since both extremes were missing the common ground of all
beliefs found in myth.

At age twenty-eight Campbell was struggling to find a way to balance
the spiritual and mystical aspects of life which he believed existed with the
material and natural realities so often set in opposition to a mystical, unseen
world. In response to this challenge he spent weeks thinking through his
philosophical approach and cross-examining himself on what he believed
about life, humanity, religion, and happiness. He constructed a credo that
would guide his thinking throughout his life. It consisted of six principles:

1) For us the universe must be an aesthetic end-in-itself. (We are to respond to its wonder and mystery, but to attempt to manipulate the
gods is out.)

2) Experience, and not the church, is our most dependable authority.

3) We are mortal fragments of man—experiments toward the Super-
man—and every act or speech of ours will live forever in the larger self.

4) To exist is to be in process.

5) Happiness lies in bringing all of our powers to wrest from each changing situation its full and unique meaning.

6) Integration of self is my major business; it is based upon a diligent attention to values.[59]

While this creed lacked doctrinal specifics and was vague on goals, it did
serve as a set of guidelines to keep Campbell from slipping off into the kind
of dogma that he saw as responsible for much of the religious turmoil in the
world. Each of these guidelines invites brief analysis.

The first concept would later develop into what Campbell understood
to be the first function of mythology, to awaken a sense of wonder and awe.
Humanity stands as a spectator, a responder, to the great mystery of the
universe. However one understands the "gods," humans are lesser creatures

58. Ibid.

59. Larsen and Larsen, *Joseph Campbell*, 160–61.

and so are students and not teachers of them. It is worth noticing that even though by this time Campbell has decided to abandon his Catholic upbringing and to discard much of its religious dogma, he nevertheless speaks of life in terms of wonder, mystery, and the gods.

His second and third tenets clarify where the final authority lies for Campbell. Instead of an outside source, such as a church or the Bible, Campbell's last word is self and how one interprets the experience of the moment. The individual self is sufficiently able to determine truth from error and reality from symbol in order to find happiness and decide the best course for life.

His fourth and fifth principles remind us that change is the one constant and happiness can be found only by accepting change and using it to one's advantage. The exigencies of life are such that the best one can do is find deeper meaning in any given moment—birth, pain, joy, sorrow, death—and realize that deeper principles are at work beyond the surface. To some individuals these are the workings of a loving and sovereign creator,[60] while to others it's the natural order of the universe, but both individuals must make the effort to see beyond the moment and discover the mystery that is life.

Campbell's final principle is integration based on personal values. Each individual must incorporate what he knows with what he experiences and then seek to find from the experience how to be a better person. As he wrote in a personal note, "I don't want to write about books, what I want is life—Life and Ideas."[61] Since no one can speak with authority about things outside and beyond experience, they must remain a mystery. "Who then, may speak to you, or to any of us, of the being or nonbeing of God, unless by implication to point beyond his words and himself and all he knows, or can tell, toward the transcendent, the experience of mystery."[62]

The challenges presented by the distinctive mysteries of religion and Campbell's desire to find commonality among the faiths is a tension found throughout his writings. He admits such distinctives, exist, but he always seeks a way to harmonize the unique qualities. For instance, when writing about the discipline of meditation he observes:

> There are two orders of meditation: discursive meditation and ordered meditation. In discursive meditation, such as that advocated by Ignatius Loyola, you consider some religious

60. "And we know that for those who love God all things work together for good, for those who are called according to his purpose" (Rom 8:28).

61. Larsen and Larsen, *Joseph Campbell*, 161.

62. Campbell, *Thou Art That*, 13.

scene—the Seven Sorrows of the Blessed Virgin or the story of the Crucifixion—arranging it as one would a stage set in the imagination. This is a protective prelude to one order of meditation. Another order of meditation is explosive because it carries you beyond all names, forms, and concepts. And then you cannot get back. If, however, you have engaged for several years in discursive meditation first, it serves as an intermediary state by which you can get back. In places in which meditation has been practiced for a long time—in contemplative orders, for example—this is well understood.[63]

Campbell identifies two orders of meditation, discursive and ordered, but one order serves as an intermediary state for the other and harmony is found. Discursive meditation can serve as a prelude to ordered meditation, preparing and grounding the practitioner for a more explosive and esoteric form of meditation.

Of all the mysteries of Christianity that stand apart and resist being harmonized with other faiths, perhaps none is greater than the claims Jesus Christ makes about himself. In response to a question posed by one of his disciples Jesus says, "I am the way, and the truth, and the life. No one comes to the Father except through me."[64] This same message is maintained by his disciples during the early church, "'This Jesus is the stone that was rejected by you, the builders, which has become the cornerstone. And there is salvation in no one else, for there is no other name under heaven given among men by which we must be saved.'"[65] Christ and his immediate followers made it clear that following him is an exclusive proposition. He is not one way among many; he stands apart and alone. Campbell addresses this question when he writes:

Let us find the way to mystery through a meditation on the birth, life, and death of Jesus. In this regard, the first century question, whether Christianity was *a* mystery religion or *the* mystery religion of which all the others were re-figurements is relevant. The many symbols, such as the animals of the Egyptian mystery religions breathing their spirit on the infant Jesus—the bull of the God Osiris in the ass of his brother Set, there in the manger—suggest their early understanding that this was indeed

63. Ibid., 14.

64. John 14:6.

65. Acts 4:11–12.

so. So, too, in the same nativity scene, the Magi wear the hat of Mithra as they pay homage.[66]

Campbell understands the characters present at the nativity (or as he calls them, the symbols); as reflecting the symbolism of other religious traditions being used by the gospel writers in a way to show the superiority of Christianity over other religions. But Campbell is careful to point out that such superiority is only perceived by the authors, a practice common to any who consider their faith the only true faith. But as he makes plain the Christ-child is an archetype, and not one uncommon to other mythical traditions, for according to Campbell, "It is clear that, in Orpheus and Christ, we have exactly the same archetype, with the motif of leaving the physical world, still symbolized with a cross in astronomy, for the spiritual. They leave the earth, symbol of Mother, to go to the realm of the Father."[67]

Instead of Jesus Christ being the one exclusive way to God, for Campbell, Jesus is the one *Christians believe* to be the one true way to God. His claims of exclusivity and his disciples' claims of his uniqueness are subservient to the greater transcending principles of myth and archetype. Since many beliefs contain mysteries of death and ascension, what Christianity professes is similar to what other faiths claim.

Christianity as Mystery: C. S. Lewis

As a supernaturalist, C. S. Lewis was comfortable with mystery. For him, mystery makes sense in matters of faith. In an essay discussing the call for women in the priesthood, "Priestesses in the Church?" Lewis takes up the matter of expecting mystery stating:

> This is what common sense will call 'mystical.' Exactly. The Church claims to be the bearer of a revelation. If that claim is false then we want not to make priestesses but to abolish priests. If it is true, then we should expect to find in the Church an element which unbelievers will call irrational and which believers will call supra-rational. There ought to be something in it opaque to our reason though not contrary to it—as the facts of sex and sense on the natural level are opaque. And that is the real issue. The Church of England can remain a church only if she retains this opaque element. If we abandon that, if we retain only what can be justified by standards of prudence and convenience at the

66. Campbell, *Thou Art That*, 14. Mithra is the Zoroastrian divinity of oaths and contracts as well as the guardian of cattle and harvest and protector of truth.

67. Ibid.

> bar of enlightened common sense, then we exchange revelation
> for that old wraith Natural Religion.[68]

Lewis understood a supernatural existence beyond this world with the revelation of the Bible as the means by which we come to understand that other world. It wasn't a case of people in this world making up or projecting their aspirations or fears into a fantasy world of gods and spirits; it was a real and loving God existing beyond space and time communicating His will to His creation in language they could understand. And when such communication happens mystery is expected since God is speaking of things humans cannot fully comprehend in language they can understand. "But we can at least comprehend our incomprehension, and see that if there is something beyond personality that *ought* to be incomprehensible in that sort of way."[69]

Since mystery was a component of Christianity, it was not a problem for Lewis, nor did he think it should be a problem for people who wanted to seriously consider and understand the Christian faith. The problem with most critics was their dismissal of Christianity based on an immature exposure to it while at the same time fawning over other beliefs as more enlightened. In speaking of pantheism he writes:

> The true state of the question is often misunderstood because people compare an adult knowledge of Pantheism with a knowledge of Christianity which they acquired in their childhood. They thus get the impression that Christianity gives the "obvious" account of God, the one that is too easy to be true, while Pantheism offers something sublime and mysterious. In reality, it is the other way around.[70]

Lewis was convinced that people who dismissed the mysterious elements of Christianity were doing so without taking the narrative accounts seriously and by simply throwing it in with every other religious tradition as if they were all the same. But Lewis understood Christianity as different from all other faiths. Since its mysteries were not to be understood as separate from everyday experiences, they were the result of a world created by an infinite God and manifested in everyday life among finite creatures. He identified the difficulty people had with mystery as two-fold: their erroneous interpretation of such mysteries and the underlying cause for their misunderstanding: rebellion against God.

---

68. C. S. Lewis, "Priestesses in the Church?" in *God in the Dock*, 238.

69. Lewis, *Miracles*, 85; italics in original.

70. Ibid., 84.

Lewis saw the danger in mystery as one of obscuring the reality of its meaning. A mystery needs context to be understood correctly. So Christian mysteries need to be interpreted in a context of the entire Bible, theology, and Christian doctrine. One is not free to simply make it up.

> Again, we may find a violence in some of the traditional imagery which tends to obscure the changelessness of God, the peace, which nearly all who approach Him have reported—the "still small voice." And it is here, I think, that the pre-Christian imagery is least suggestive. Yet even here, there is danger lest the half conscious picture of some huge thing at rest—a clear, still ocean, a dome of "white radiance"—should smuggle in ideas of inertia or a vacuity. The stillness in which the mystics approached him is intent and alert—at the opposite pole from sleep or reverie. They are becoming like Him. Silences in the physical world occur in empty places: but the ultimate Peace is silent through very density of life. Saying is swallowed up in being. There is no movement because his actions (which is Himself) is timeless. You might, if you wish, call it movement at an infinite speed, which is the same thing as rest, but reached by a different—perhaps a less misleading—way of approach.[71]

Lewis challenged the natural tendency of making gods in our own image. One needs revelation from outside of self—revelation from God—to understand God. Lewis would concur with the Apostle Paul, "For who knows a person's thoughts except the spirit of that person, which is in him? So also no one comprehends the thoughts of God except the Spirit of God."[72] As natural and appealing as it is to explain mystery with human reasoning, Lewis would argue that the mysteries of Christianity are God's mysteries and can only be explained by God.

Dismissing God's explanation and substituting one based on what seems reasonable to human understanding needs to be questioned. Why is rejection of the Christian explanation of its mysteries so common? Some would respond it's because the Christian answer requires a belief in a nonexistent supernatural realm. Lewis would disagree; it's not a matter of mind and science, it's a matter of the human heart not wanting to be held accountable by its Creator. Again, when speaking against pantheism Lewis observes,

> Men are reluctant to pass over from the notion of an abstract and negative deity to the living God. I do not wonder. Here lies the deepest tap-root of Pantheism and of the objection to

71. Ibid., 93.

72. 1 Cor 2:11.

traditional imagery. It was hated not, at bottom, because it pictured Him as a man but because it pictured Him as king, or even as warrior. The Pantheist's God does nothing, demands nothing. He is there if you wish for Him, like a book on a shelf. He will not pursue you. There is no danger at any time heaven and earth should flee away at his glance. If He were the truth, then we could really say that all the Christian images of kingship were a historical accident of which our religion ought to be cleansed. It is with a shock that we discover them to be indispensable. You have had a shock like that before, in connection with smaller matters—when the line pulls your hand, when something breathes beside you in the darkness. So here; the shock comes at the precise moment when the thrill of *life* is communicated to us along the clue we have been following.[73]

Lewis contends the "problem" with mystery in the Christian faith is not that things happen that can't be reasonably explained; that is to be expected. The problem is that behind such events is a being humanity cannot understand unaided by His (Her or Its) assistance.

Lewis argued that historic Christianity is in a no-win position regarding mystery. On the one hand when the mysteries are understood symbolically as advocating desirable qualities such as love and peace (which it does in fact advocate), there is nothing that sets it apart from any great religion. But when it speaks of its unique distinctions, such as salvation through faith in Jesus Christ alone, it is considered unreasonable and barbaric with the result that, "Sadly, the debate about Christianity has shifted from 'is it true' to 'was anyone offended.'"[74] As Lewis notes:

> At every point Christianity must correct the natural expectations of the Pantheist and offer something more difficult, just as Schroedinger has to correct Democritus. At every moment he has to multiply distinctions and rule out false analogies. He has to substitute the mappings of something that has a positive, concrete, and highly articulate character for the formless generalities in which Pantheism is at home. Indeed, after the discussion has been going on for some time, the Pantheist is apt to change his ground and where he before accused us of childless naïveté now to blame us for the pedantic complexity of our "cold Christs and tangled Trinites." And we may well sympathize with him. Christianity, faced with popular "religion" is continuously troublesome. To the large well-meant statements of "religion" it finds

73. Lewis, *Miracles*, 93–94.
74. Mark Driscoll in Carson, *The Intolerance of Tolerance*, back flyleaf.

itself forced to apply again and again, "Well, not quite like that."
This troublesomeness does not of course prove it to be true; but
if it were true it would be bound to have this troublesomeness.[75]

Mystery, along with debates about mystery and fact, are expected in matters
of faith and they present challenges. But such challenges need to be accepted
as a necessary part of the belief system. However one explains such mysteries one is not free to recreate the faith with only the acts or events one finds
believable.

Lewis understood this need to explain away or recreate certain mysteries not as a lack of religion, or even as an opposition to religion, but as
the replacement of one religion with another; the offensive religion being
replaced with one more suitable to the tastes of the individual. He writes:

> We who defend Christianity find ourselves constantly opposed
> not by the irreligion of our hearers but by their real religion.
> Speak about beauty, truth and goodness, or about a God who
> is simply the indwelling principle of these three, speak about
> a great spiritual force pervading all things, a common mind of
> which we all are parts, a pool of generalised spirituality to which
> we can all flow, and you will command friendly interest. But the
> temperature drops as soon as you mention a God who has pur-
> poses and performs particular actions, who does one thing and
> not another, a concrete, choosing, commanding, prohibiting
> God with a determinate character. People become embarrassed
> or angry. Such a conception seems to them primitive and crude
> and even irreverent. The popular "religion" excludes miracles
> because it excludes the "living God" of Christianity and believes
> instead in a kind of God who obviously would not do miracles,
> or indeed anything else.[76]

Lewis contends the real issue with those who oppose or redefine mysteries
they find offensive is not simply the moral implication of some mysteries, or
that mystery cannot be explained in naturalistic terms; it's the implication
that there is a Being behind the mystery; a Being before whom each person
will one day appear and give an account and, while this point is true of many
religions, Lewis found it especially the case regarding his own encounter
with Christianity:

> It is always shocking to meet life where we thought we were
> alone. "Look out!" we cry, "it's *alive*." And therefore this is the
> very point at which so many draw back—I would have done

75. Lewis, *Miracles*, 85.
76. Ibid., 86.

so myself if I could—and proceed no further with Christianity. An "impersonal God"—well and good. A subjective God of beauty, truth and goodness, inside our own heads—better still. A formless life-force surging through us, a vast power which we can tap—best of all. But God Himself, alive, pulling at the other end of the cord, perhaps approaching at an infinite speed, the hunter, King, husband—that is quite another matter. There comes a moment when the children who have been playing at burglars hush suddenly: was that a *real* footstep in the hall? There comes a moment when people who have been dabbling in religion ("Man's search for God"!) suddenly draw back. Supposing we really found him? We never meant it to come to *that*! Worse still, supposing He had found us?

So it is a sort of Rubicon. One goes across; or not. But if one does, there is no manner of security against miracles. One may be in for *anything*.[77]

Lewis shifts attention from the theoretical to the relational, from the comfortable abstract to the unsettling personal, contending that humanity's greatest mystery is not specific mysteries of any given faith, or even the greater "mystery of humanity" itself. The greatest unknown is the Creator who desires to be known as He is. In the Christian tradition, this Being seeks to be known through relationship; it's not just a belief system but a bond, a connection, with the believer. This distinction between a "personal" and a "religious" Christianity is critical to Lewis's thinking. He states:

But "religion" also claims to base itself on experience. The experiences of the mystics (that ill-defined but popular class) are held to indicate that God is the God of "religion" rather than of Christianity; that He—or It—is not a concrete Being but "being in general" about which nothing can be truly asserted. To everything which we try to say about Him, the mystics tend to reply, "Not thus." What all these negatives of the mystics really mean I shall consider in a moment: but I must first point out why it seems to me impossible that they should be true in the same sense popularly understood.[78]

Lewis was troubled by the suggestion of some that since not everything can be known about God then nothing can be known. Further complicating the issue is the idea that each individual is free to make up what the mysteries of

77. Ibid., 93–94; italics in original.
78. Ibid., 86.

the faith mean with the result that contradictions are considered logical and everyone is correct. He found such a position untenable.

Lewis argues that this emphasis on a desired commonality of all religious mysteries has a long history and is the result of the assumption that each generation is more progressive and educated than all previous ones. As each generation passes down the stories, they become improved upon, advanced, more divine and insightful than the traditional belief. As he explains it:

> According to this picture, Man starts by inventing "spirits" to explain natural phenomena; and at first he imagines the spirits to be exactly like himself. As he gets more enlightened they become less manlike, less "anthropomorphic" as the scholars call it. Their anthropomorphic attributes drop off one by one—first the human shape, then human passions, then personality, will, activity—in the end every concrete or positive attribute whatever. There is left in the end a pure abstraction—mind as such, spirituality as such. God, instead of being a particular entity with a real character of its own, becomes simply "the whole show" looked at in a particular way or the theoretical point at which all the lines of human aspiration would meet if produced to infinity. And since, on the modern view, the final stage of anything is the most refined and civilised stage, this "religion" is held to be more a profound, more spiritual, and more enlightened belief than Christianity.[79]

So these "spirits," along with all matters mysterious, are simply the result of human reasoning applied to unexplainable natural phenomena. In time, as human intelligence develops and knowledge increases, it arrives at the deepest and most profound point where it is able to explain all mysteries in a way reasonable to the largest number of "civilized" people.

To explain the way humanity conceives the nature and character of God and then changes this original understanding into something less, Lewis constructed a mythical account concerning limpets, a form of snail, who first encountered a human being. How is the creature to explain such an encounter? He states:

> Let us suppose a mystical limpet, a sage among limpets, who (rapt in vision) catches a glimpse of what Man is like. In reporting it to his disciples, who have some vision themselves (though less than he) he will have to use many negatives. He will have to tell them that Man has no shell, is not attached to a rock, is not

---

79. Ibid., 82.

surrounded by water. And his disciples, having a little vision of their own to help them, to get some idea of Man. But then there come erudite limpets, limpets who write histories of philosophy and give lectures on comparative religion, and who have never had any vision of their own. What they get out of the prophetic limpets words is simply and solely the negatives. From these, uncorrected by any positive insight, they build up a picture of Man as a sort of amorphous jelly (as he has no shell) existing nowhere in particular (he is not attached to a rock) and never taking nourishment (there is no water to drift it toward him). And having a traditional reference for Man they conclude that to be a famished jelly in a dimensionless void is the supreme mode of existence, and reject as crude, materialist superstition any doctrine which would attribute to Man a definite shape, a structure, and organs.[80]

This is the situation where modern people find themselves regarding Christianity. God has revealed Himself thorough the Bible and in the man, Christ Jesus. But since much of this truth is mysterious because it lies beyond the ability of natural law and human understanding for deity to inhabit humanity, humans, like limpets, must describe God by a process of removing the mysterious elements and leaving only what seems reasonable to human understanding; in this case, removing the human in favor of the divine:

Great prophets and saints have an intuition of God which is positive and concrete in the highest degree. Because, just touching the fringes of His being, they have seen that he is plentitude of life and energy and joy, therefore (and for no other reason) they have to pronounce that He transcends those limitations which we call personality, passion, change, materiality, and the like. The positive quality in him which repels the limitations is their only ground for all the negatives. But when we come limping after and try to construct an intellectual or "enlightened" religion, we take over these negatives (infinite, immaterial, impassable, immutable, etc.) and use them unchecked by any positive intuition. At each step we have to strip off from our idea of God some human attribute.

But the only real reason for stripping off the human attribute is to make room for putting in some positive divine attribute. In St. Paul's language, the purpose of all this unclothing is not that our idea of God should reach nakedness but that it should be re-clothed. But unhappily we have no means of doing the

80. Ibid., 89.

re-clothing. When we have removed from our idea of God some puny human characteristic, we (as merely erudite or intelligent enquirers) have no resources from which to supply that blindly real and concrete attribute of Deity which ought to replace it.

Thus at each step in the process of refinement our idea of God contains less, and the fatal pictures come in (an endless, silent sea, an empty sky beyond all stars, a dome of white radiance) and we reach at last near zero and worshiping nonentity.[81]

This point of reaching zero and worshipping nonentity is what Lewis understood as the natural result of humanity seeking to make sense of mystery without the aid of divine revelation. To assume that no God exists leaves one free, yet forced, to make sense of the aspects of faith that lie beyond human understanding. But if one begins with the assumption that God does exist, then such mysteries take on a very different meaning. They no longer need an explanation; they can be understood by context and the revealed meaning.

But as Lewis points out, when unaided by revelation human reasoning on its own

> ... can hardly help following this path. That is why the Christian statement that only He who does the will of the father will ever know the true doctrine is philosophically accurate. Imagination may help a little: but in the moral life, and (still more) in the devotional life we touch something concrete which would once begin to correct the growing emptiness of our idea of God. One moment even of feeble contrition or blurred thankfulness will, at least in some degree, head us off from the abyss of abstraction. It is Reason herself which teaches us not to rely on Reason only in this matter. For Reason knows that she cannot work without materials. When it becomes clear that you cannot find out by reasoning whether the cat is in the linen-cupboard, it is Reason herself who whispers, "Go and look. This is not my job: it is a matter for the senses." So here. The materials for correcting our abstract conception of God cannot be supplied by Reason: she will be the first to tell you to go and try experience—"Oh, taste and see! For of course she will have already pointed out that your present position is absurd. As long as we remain Erudite Limpets we are forgetting that if no one had ever seen more of God then we, we should have no reason even to believe Him immaterial, immutable, impassable and all the rest of it. Even that negative knowledge which seems to us so enlightened is only a

81. Ibid., 89–90.

relic left over from the positive knowledge of better men—only the pattern which that heavenly wave left on the stand when it retreated.[82]

As Lewis argues, when human reason is respected it is evident that mystery lies beyond what reasoning is designed to understand. Reason has limits, it "cannot work without materials," it can only fathom matters within space and time. And since mystery involves matters beyond space and time one must turn to other avenues such as faith and belief to aid reasoning. Mystery, Lewis would argue, is a matter of faith seeking understanding.

COMPARATIVE VIEWS OF CHRISTIANITY AS MYTH

Does myth have a place in Christianity? In spite of their different conclusions both Joseph Campbell and C. S. Lewis found myth to be important alongside mystery and history in the Christian faith. As noted above, both men realized that Christianity is rooted in human history. For Campbell, myth is what gives practical and relevant meaning to both the history and mystery of the Christian faith; myth enables one to make sense of the supernatural aspects of the faith. In fact, without myth, with only a natural reading of the Bible, interpreting the supernatural literally instead of symbolically can be harmful. In speaking of taking the supernatural elements of the Bible literally, that is, taking the symbolic as literal, Campbell cautions, "However, today such claims can no longer be taken seriously by anyone with even a kindergarten education. And in this there is serious danger."[83]

For some Christians myth is a necessary tool for interpreting certain parts of the Bible and understanding the true message of the Christian gospel. But to other believers myth undermines a proper interpretation by relegating the historical to the fictional. To these followers, a mythical or symbolic interpretation of historical events such as the physical resurrection of Jesus Christ destroys Christianity and empties the gospel of its message and meaning. These believers point to the Apostle Paul's admonition, "And if Christ has not been raised, then our preaching is in vain and your faith is in vain. We are even found to be misrepresenting God, because we testified about God that he raised Christ, whom he did not raise if it is true that the dead are not raised. For if the dead are not raised, not even Christ has been

---

82. Ibid., 90–91.
83. Campbell, *Myths to Live By*, 10.

raised. And if Christ has not been raised, your faith is futile and you are still in your sins."[84] To such followers, myth erodes the truth claims of the faith.

As noted earlier, Joseph Campbell was raised in a Roman Catholic faith that maintained the miraculous as historical. But through his studies and travels he came to conclude that a historical reading of the Bible misses the true meaning of the narrative by confusing the literal and metaphorical interpretations of its stories. C. S. Lewis, though born into a home that attended the Church of Ireland, would, by the age of fifteen, drift from those beliefs, dabble in the occult, and finally claim to be an atheist. As he wrote of this time,

> I was at this time living, like so many Atheists or Antitheists, in a whirl of contradictions. I maintained that God did not exist. I was also very angry with God for not existing. I was equally angry with Him for creating a world.[85]

But in time Lewis would return to a religious belief, first to a theistic and then specifically to the Christian faith, and from this worldview he would argue for a place for myth in Christianity. Yet he also believed in the historicity of the gospel accounts. How did he reconcile myth and Christianity?

This section views these questions by explaining what Lewis meant by Christianity as "true myth" and by explaining Campbell's journey from a religion that claimed "The task of giving an authentic interpretation of the Word of God, whether in its written form or in the form of Tradition, has been entrusted to the living, teaching office of the Church alone"[86] to one where individual interpretation and common universal mythical themes offered a better way to understand the stories and symbols of the faith.

For the Bible to be meaningful, providing guidance to moderns, and for Christianity to remain a viable faith with meaning in a technological age, it is necessary to understand the place of myth. What is myth's proper role in a faith many conclude is lived out in a specific time and place? Can one, at the same time, allow for elements of the symbolic and allegorical without letting such symbolism turn the entire gospel narrative into fiction?

---

84. 1 Cor 15:14–17.

85. Lewis, *Surprised by Joy*, 115.

86. *Catechism of the Catholic Church*, 27.

Christianity as Myth: Joseph Campbell

In the "Editor's Foreword" to *Thou Art That: Transforming Religious Metaphor*, noted Campbell scholar Eugene Kennedy carefully explains what Joseph Campbell set out to do regarding Christianity as myth:

> In the same way, Joseph Campbell reacquaints Christians with the aura of meanings that hover about the religious incidents and stories of the New Testament. As in treating Jewish history, it is this aura—that is, in the connotations that by their nature blossom out of metaphors—that the deepest significance of the stories of Jesus' life and work are to be found.[87]

Campbell never intended to introduce some new approach to understanding the Christian faith. He was seeking to reintroduce the original interpretation to a technologically advanced culture that still needed transcending principles to guide it into the future but had lost its way due to the influences of a religion that misunderstood the original meaning and message. The correction for this error was myth. But myth not as a replacement for the Christian message, or a challenge to it, instead myth was to be understood as the means of communicating the message; a timeless way for the lessons of the Christian faith to be conveyed. The *truth* of Christian doctrine should not be confused with the *means* by which such doctrine is taught. To speak of Christianity as myth should not, according to Campbell, be interpreted to mean the message of Christianity is not true. As Kennedy further explains,

> To describe the testaments as myth is not, as Campbell points out, to debunk them. The contemporary impression of myth as falsehood has, as Campbell illustrates in these pages by recalling an obnoxious and ill-informed interviewer, lead people to think of them as fantasies passing as truth. But mythology is a vessel of the truth that is far more reliable than census and almanac figures, which, subject to time as myth is not, are out of date as soon as they are printed. Joseph Campbell's purpose in exploring the biblical myths is not to dismiss them as unbelievable but to lay open once again their living and nurturing core.[88]

Not only does a mythical reading of the Bible *not* demean its message or veracity, but to read it any other way is to confuse and obscure the original intent and purpose. Kennedy writes:

---

87. Eugene Kennedy, "Editor's Foreword" in Campbell, *Thou Art That*, xiv.
88. Ibid., xv.

Many elements of the Bible seem lifeless and unbelievable because they have been regarded as historical facts instead of metaphorical representations of spiritual realities. They have been applied in a concrete way to great figures, such as Moses and John the Baptist, as if they were real-time accounts of their actions. That this heavy emphasis on the historical rather than the spiritual should have continued into the twenty-first century illustrates the lag-time that the leaders of institutional religions have allowed to open up between their static ideas in the rapidly developing understandings of solid new scholarship. A failure to follow Pope John XXIII's injunction to "read the signs of the times" leaves them behind even their own times.[89]

Instead of setting myth in opposition to history and truth, Campbell wanted myth to be the means by which one discovers truth unhindered by a historical literalism that not only prevents understanding the Bible but one that was never intended as the way to read the Bible. Kennedy summarizes Campbell's thinking this way:

The best thing one can do with the Bible is to read it spiritually rather than historically. Read the Bible in your own way, and take the message because it says something special to each reader, based on his or her own experience. The gift of God comes in your own terms. God, pure and in himself, is too much. Carl Jung said, "Religion is a system to defend us against the experience of God." It may be a species of impudence to think that the way you understand God is the way God is.[90]

Such a "spiritual" reading sets the Bible free from a single interpretation based on the traditional historical understanding and allows the reader the freedom to find the deeper, symbolic lessons of the text that best suits his or her immediate need.

Thus, the Virgin Birth, as the reader will learn, does not refer to the biological condition of Mary, the mother of Jesus, but to a rebirth of the spirit everyone can experience. The Promised Land refers not to a geographical location but to the territory of the human heart that anyone can enter.[91]

89. Ibid.
90. Ibid., 60.
91. Ibid., xvii.

And so myth, often misunderstood as having nothing to do with truth or, worse, as being false, is a morally neutral means of conveying truth. Kennedy explains,

> Although the word is popularly used to denote falsehood, myth is actually a perennial vehicle for expressing truth. Human beings have always been told, in mythic forms, the stories they want to be remembered and passed on—such as the Arthurian legends or the enduring biblical tales—to distinguish them from fashions, fads, and the constantly changing facts of almanacs or the *Guinness Book of World Records*. Myths and symbol are fundamental and essential properties of all religions; they are the special language of religious experience.[92]

Myth, according to Campbell, is the one sure method of communicating the transcending lessons of the Bible—and not the Bible only, but all religions.

> Joseph Campbell has devoted his life to their [myths] study, detecting recurrent themes and motifs in the varied mythologies of different cultures that suggest that a single underground spring of religious experience nourishes them all. According to Campbell, what appears to be diverse religious traditions are actually different expressions of a unitary experience that is shared across all cultures.[93]

Campbell does not single out Christianity as mythical since he argues that myth is the common thread running through all religions, including Christianity, which serves as a common bond holding all religions and all of humanity together by pointing out the common signs and symbols indigenous to all faith. "[M]yth is not a lie. A whole mythology is an organization of symbolic images and narratives, metaphorical of the possibilities of human experience and the fulfillment of a given culture at a given time."[94]

All the religions of the world have myth as a common denominator. The challenge is that the adherents of each religion do not look deep enough into their faith or wide enough to see the faiths of others and so fail to see the mythical themes running throughout all beliefs. Most people, especially Christians, have only a shallow understanding of their faith based on a literal reading of the Bible, so they are closed off to the contributions made by other faiths that would give them a better understanding and appreciation of their own Christian faith, as well as the faith of those with whom

92. Eugene Kennedy, "Appendix: A Discussion," Campbell, *Thou Art That*, 102.

93. Ibid.

94. Campbell, *Thou Art That*, 1.

they differ. Campbell understood the problem between religions as one of perspective.

> There are two orders of religious perspective. One is ethical, pitting good against evil. In the biblically grounded Christian West, the accent is on ethics, on good against evil. We are thus bound by our religion itself to the field of duality. The mystical perspective, however, views good and evil as aspects of one process. One finds this in the Chinese yin-yang sign, the *dai-chi*.
>
> We have, then, these two totally different religious perspectives. The idea of good and evil absolutes in the world after the fall is biblical and as a result you do not rest on corrupted nature. Instead, you correct nature and align yourself with the good against evil. Eastern cults, on the other hand, put you in touch with nature, where what Westerners call good and evil interlock. But by what right, this Eastern tradition asks, do we call these things evil when they are of the process of nature?[95]

The fault of all religious misunderstanding begins with this duality of religious perspective and Campbell devoted his life to finding a way to bridge these two views. He shares that it was during a trip to Japan that he experienced a critical shift in his thinking that caused him to see the two views clearly, as well as to see that individuals were looking too closely at their faith. They needed to step back away from the specific doctrines and religious language and see the bigger scope of commonality found in transcendence.

> I was greatly impressed when I was first in Japan to find myself in a world that knew nothing of the Fall in the Garden of Eden and consequently did not consider nature corrupt. In the Shinto Scriptures one reads that the processes of nature cannot be evil. In our tradition, every natural impulse is sinful unless it has been purified in some manner.
>
> In some artistic representations, one sees the Deity and at his right stand the three Graces. The muses are close because art clothes mystery. The final revelation is the naked mystery itself. The first of the three Graces is Euphrosyne, or rapture, sending forth the energy of Apollo into the world. The second is Aglaia, splendor, bringing the energy back. Then, embracing the two, we find Thalia, abundance. One recognizes that these are the functions of the Trinity in the Christian biblically-based tradition in which the same powers are given a masculine form.[96]

95. Ibid., 16; italics in original.
96. Ibid.

What Christianity has in common with other religions is preeminent to Campbell; the Christian faith was unique in the specific ways it composed the details of its myths. Once Christians can appreciate these myths, myths they have in common with other religions, along with the universal moral lessons inherent in other faiths, there can be a greater appreciation of other faiths and greater harmony throughout a world rife with religious differences and wars. What believers need to do is see beyond their myopic view of Christianity, its signs, symbols, and language, and realize that beyond all such barriers are transcending spiritual truths that will draw them closer to those of other faiths and deepen their own spiritual experience. Speaking of the Christian doctrine of the Trinity and similar ideas in other religions, Campbell explains:

> Finally, it does not matter whether you are going to name them male and female. Transcendence is beyond all such naming. This symbol refers to what might simply be called total meditation. Father is Thalia, the abundance who unites the other two. The Son is Euphrosyne, the rapture of love that pours itself into the world. The Holy Spirit, the Paraclete, is Aglaia, who carries us back. The energy itself stems from Apollo, who in the Christian tradition is the one Divine substance of which the three of the Trinity are personalities.
>
> Remember my earlier statement that the experience of mystery comes not from expecting it but through yielding all your programs, because your programs are based on fear and desire. Drop them and the radiance comes.[97]

Historic Christianity is in essence its own worse enemy. Maintaining a hermeneutic that insists Biblical stories and characters actually existed is to misplace the focus of the faith and to unnecessarily set up barriers that further divide devout people from one another. Better to heed a gospel message of love and brotherhood conveyed in symbols, one that enhances humanity in its divinity and diversity, by interpreting the Christian message as myth. This approach enhances personal faith and allows for a greater expansion of understanding others who are equally devout to different beliefs. Meaning cannot be fixed to just one idea; what is true for one is not necessarily true for another. In a world of religious signs and symbols, each believer must be able to see beyond the text and detect a greater message:

---

97. Ibid., 16. Thalia, Euphrosyne, and Aglaea were the "three graces" and daughters of Zeus. Thalia was the goddess of festivity; Euphrosyne the goddess of mirth; and Aglaea the goddess of beauty and adornment.

How, in the contemporary period, can we evoke the imagery
that communicates the most profound and most richly developed sense of experiencing life? These images must point past
themselves to that ultimate truth which must be told: that life
does not have any one absolutely fixed meaning. These images
must point past all meanings given, beyond all definitions and
relationships, to that really ineffable mystery that is just the
existence, the being of ourselves and of our world. If we give
that mystery an exact meaning we diminish the experience of
its real depth. But when a poet carries the mind into a context of
meanings and then pitches it past those, one knows that marvelous rapture that comes from going past all categories of definition. Here we sense the function of metaphor that allows us to
make a journey we cannot otherwise make, past all categories
of definition.[98]

Mystery must not be understood as having an exact meaning; one
must instead seek the experience, for in the experience of the moment is
the real depth of spirituality. Christianity has to be interpreted mythically
and not literally because that is how it was intended to be interpreted and
because only through myth can Christianity find relevance in the global
community and in the technologically driven culture of the West. Also true
is that myth speaks to the human mind in ways philosophy and logic cannot. Dinkler writes:

It has been pointed out . . . that myth issues from an activity
of the human mind or psyche distinct from, and independent
of, that which produces philosophy or speculative thought, and
that its most natural medium is artistic fancy. Accordingly, we
must expect to find in biblical poetry a constant undercurrent of
mythopoeic imagery, suggestion, and association. Furthermore,
the comparative study of folk literature has shown that traditional saga tend likewise to be tinged with the logical coloration,
historical persons (e.g. Arthur of Britain) and events being thus
assimilated to ideal, mythic characters and situations.[99]

Campbell's claim of Christianity as myth is deeper and far more complicated
than relegating it to a children's bedtime story. His argument is that myth
brings Christianity into its own by bringing together truth with the best
means of expressing that truth since myth alone is the best way forward out

98. Ibid., 8–9.
99. Dinkler, "Myth in the NT," in *Interpreter's Dictionary of the Bible*, 485.

of a wooden literalism that results in a moribund faith that is both parochial and irrelevant for most of the modern world.

Nowhere does Campbell deny the historicity of certain people and events in the Bible. As he notes, "Historical themes in the Bible became actually historical, rooted in real events, with Chronicles and Kings. These are based on genuine Chronicles in the treasuries of the royal house of David, from about 1000 B.C." But even here he hesitates to agree with a thoroughly historical interpretation of even these events for he adds:

> Although they are historical, there is still a good deal of legend in them. Purely legendary events are also found even in much later stories. Although there is a marked interest on the part of archaeologists in actually dating these things, such dating cannot have anything to do with the early Book of Genesis, before chapter twelve. The datings can began to handle the periods of Abraham, Jacob, and Joseph but, as I have observed, one doesn't try to find true history until Kings and Chronicles. In Judges, the legends are transparently clear. Joshua's stopping the sun is a legend, not history. That the sun cannot literally be stopped does not detract from it as a legendary event, whose meaning and purpose add great value to what has been experienced by the Jewish people.[100]

Specific incidents may be historical depending on their credibility in a scientific worldview. Campbell does not dispute that a character such as Joshua may have lived, but he obviously could not alter the earth's rotation around the sun. So Joshua is historical, but his story is not. But none of this should concern the reader since "The central myth in the Bible is that of exile,"[101] and so to illustrate this theme the Biblical authors resort to stories of unbelievable acts (miracles) to capture the reader's attention and demonstrate this central theme.

Campbell's understanding of Christianity as myth was multi-dimensional; the Jewish and Christian faith grew out of historical figures and events, but the people and occurrences in the Bible are to be understood symbolically as teaching lessons greater than they at first appear. Campbell does not replace the literal with the symbolic.

> Yes, [symbols] do represent historical facts. A symbol doesn't just point to something else. As Thomas Merton wrote, a symbol contains a structure that awakens our consciousness to a new awareness of the inner meaning of life and reality itself.

100. Campbell, *Thou Art That*, 57.
101. Ibid.

Through symbols we enter emotionally into contact with our deepest selves, with each other, and with God—a word that is to be understood as a symbol. When theologians spoke of God's being dead, a decade or so ago, just as the space age began, they were really saying that their symbols were dead.[102]

The central focus of the Christian message has to do with this inner meaning of life and reality. The problem with a literal interpretation of the Bible is that it is one-dimensional, resulting in little more than a record of supposed events that occurred millenniums ago to a people who did not understand what later science could explain. Such unbelievable stories read literally can serve no purpose to readers who encounter them outside a time of writing when myth played a normative role in the culture. Unlike those primitive cultures that looked outside of self to worlds of gods and spirits to aid them to understand life, individuals living in a technological society need instead to look deep within to find such guidance.

A mythology may be understood as an organization of metaphorical figures connotative of states of mind that are not finally of this or that location or historical period, even though the figures themselves seem on their surface to suggest such a concrete localization. The metaphorical language of both mythology and metaphysics are not denotative of actual worlds or gods, but rather connote levels and entities within the person touched by them. Metaphors only seem to describe the outer world of time and place. Their real universe is the spiritual realm of the inner life. The Kingdom of God is within you.[103]

Interpreting Christianity as myth is to understand the Christian message in its fullest and most meaningful way. Such an interpretation places Christianity among all the other great religions with similar messages and symbols and frees it from the parochial and sectarianism that religion has made of it. As Campbell states,

The exclusivism of there being only one way in which we can be saved, the idea that there is a single religious group that is in sole possession of the truth—that is the world as we know it that must pass away. What is the kingdom? It lies in our realization of the ubiquity of the divine presence in our neighbors, and our enemies, in all of us.[104]

102. Ibid., 109.
103. Ibid., 6–7.
104. Ibid., 107.

Myth answers not only how to understand Christianity, but it also addresses how a world of various and opposing religions can finally come to an understanding of unity.

Humans are by nature religious. People the world over are drawn to believe in another existence, an existence similar to this world but one free of the pain, confusion, and suffering that is so common in this world. Campbell understood that to a large segment of humanity Christianity offers that hope, and for these people the Christian message found in the Bible explains both the brokenness of the current situation and offers the needed direction to a spiritual unity that can tie Christians to all of humanity. By using symbols common to all Christians, Campbell explains the problem and the solution:

> When Man ate of the fruit of the Tree, he discovered himself in the field of duality instead of the field of unity. As a result, he finds himself out, in exile. The two cherubim placed at the gate are there representative of the world of the pairs of opposites in which, having been cast out of the world of unity, he is now located. You are kept in exile by your commitment to that world.
>
> Christ goes past that—"I and the father are one"—back into the realm of unity from which we have been expelled. *These* are mysteries. Here is an echo and a translation into another set of images of what we ourselves are experiencing. What comes forth now with the grain, as particles of that one life that informs all things, is the revelation of the spiritual unity in all its aspects. It also is the revelation that one life can be personified as a Deity, as in the Christian tradition, and everything comes from the Deity. But the personification is not what is important. What we have is a trans-theological, transpersonified revelation.[105]

Christianity, understood traditionally, limits its own message and divides its followers, but Christianity as myth widens its message by emphasizing what it has in common with other faiths and forming common bonds among all people.

Christianity as Myth: C. S. Lewis

For C. S. Lewis, Christianity is a true myth; "a myth which is also a fact."[106] For him the events in the Bible, including miraculous events such as Christ's virgin birth, sinless life, substitutionary death, and physical resurrection,

---

105. Ibid., 15.

106. Lewis, "Myth Became Fact," in *God in the Dock*, 66.

were those of "a historical person crucified (it is all in order) *under Pontius Pilate.*"[107] This blending together of two ideas often seen as diametrically opposed—myth and fact—enabled Lewis to reconcile what many considered irreconcilable; the supernatural and the natural, the universal allure of myth with the historical convictions Lewis held concerning the gospel accounts. "The decisive insight was that Christianity was not a set of doctrines or moral principles, but a controlling grand narrative — a myth, in the true sense of the term — which generated and sustained such ideas and values."[108]

Both Joseph Campbell and C. S. Lewis understood a place for myth within the faith, the question is: What place? Does accepting myth's role radically change one's understanding of the Christian faith and reading of the Bible from what has been accepted for thousands of years, or does myth serve as the bridge that holds together the tension of history and mystery of the ancient faith thus making the message relevant for all people everywhere?

In his classic work, *Mere Christianity*, C. S. Lewis offered an uncompromising either/or ultimatum on the claims Christ made about himself:

> I am trying here to prevent anyone saying the really foolish thing that people often say about Him: "I'm ready to accept Jesus as a great moral teacher, but I don't accept his claim to be God." That is the one thing we must not say. A man who was merely a man and said the sort of things Jesus said would not be a great moral teacher. He would either be a lunatic — on the level with the man who says he is a poached egg — or else he would be the Devil of Hell. You must make your choice. Either this man was, and is, the Son of God, or else a madman or something worse. You can shut him up for a fool, you can spit at him and kill him as a demon or you can fall at his feet and call him Lord and God, but let us not come with any patronising nonsense about his being a great human teacher. He has not left that open to us. He did not intend to.[109]

If this was the only quote from Lewis about Jesus or the Christian faith one could reasonably conclude he had little use for myth in Biblical Christianity; but elsewhere Lewis argues strongly that myth plays an important role for the believer who wants to understand the gospel narrative.

---

107. Ibid., 67; italics in original.

108. McGrath, *The Intellectual World of C. S. Lewis*, 62.

109. Lewis, *Mere Christianity*, 55–56.

As discussed earlier, Lewis was born into a religious family that supported the Church of Ireland. From his earliest years he was familiar with the doctrines, rituals, language, and practices of a religious environment, but by his early teens he had grown disenchanted with the church and the Christian faith. But by the time he entered his early thirties Lewis began to perceive the inadequacy of his agnosticism and by the summer of 1929 he renounced agnosticism and professed himself not as a Christian, but as a theist, believing in the existence of God. Lewis's friend and biographer, Walter Hooper, explains the context stating that,

> 'a realization of the truth in mythologies triggered Lewis's conversion' to Christianity: This came about after a long discussion in 1931 with Tolkien and Hugo Dyson which continued until four o'clock in the morning. At the end of this marathon discussion Lewis believed that myths were real and that facts took the shine off truth, emptying truth of its glory. Thereafter he became an excellent Christian apologist.[110]

The impact of this meeting, which took place on September 19, 1931, is evident a month later when, as noted earlier, Lewis, writing to his good friend Arthur Greeves in a letter dated October 18, 1931, shares:

> Now the story of Christ is simply a true myth: a myth working on us in the same way as the others, but with this tremendous difference that it really happened: and one must be content to accept it in the same way, remembering that it is God's myth while the others are men's myths: i.e. the Pagan stories are God expressing Himself through the minds of poets, using such images as He found there, while Christianity is God expressing Himself through what we call 'real things.' Therefore it is true, not in the sense of being a 'description' of God (that no finite mind could take in) but in the sense of being the way in which God chooses to (or can) appear to our faculties. The 'doctrines' we get out of the true myth are of course less true: they are translations into our concepts and ideas of that wh. [sic] God has already expressed in a language more adequate, namely the actual incarnation, crucifixion, and resurrection. Does this amount to a belief in Christianity? At any rate I am now certain (a) That this Christian story is to be approached, in a sense, as I approach the other myths. (b) That it is the most important and full meaning. I am also nearly certain that it really happened.[111]

110. Pearce, *Tolkien*, 57.

111. Hooper, *The Collected Letters of C. S. Lewis*, 1:977; italics in original.

Though Lewis is cautious, as evident by his use of "nearly," this is no longer the man who maintained that God did not exist. Understanding myth enabled him to pass from unbelief to belief, not just in God, but in the gospel presentation of a supernatural Jesus Christ.

Lewis had invited J. R. R. Tolkien and Hugo Dyson, Lecturer in English Literature at Reading University, to dine with him at Magdalene College and it was this meeting that was such a watershed for him. Following their meal, the three men went for a walk beside a river and discussed the purpose of myth. Being at first critical of myth:

> Lewis explained that he felt the power of myths but that they were ultimately untrue. As he expressed it to Tolkien, myths are 'lies and therefore worthless, even though breathed through silver.'
>
> 'No,' said Tolkien. 'They are not lies.'
>
> At that moment, Lewis recalled, there was 'a rush of wind which came so suddenly on the still, warm evening and sent so many leaves pattering down that we thought it was raining. We held our breath.'
>
> Tolkien resumed, arguing that myths, far from being lies, were the best way of conveying truths which would otherwise be inexpressible. We have come from God, Tolkien argued, and inevitably the myths woven by us, though they contain error, reflect a splintered fragment of the true light, the eternal truth that is with God. Myths may be misguided, but they steer however shakily toward the true harbour, whereas materialistic 'progress' leads only to the abyss and the power of evil.[112]

As the two men shared with Lewis that the gospel myth was similar to others except that it really happened in time and space, it further confirmed an event that took place five years earlier following Lewis's reading of G. K. Chesterton's *The Everlasting Man*. As noted earlier it was following that conversation that Lewis observed:

> I had not long finished The Everlasting Man when something far more alarming happened to me. Early in 1926 the hardest boiled of all the atheists I ever knew sat in my room on the other side of the fire and remarked that the evidence for the historicity of the Gospels was really surprisingly good. "Rum thing," he went on. "All that stuff of Frazer's about the Dying God. Rum thing. It almost looks as if it really happened once." To understand the shattering impact of it, you would need to know the man (who

---

112. Pearce, *Tolkien*, 57–58. See also 969–72.

has certainly never since shown any interest in Christianity). If he, the cynic of cynics, the toughest of the toughs, were not—as I would still have put it—"safe," where could I turn? Was there no escape?[113]

So even though there were moments when Lewis made certain realizations, they were part of a cumulative effect that took place over years.

Building on this philosophy of myth, Tolkien and Dyson went on to express their belief that the story of Christ is simply a true myth; a myth that works in the same way as the others, but a myth that really happened. This revelation changed Lewis's entire conception of myth and Christianity. In fact, this line of reasoning struck a particular note of poignancy with Lewis because he had examined the historicity of the Gospels and had come to the almost reluctant conclusion that he was 'nearly certain that it really happened.'

As Lewis listened to Tolkien and Dyson, unable to find a weakness in their arguments, he began to realize that what they were saying made good sense. Tolkien had

shown that pagan myths were, in fact, God expressing himself through the minds of poets, using the images of their 'mythopoeia' to reveal fragments of His eternal truth. Yet, most astonishing of all, Tolkien maintained that Christianity was exactly the same except for the enormous difference that the poet who invented it was God Himself, and the images He used were real men and actual history. The death and resurrection of Christ was the old 'dying god' myth except that Christ was the real Dying God, with a precise and verifiable location in history and definite historical consequences. The old myth had become a fact while still retaining the character of a myth.[114]

Lewis's unbelief was being replaced with belief and the Christian message was gradually making sense. Lewis was so moved by this evening stroll and conversation that three days later, in a letter dated September 22, 1931, he wrote to his friend Arthur Greeves, and said that after the walk, "We continued (in my room) on Christianity: a good long satisfying talk in which I learned a lot: then discussed the difference between love and friendship—and then finally drifted back to poetry and books."[115] Shortly after, in a letter dated October 1, he confessed:

113. Lewis, *Surprised by Joy*, 223–24.
114. Pearce, *Tolkien*, 59.
115. Hooper, *The Collected Letters of C. S. Lewis*, 1:970.

'I have just passed on from believing in God to definitely believing in Christ—in Christianity. I will try to explain this another time. My long night talk with Dyson and Tolkien had a good deal to do with it.'[116]

What happened to Lewis that evening was a complete shift in worldview, a crisis of faith; he had moved from atheism to theism and then to Christianity. Pearce observes:

> Building on this philosophy of myth, Tolkien explained to Lewis that the story of Christ was the true myth at the very heart of history and at the very root of reality. Whereas the pagan myths were manifestations of God expressing Himself through the minds of poets, using the images of their "mythopoeia" to reveal fragments of His eternal truth, the true myth of Christ was a manifestation of God expressing Himself through Himself, with Himself and in Himself. God, in the Incarnation, had revealed Himself as the ultimate Poet who was creating reality, the true poem or true myth, in His own image. Thus, in a divinely inspired paradox, myth was revealed as the ultimate realism.
>
> Such a revelation changed Lewis's whole conception of Christianity, precipitating his conversion.[117]

In the October 18 letter, Lewis shares that the stumbling block to his coming to faith in Christ was primarily understanding the Christian doctrine of redemption and the substitutionary death of Jesus Christ on behalf of sinful humanity which caused him to remain aversive to the gospel message. Prior to his believing in Christ, Lewis found the doctrine and the expressions used to describe it as "either silly or shocking."[118] Lewis writes:

> My puzzle was the whole doctrine of Redemption: in what sense the life and death of Christ 'saved' or 'opened salvation to' the world. I could see how miraculous salvation might be necessary: one could see from ordinary experience how sin (e.g. the case of a drunkard) could get a man to such a point that he was bound to reach Hell (i.e., complete degradation and misery) in this life unless something quite beyond natural help or effort stepped in. And I could well imagine a whole world of being in the same state and similarly in need of miracle. What I couldn't see was how the life and death of Someone Else (whoever he was) 2000 years ago could help us here and now — except in so far as his

116. Ibid., 974.

117. Pearce, *Literary Giants*, 243.

118. Hooper, *The Collected Letters of C. S. Lewis*, 1:976.

example helped us. And the example business, tho' true and important, is not Christianity: right in the center of Christianity, in the Gospels and St. Paul, you keep on getting something quite different and very mysterious expressed in those phrases I have so often ridiculed ('propitiation' — 'sacrifice' — 'the blood of the Lamb').[119]

Now that Lewis could see how the death of Someone Else could help us here and now, he needed a way to explain it to others and from talking to Tolkien and Dyson he realized that myth was that means.

Tolkien's reasoning that myths were not lies, but were the best way of conveying otherwise inexpressible truths, is what convinced Lewis. The idea that myths may be misguided but can nevertheless steer shakily toward the harbour, suggested to Lewis that one need not look at myth and truth as an either/or proposition. Instead, one could look at them as a both/and; myth is a means of conveying truth.

From his earliest years Lewis had a lifelong love for myths and the worlds they described. As he wrote in *The Problem of Pain*, "I have the deepest respect even for Pagan myths, still more from myths in Holy Scripture."[120] But it wasn't just myth as a genre that drew his interest, nor was it the question of the historicity of the story that was paramount. It was the power of the story that captured his attention. As he says when speaking of poetry:

Hence it is irrelevant whether the mood expressed in a poem was truly and historically the poet's own or one that he also had imagined. What matters is his power to make us live it . . .

This, so far as I can see, is the specific value or good of literature considered as Logos; it admits us to experiences other than our own. They are not, any more than our personal experiences, all equally worth having. Some, as we say, 'interest' us more than others. The causes of this interest are naturally extremely various and differ from one man to another; it may be the typical (and we say 'How true!') or the abnormal (and we say 'How strange!'); it may be the beautiful, the terrible, the awe-inspiring, the exhilarating, the pathetic, the comic, or the merely piquant. Literature gives the entree to them all.[121]

The power of poetry was in the author's ability to make the reader live the poem. Myth too had a power of its own and, irrespective of how the myth originated, its power to convey truth or change a life originated with God.

119. Ibid.; italics in original.
120. Lewis, *The Problem of Pain*, 66.
121. Lewis, *An Experiment in Criticism*, 139–40; italics in original.

Lewis understood the mythical element in Christianity was found throughout the Old Testament as far back as creation. Myth was always a means for God to speak to the human race. To people with or without special revelation, such as the Bible, myth served as one way for humanity to know what God desired of it.

In speaking of the "fatal flaw" in the human race that "always brings the selfish and cruel people to the top," Lewis notes God did three things:

> First of all He left us conscience, the sense of right and wrong: and all through history there have been people trying (some of them very hard) to obey it. None of them ever quite succeeded. Secondly, he sent the human race what I call good dreams: I mean those queer stories scattered all through the heathen religions about a god who dies and comes to life again and, by his death, has somehow given new life to men. Thirdly, He selected one particular people and spent several centuries hammering into their heads the sort of God He was—that there was only one of Him and that he cared about right conduct. Those people were the Jews, and the Old Testament gives an account of the hammering process.[122]

So, along with conscience and the Jewish people, God used the myth of a person dying and rising again to give new life to people as a way of preparing the human race for the coming of Jesus Christ. When Christ appears in space and time as a newborn infant this myth takes on flesh. Lewis writes:

> Then comes the real shock. Among these Jews there suddenly turns up a man who goes about talking as if He was God. He claims to forgive sins. He says He has always existed. He says He is coming to judge the world at the end of time. Now let us get this clear. Among Pantheists, like the Indians, anyone might say that he was a part of God, or one with God; there would be nothing very odd about it. But this man, since He was a Jew, could not mean that kind of God. God, in their language, meant that Being outside the world Who had made it and was infinitely different from anything else. And when you have grasped that, you will see that what this man said was, quite simply, the most shocking thing that has ever been uttered by human lips.[123]

Instead of arguing that it was a coincidence that a story of someone dying for others spread among cultures and that Christians simply applied it to

122. Lewis, *Mere Christianity*, 54.
123. Ibid.

their founder, Lewis maintained that the story originated in the goodness of God as a precursor of what was to come.

This then, to Lewis, is the purpose of myth. Myth is extra-literary, and even though by necessity it is comprised of words, the purpose of myth is to serve as a means of conveying power. In his *An Experiment in Criticism* he explains:

> There is, then, a particular kind of story which has a value in itself—a value independent of its embodiment in any literary work. The story of Orpheus strikes and strikes deep, of itself; the fact that Virgil and others have told it in good poetry is irrelevant. To think about it and be moved by it is not necessarily to think about those poets or to be moved by them. It is true that such a story can hardly reach us except in words. But this is logically accidental. If some perfected art of mime or silent film or serial pictures could make it clear with no words at all, it would still affect us in the same way.
>
> One might have expected that the plots of the crudest adventure stories, written for those who want only the Event, would have this extra-literary quality. But it is not so. You could not fob them off with a synopsis instead of the story itself. They want only the Event, but the event will not reach them unless it is 'written up.' Moreover, their simplest stories are far too complicated for a readable abstract; too many things happen. The stories I am thinking of always have a very simple narrative shape—a satisfactory and inevitable shape, like a good vase or a tulip.
>
> It is difficult to give such stories any name except myths, but that word is in many ways unfortunate.[124]

Even though Lewis was not comfortable with the word "myth," he realized that to make up a different word would prove more difficult. And myth, when properly understood, could serve his purpose well enough.

In his book *Miracles*, Lewis has a footnote that addresses the question of the historicity of Old Testament miracles that further unpacked his understanding of myth becoming fact in history. He writes:

> My present view—which is tentative and liable to any amount of correction—would be that just as, on the factual side, a long preparation culminates in God's becoming incarnate as Man, so, on the documentary side, the truth first appears in mythical form and then by a long process of condensing or focusing finally becomes incarnate as History. This involves the belief

---

124. Lewis, *An Experiment in Criticism*, 41–42; italics in original.

that Myth in general is not merely misunderstood history (as Eubemerus thought) nor diabolical delusion (as some of the Fathers thought) nor priestly lying (as the philosophers of the Enlightenment thought) but, at its best, a real though unfocused gleam of divine truth falling on human imagination.[125]

The message or lesson of a myth was true; it was "divine truth" conveyed to human imagination irrespective of whether the story used to convey the point actually happened. Lewis's approach put the emphasis on the lesson of the story while critics focused on the veracity of the story. Someone rising from the dead was important, the specific person who rose from the dead being necessary for the story but secondary to the meaning of the myth.

Lewis's perspective regarding myth in the Bible was comprehensive. Not only did he see myth being fulfilled in history in the physical resurrection of Jesus Christ, but he understood Christ's resurrection as the culmination of thousands of years of God speaking through myth to the Jews throughout the Old Testament. He writes:

> The Hebrews, like other people, had mythology: but as they were the chosen people their mythology was the chosen mythology— the mythology chosen by God to be the vehicle of the earliest sacred truths, the first step in that process which ends in the New Testament where truth has become completely historical. Whether we can ever say with certainty where, in this process of crystallisation, any particular Old Testament story falls, is another matter. I take it that the memoirs of David's court come at one end of the scale and are scarcely less historical than St. Mark or Acts; and that the Book of Jonah is at the opposite end. It should be noted that on this view (a) Just as God, in becoming Man, is "emptied" of his glory, so the truth, when it comes down from the "heaven" of myth to the "earth" of history, undergoes a certain humiliation. Hence the New Testament is, and ought to be, more prosaic, in some ways less splendid, than the Old; just as the Old Testament is and ought to be less rich in many kinds of imaginative beauty than the Pagan mythologies. (b) Just as God is none the less God by being Man, so the Myth remains Myth even when it becomes Fact. The story of Christ demands from us, and repays, not only a religious and historical but also an imaginative response. It is directed to the child, the poet, and the savage in us as well as to the conscience and to the intellect. One of its functions is to break down dividing walls.[126]

125. Lewis, *Miracles*, 133–34n1; italics in original.
126. Ibid.; italics in original.

So Lewis contends that God was working through myth from the very beginning of humanity in what he called a "process of crystallisation" that gradually became less fantastic (manna falling from heaven) and more physical (restoring sight to blind eyes), culminating in the ultimate combination of myth and fact, the resurrection of one who died. It was this desire of the Creator to communicate to all people everywhere throughout human history that necessitated the use of myth, since myth was the perfect means to tie together the religious, historical, and imaginative and could speak to everyone on some level.

Another consideration that factored into Lewis's defense of myth was the detrimental influence upon myth of Naturalism, the idea that natural laws as opposed to supernatural laws governed the universe. Lewis argued that Naturalism was a relatively new way of looking at the world. For much of human history the idea of the natural being affected by the supernatural was the norm and this shift in thinking that relegated myth to a lesser place than previously held was, in Lewis's mind, not necessarily an advancement in human progress:

> The state of affairs in which ordinary people can discover the Supernatural only by abstruse reasoning is recent and, by historical standards, abnormal. All over the world, until quite modern times, the direct insight of the mystics and the reasonings of the philosophers percolated to the mass of the people by authority and tradition; they could be received by those who were no great reasoners themselves in the concrete form of myth and ritual and the whole pattern of life. In the conditions produced by a century or so of Naturalism, plain men are being forced to bear burdens which plain men were never expected to bear before. We must get the truth for ourselves or go without it.[127]

This substitution of myth, ritual, and tradition with individual authority led to the gradual demise of myth, a shift Lewis found catastrophic; nevertheless, he realized there were reasons behind such changes and suggested two. He argues:

> It might be that humanity, in rebelling against tradition and authority, has made a ghastly mistake; a mistake which will not be the less fatal because the corruptions of those in authority rendered it very excusable. On the other hand, it may be that the Power which rules our species is at this moment carrying out a daring experiment. Could it be intended that the whole mass of the people should now move forward and occupy for

127. Ibid., 42.

themselves those heights which were once reserved only for the sages? Is the distinction between wise and simple to disappear because all are now expected to become wise? If so, our present blunderings would be but growing pains. But let us make no mistake about our necessities. If we are content to go back and become humble plain men obeying a tradition, well. If we are ready to climb and struggle on till we become sages ourselves, better still. But the man who will neither obey wisdom in others nor adventure for her himself [sic] is fatal. A society where the simple many obey the few seers can live: a society where all were seers could live even more fully. But a society where the mass is still simple and the seers are no longer attended to can achieve only superficiality, baseness, ugliness, and in the end extinction. On or back we must go; to stay here is death.[128]

So while Lewis could understand and identify some causes for the demise of myth in civilization, he wondered if the ultimate mythmaker was not up to some kind of an experiment. But whatever the cause, he saw the passing of myth as detrimental to a happy and healthy society.

For Lewis, myth was a shadow of reality, not real, yet with meaning, for through myth God was communicating to humanity. The pagan myths revealed the story through imperfect beings in a supernatural world. But the gospel message was the substance revealed in time and space through people and ultimately through the perfect person, Jesus Christ of Nazareth. "The Word was God . . . and the Word became flesh and dwelt among us."[129]

Lewis's approach to myth is similar to someone having a thought that is truthful but unexpressed. To convey the idea to another it needs to be communicated. Once the idea is spoken (or written) it is manifested so others can consider the message. Whether it is spoken or written does not matter; what is important is that the idea, the truth, is conveyed. Out of a desire to communicate his mind to humanity God used a means that could convey the supernatural elements of the "other world" in language and ideas understood by humanity. To Lewis that means of communication is myth.

CONCLUSION

Myths have always served as a way of putting the fantastic into a context of the believable. Fear becomes a person (witch), danger a creature (dragon),

128. Ibid., 42–43.
129. John 1:1, 14.

and the tragedy of an unexplainable loss makes sense when seen from the perspective of the gods who had reasons for inflicting such harm.

> Far from being merely fantastic or cultish, myths are a treasure of realities—a kaleidoscope which, depending upon the age and experience of the reader, reflects and illuminates his experiences, fantasies, hopes, and fears. Myths have continued to capture the imagination and the soul of man for thousands of years because they depict and reveal behavior and problems common to all human beings. They deal with people who could be alive today, reminding us that human nature has not changed much throughout the long course of history. Thus the ancient myths speak clearly to modern man. They focused directly upon the nature of man as he was in the past, as he is in the present, and as he will continue to be in the future. They examine how man copes with his physical, social, religious, and political environment.[130]

As long as human beings reflect on the past, wonder about the future, and face disappointment and catastrophe in the present, myth will serve as a means to make sense of them. And while myth may not completely satisfy the rational side of humanity, it puts into language and concepts the ideas necessary to bring peace and hope into situations void of both.

Joseph Campbell and C. S. Lewis were both raised in homes with a strong faith tradition. Campbell in Roman Catholicism, Lewis in the Church of Ireland. And both men stepped away from their faith for years and explored other answers to the great questions of life. Lewis later returned to faith, first as a theist, and later as a Christian, and from that perspective he looked at how to best answer the great questions of meaning. And the supernatural was a necessary part of his answer since it was a part of life and faith. Lewis urged:

> Do not attempt to water Christianity down. There must be no pretence that you can have it with the Supernatural left out. So far as I can see Christianity is precisely the one religion from which the miraculous cannot be separated. You must frankly argue for supernaturalism from the very outset.[131]

From the moment of his conversion he concluded that the God who created history also accomplished His will in it through what are called miracles. Once the supernatural was assumed everything made sense and myth

---

130. Rosenberg and Baker, *Mythology and You*, 1–2.

131. Lewis, "Christian Apologetics," in *God in the Dock*, 99.

became a means used by God and humans to express and describe how these two worlds could become as one.

Joseph Campbell never returned to the faith of his youth.[132] His studies, travels, and explorations of other religions led him to conclude that the idea of the miraculous conflicted with history since history was subject to and explained by natural laws and scientific discoveries. And within the created order, in the heart of every individual, there was an unexplainable quality of life that each person of any religion or no religion could connect with to help find meaning in a less than ideal world. He wrote:

> But now, on the other hand (and here is the great point): that which is thus ultimately transcendent of all definition, categories, names, and forms, is the very substance, energy, being, and support, of all things, including ourselves: the reality of each and all of us. Transcendent of definition, transcendent of enclosure, it is yet immanent in each.[133]

For Campbell and Lewis, the subject matter they studied was often the same, but the conclusions they drew from their studies only had partial overlapping. There was significance in the content of their studies, but the importance and significance was weighted differently by each author.

132. The Larsens note that in August, 1987, Campbell was admitted to St. Francis Hospital in Honolulu with cancer of the esophagus. While there the hospital chaplain, Father Kieran Murray, asked to pray with him. "After the prayer concluded, to Jean's astonishment Joseph crossed himself. The priest registered the devotional act immediately, and asked if Campbell would like confession. 'I should not,' Campbell said, and smiled, indicating that he was not a practicing Catholic" (Larsen and Larsen, *Joseph Campbell*, 558).

133. Campbell, *The Flight of the Wild Gander*, 196.

6

C. S. Lewis and Joseph Campbell on the Role of Myth in a Technological Society

CULTURE IS COMPRISED OF individuals, and myth, like religion, influences on both an individual and societal level. Even in a technological society in which many people, and perhaps a majority, believe themselves and their society beyond its influence, myth remains a building block in literature, art, music, and advertising. And like religion, myth has both benefitted and hindered cultural advancement. It can be used and abused, serving as a means to bring order to a society or a form of destructive propaganda as citizens are subtly brainwashed, or coerced, by having their values conditioned by what they are told "everyone believes."

This chapter discusses the influence of myth upon the individual and the culture in a technological society. In so doing, it addresses several questions: How much does myth permeate and affect culture and how much does culture influence myth? Are there major storylines universal to myth even when the specific characters, context, and dialogue differ? Does culture influence myth to the same degree myth influences culture?

MYTH AND THE SIGNIFICANCE WITH RELIGION

Joseph Campbell and C. S. Lewis had a great interest in myth's role in culture and both men recognized its subtle and not-so-subtle influence. As one of the foremost contemporary authorities on mythology, Campbell was familiar with ancient and modern myths. He observed how certain themes appeared from one culture to another and how myth could be adapted in a modern context. Myths were timeless since "Myths are stories of our search through the ages for truth, for meaning, for significance."[1]

Like Campbell, C. S. Lewis also recognized the transcending nature of myth, that "myth transcends thought."[2] And like Campbell, Lewis understood how similar myth is to religion. Speaking of his Christian theology Lewis admitted, "We must not be ashamed of the mythical radiance resting on our theology. We must not be nervous about 'parallels' and 'Pagan Christs': they *ought* to be there."[3] Lewis understood the supernatural aspects of Christianity and myth and recognized the advantages in bringing the two together and allowing the one to help understand the other.

Myth, like religion, is timeless and universal. Some go so far as to argue myth *is* religion.[4] Since early in human history, people looked to both for daily guidance and for answers to the great questions of life such as: Is there any purpose beyond the immediate to life or tragedy? Can one make sense of death, especially the death of the young and innocent? What becomes of justice in the face of injustice? Can satisfactory reasons be found for the prosperity of the wicked or suffering of the innocent? Such questions remain as relevant—and answers as elusive—today as ever despite developments in education, science and technology.

Human beings have always been mythmakers. "All ancient peoples seem to have had their mythologies. In them they defined reality in terms of a transcendent world available only to the imagination."[5] Archaeologists point to ancient graves containing weapons, tools, and the bones of sacrificed animals, all of which suggest a belief in a future world similar to or better than their own.[6] Humans have always sought to know more about life above and beyond the here and now. Joseph Campbell observes:

> Mythology is apparently coeval with mankind. As far back, that is to say, as we have been able to follow the broken, scattered, earliest evidences of the emergence of our species, signs have been found which indicate that mythological aims and concerns were already shaping the arts and world of Homo sapiens.[7]

---

1. Campbell, *The Power of Myth*, 5.
2. Lewis, "Myth Became Fact," in *God in the Dock*, 66.
3. Ibid., 67; italics in original.
4. Hall, *Introduction to the Study of Religion*, 35.
5. Hein, *Christian Mythmakers*, 5.
6. Armstrong, *A Short History of Myth*, 1.
7. Campbell, *Myths to Live By*, 21.

As far as is known, humans appear alone as the only creatures concerned with transcendence, life after death, and practical thoughts such as caring for others beyond self and one's immediate family. Animals show no concern with the troubles or condition of animals in other parts of the world or even across the field, nor are they concerned about the suffering of others. Human beings alone are concerned with value and meaning. Humans also have the unique ability to imagine, to invent, and to conceive of things that do not exist. This is the "faculty that produces religion and mythology."[8]

This capability to imagine also serves to assure that myth and religion will remain part of the human experience. Imagination prevents science and technology from totally eradicating myth. Religious scholar Karen Armstrong notes:

> But the imagination is . . . the faculty that has enabled scientists to bring new knowledge to light and to invent technology that has made us immeasurably more effective. The imagination of scientists has enabled us to travel through outer space and walk on the moon, feats that were once only possible in the realm of myth. Mythology and science both extend the scope of human beings. Like science and technology, mythology . . . is not about opting out of this world, but about enabling us to live more intensely within it.[9]

Instead of myth being something dismissed by science and technology or as something opposed to religion, myth is able to transcend those disciplines and bring them together in a way that, for many, results in a deeper and more fulfilling life.

The enduring nature of myth is evident when one considers its implications in science, technology, and religion. For example, with respect to science, one only needs to think of the "big bang" theory in cosmology to realize it is another creation story similar to the many attributed to religion and myth, "and descriptions of such things as 'quasars,' 'quarks,' 'antimatter,' and 'black holes' among astronomers are more curious than anything the mad mind of the mythmaker ever invented."[10]

But one point that sets myth apart and places it above science is its ability to speak to matters science and technology cannot address; the need of humans to find meaning, reason, and hope in tragedy. Of the many reasons given for the continuing existence of myth, its ability to offer hope in crisis is vital.

8. Armstrong, *A Short History of Myth*, 2.

9. Ibid., 3.

10. Hall, *Introduction to the Study of Religion*, 43.

As far back as the time of the psalmist Asaph, the cry of injustice has been heard, "For I was envious of the arrogant when I saw the prosperity of the wicked. For they have no pangs until death; their bodies are fat and sleek. They are not in trouble as others are; they are not stricken like the rest of mankind . . . All in vain have I kept my heart clean and washed my hands in innocence. For all the day long I have been stricken and rebuked every morning."[11] For Asaph, the answer was found when he "went into the sanctuary of God; then I discerned their end."[12] Asaph concluded there was a God in heaven who ruled and reigned and this God would someday see to it that the guilty were punished and the innocent were vindicated.

But what about people outside of Asaph's belief system, of what came to be known as Judaism? What Asaph believed offered him a way to reconcile the injustices of life with the sovereign rule of a perfect God. It was a matter of God's concern, time, and perspective. Asaph's religious perspective represented a culturally and historically specific context, but his questions are universal. What of the Hindu, Muslim, Buddhist, and Christian? And what of those who find any suggestion of religious belief no help at all? In technological cultures science has a way of rendering religious beliefs to a level of unthinking sentimentalism. In the absence of a god or doctrine, how is one to cope with such mysteries? For many people the answer lies partly or wholly in the realm of myth.

C. S. Lewis and Joseph Campbell wrestled with such questions, and both men concluded that myth provided a nearly perfect way to express the inexpressible and to put into human terms and understanding that which brings reason out of chaos. Myth provides a way to speak in language typically reserved for religion without the constraints of any specific faith. And unlike religion, myth adapts to any culture. Instead of imposing upon people a set of beliefs or absolute truths from the "top down," myth originates from the human mind and conveys lessons and morals that translate to the surrounding culture. So both men saw three great advantages of myth over religion: (1) It provides the depth needed to tackle the most difficult questions of origin, life, and death. (2) It has the breadth to encompass all humanity and every culture from the most primitive to the most advanced, the religious and irreligious. And finally, (3) Myth achieves these goals without the divisiveness that accompanies religion with its claims of absolute truth or speaking on behalf of one true God.

Because there are areas of agreement between myth and religion, the greater challenge for the contemporary relevance of myth has been science.

11. Ps 73:3–14.

12. Ps 73:17.

But even this dispute has lessened as the perception of myth has changed over the centuries. As Segal observes:

> There is one genuine difference between nineteenth- and twentieth-century theories. Nineteenth-century theories tended to see the subject matter of myth as the natural world and to see the function of myth as either a literal explanation or a symbolic description of that world. Myth was typically taken to be the 'primitive' counterpart to science, which was assumed to be wholly modern. Science rendered myth not merely redundant but outright incompatible, so that moderns, who by definition are scientific, had to reject myth. By contrast, twentieth-century theories have tended to see myth as almost anything but an outdated counterpart to science, either in subject matter or in function. Consequently, moderns are not obliged to abandon it for science.[13]

Once it is recognized that myth addresses questions different from those asked of science, the two disciplines are not so incompatible. When asked if he thought myth and science were in conflict Campbell responded,

> No, they don't conflict. Science is breaking through now into the mystery dimensions. It's pushed itself into the sphere the myth is talking about. It's to the edge . . . the interface between what can be known and what is never to be discovered because it is a mystery that transcends all human research.[14]

The marvel of myth, and a reason for its longevity, is its ability to blend the true and experiential with the fantastic and miraculous. "Myth is . . . at its best, a real though unfocused gleam of divine truth falling on human imagination."[15] If myths were simply childish stories or short-term explanations to immediate problems with no ties into the human condition, they would likely become irrelevant and not be passed on. If they were devised simply to entertain children or identify one tribe from another, it is hard to see how they would be handed down from generation to generation or how they would adopt to new and very different cultures. Nor is it the case that myths originated and thrived only in pre-modern cultures. Ancient cultures as technologically advanced in their day as the Minoan civilization that created an alphabet and calendar found such inventions inadequate to meet deeper needs and so their culture too became a source of myth.

13. Segal, *Myth*, 3.

14. Campbell, *The Power of Myth*, 132.

15. Lewis, *Miracles*, 134.

But true myth is a blend of religion, philosophy, and imagination that takes place in a context that resonates with everyday life. What people experience in this life is portrayed in myth. Granted, people do not turn into animals, but caterpillars do turn into butterflies and small ugly creatures do become large beautiful birds; so some idea of metamorphosis is believable. And while people cannot vanish into thin air or turn children into animals, shamans and magicians have been mesmerizing people from the earliest times into thinking they could. The people who dismiss myth as the belief of the gullible, fail to see how close they are to believing it when entertained by sleight of hand and special effects. And anyone who thinks deeply about the wonder of birth and mystery of death is meditating about myth.

Another reason myth lives on is seen in the observation of the Preacher in Ecclesiastes when he says, "What has been is what will be, and what has been done is what will be done, and there is nothing new under the sun. Is there a thing of which it is said, 'See, this is new'? It has been already in the ages before us."[16] Myths rely on the fact that human nature changes very little despite the influences of education, technology, and culture. The challenges of simply being human with a capability to think, to inquire, to imagine, and to face disappointment and tragedy has changed little in human history; so myth endures since it can speak to the past, the present, and the future of people everywhere. Myth exists because myth is part of the human experience. "The themes [of myth] are timeless, and the inflection is to the culture."[17]

But as much as advocates see myth as a common thread running throughout all humanity with the potential of drawing all people together, myth is not without problems and challenges, starting just with its definition. As English professor Michael Sexton quipped, "The word *myth* belongs with the terms that Humpty Dumpty says deserve extra pay for doing so much work."[18] To critics, myth cannot be taken seriously since it serves as a poor substitute to truth and experience. Myth belongs in the realm of child rearing along with games, fables, and bedtime stories; it is a means of offering hope and comfort to those who lack the maturity to face the difficult questions of life. But as individuals mature, they must learn to benefit from the morals and life-lessons of such stories while putting away any idea that such stories are credible. But Campbell and Lewis both disagree and argue that myth should be taken seriously because it is a reflection of truth and experience rather than being a substitute for each.

16. Eccl 1:9–10.

17. Campbell, *The Power of Myth*, 11.

18. Hall, *Introduction to the Study of Religion*, 35; italics in original.

The idea of "outgrowing myth" is the solution proposed by those averse to myth. Critics do not think myth has no place in a society; their concern is when myth is taken seriously by adults as offering helpful and reasonable answers to questions regarding the meaning of life, death, hope, and tragedy. Few critics maintain that a myth is a lie, a deliberate attempt to deceive or withhold truth. The concern is that belief in myth is naïve and thus detrimental; myth attempts to do too much (to give comprehensive explanations to great philosophical questions) with too little (stories of gods and goddesses, dragons and miraculous events). One cannot always believe the stork brought the baby.

So, what, for Campbell and Lewis, is the place for myth in a culture dominated by science and technology? Is it similar to religion or closer to philosophy? Can myth exist comfortably in a society dominated by materialists, secularists, or atheists? Is myth specifically religious or does it swallow up religion in some grand meta-narrative that makes religion a sub-text of myth? Or is myth nothing more than what it means to be human? Does myth preserve the unwritten rules of life telling each culture and individual how to live in ways that insure a fulfilled and happy existence? What significance does myth hold for the individual and culture?

MYTH AND THE SIGNIFICANCE OF THE INDIVIDUAL

Campbell and Lewis agree that, among other things, for those who accept them, myths set forth guidelines for living and personal behavior. As a child learns of the activities and attitudes of the deities, a moral tone is conveyed and expectations of individual behavior become standardized. An individual who must live with others cannot be free to make up moral behavior that suits only individual desires and expectations. In myth, one is able to identify ethical situations that occur in life and be presented with a number of available options by way of response. Myths are stories in which humans are rewarded and punished enabling the individual to know what is accepted behavior in an orderly and well-structured society. When asked if accepted cultural behavior could be regarded as mythology, Campbell responded, "An unstated mythology, you might say. This is the way we use fork and knife, this is the way we deal with people, and so forth. It's not all written down in books."[19]

But not only do myths set forth standards of morality and acceptable behavior, they also address questions asked universally concerning life and meaning. Jennings observes, "With the communication and sharing

19. Campbell, *The Power of Myth*, 8.

of experiences, humans create a shared symbolic reality and try to answer questions that have seemed to plague humankind for all time—to discover a 'truth' or message in similar experiences.[20]

In her book, *In Other Worlds: SF and the Human Imagination*,[21] Margaret Atwood discusses eight questions every person asks when considering life and meaning.[22]

1. *Where did the world come from?*

As Lewis comments, this question is universal:

> I suspect that many people assume that some clear doctrine of creation underlies all religions: that in Paganism the gods, or one of the gods, usually created the world; even that religions normally begin by answering the question, "Who made the world?"[23]

Irrespective of whether the conclusion is creation out of nothing, the result of preexisting materials, or the outcome of a sexual act between gods, every individual (and culture) looks down the corridor of human history for a beginning of existence. How did the earth, sun, stars, and moon come into existence? What causes the wind to blow, the tides to come in and out, the sun and moon to rise and set? Such questions transcend time and culture, and myth can provide answers that make sense. As Lewis says, "In the enjoyment of a great myth we come nearest to experiencing as a concrete what can otherwise be understood only as an abstraction."[24]

2. *Where did people come from?*

Children have parents who have parents, etc., but it cannot be *ad infinitum,* so how did humanity begin? Who parented the first human and how did those parents come into being? The creation story in Genesis, of God forming man out of the dust of the earth and woman from man's rib, is well known but it is not the only creation story. Since no one can come from nothing and every beginning has to start from something how did the human race begin? How did I get here? Myth and religion offer answers to such questions, answers that sometimes sound similar. Lewis remarks,

> I have therefore no difficulty in accepting, say, the view of those scholars who tell us that account of Creation in *Genesis*

20. Jennings, "Communication and Myth," 9.
21. Atwood, *In Other Worlds.*
22. Ibid., 51–52.
23. Lewis, "The Poison of Subjectivism," in *Reflections on the Psalms,* 78.
24. Lewis, "Myth Became Fact," in *God in the Dock,* 66.

is derived from earlier Semitic stories which were Pagan and mythical. We must of course be quite clear what "derived from" means. Stories do not reproduce their species like mice. They are told by men. Each re-teller either repeats exactly what his predecessor had told him or else changes it. He may change it unknowingly or deliberately.[25]

3. Where did our people come from?

While the human race is one, it is comprised of individuals and races of different features, skin color, languages, and customs. Why and how did such differences come about? How did humanity become different tribes and people? Again, the Genesis account of the Tower of Babel offers one answer but there are others because people everywhere want to know how they became who they are. Why am I the way I am?

4. Why do bad things happen to good people?

Perhaps no question has been asked more often in the face of tragedy than "Why, God?" Even people who do not consider themselves religious find themselves wondering why or how a good and sovereign God would allow a natural disaster or senseless calamity resulting in great loss. As Campbell points out,

> I can't think of any [myths] that say if you're going to live, you won't suffer. Myths tell us how to confront and bear and interpret suffering, but they do not say that in life there can or should be no suffering.[26]

When Rabbi Harold Kushner's three-year-old son was diagnosed with a degenerative disease that took his life in his early teens it prompted Kushner to write a book with the now familiar title, *When Bad Things Happen to Good People.*[27] Whether it's the terminal illness of a child, the disaster of an innocent man such as Job, or the crucifixion of a holy man such as Jesus, people have an innate need to make sense out of such senseless acts and myth offers such answers.

5. Why do good things happen to bad people?

Equally troubling as the earlier question is making sense of the prosperity and trouble-free existence of those who are deliberately wicked and cruel. Rulers often rise to power and live a life of extravagance by sacrificing the innocent without apparent consequences. Does anything happen to

25. Lewis, "Historicism," in *Reflections on the Psalms,* 110; italics in original.

26. Campbell, *The Power of Myth,* 160.

27. Kushner, *When Bad Things Happen.*

them after death? Do the gods finally mete out justice and right all wrongs, or is life simply brief and unfair? Myth probes such questions and offers answers.

6.   *What is right behavior?*

Related to the above, and no less difficult, is the question of right and wrong behavior. To this question religious answers are usually clear and absolute. One thinks, for instance, of the Ten Commandments. But myths offer their own versions of right and wrong conduct which sometimes run contrary to religious answers. It is not uncommon in myth for lying to be commendable or killing to be heroic, but for those who start such myths, as well as those who pass them on, such answers meet a need for a standard of correct behavior. When a culture lacks traditional myths, the result is an alienation of younger generations from the culture. When Bill Moyers asked Campbell where kids growing up in today's cities get their myths he responded,

> They make them up themselves. This is why we have graffiti all over the city. These kids have their own gangs and their own initiations and their own morality, and they're doing the best they can. But they're dangerous because their own laws are not those of the city. They have not been initiated into our society.[28]

So in the absence of religion and common cultural traditions, humanity still has its myths, but such myths originate in a very small context. Instead of a large, homogeneous culture handing down myths that unify, gangs and individuals make up myths that serve to satisfy a select few with behavior that can be destructive to outsiders.

7.   *What do the gods want, or God, if it's a monotheism?*

Ultimately, the gods rule everything. From the ability to bear children to the rain and sun needed for crops, keeping the gods happy is paramount. But knowing what pleases them requires revelation or observing human behavior. Since obedience and gift giving signifies loyalty and expresses appreciation, such practices appear in myth as ways of pleasing the gods. Whether it's offering up the fruit of one's labor, performing a heroic deed, or sacrificing one's children, myth informs future generations of how to appease the unseen who see everything.

Tied in to such questions of theology is how people from different backgrounds understand the divine; as Campbell points out,

---

28. Campbell, *The Power of Myth*, 8.

[T]he ultimate function of Oriental myths, philosophies, and social forms, therefore, is to guide the individual to an actual *experience* of his identity with *that; tat tvam asi* ("Thou art that") is the ultimate word in this connection.

By contrast, in the Western sphere—in terms of the orthodox traditions, at any rate, in which our students have been raised—God is a person, the person who has created this world . . . We, therefore, do not find in the religions of the West, as we do in those of the East, mythologies and cult disciplines devoted to the yielding of an experience of one's *identity* with divinity. That, in fact, is heresy. Our myths and religions are concerned, rather, with establishing and maintaining an experience of relationship—and this is quite a different affair.[29]

Unlike monotheistic religions that impose one view of the divine upon everyone, myth allows questions of divinity to be answered in ways that consider the cultural context. As Lewis observes, "I suspect that men have sometimes derived more spiritual sustenance from myths they did not believe than from the religion they professed."[30] Whether one is seeking an experience or an identity with the divine, both are found in myth.

8. *What are the right relationships between men and women?*

This question is also timeless as the sexes continue to wrestle with matters of equality and the roles of gender. Even in cultures that look with disdain on the inequality of men and women practiced in other cultures, the place of gender remains controversial. Is woman man's equal or is she superior or inferior to him? Does it matter if a myth comes out of a patriarchal culture or does myth reveal the mind of the gods who transcend (rather than reflect) culture? No closer relationship exists than between man and woman so it is imperative to a happy and satisfying life to know the creator's intent. When speaking about the closest relationship between a man and woman, that of marriage, Campbell explains it in mythological terms,

Myth helps you to put your mind in touch with this experience of being alive. It tells you what the experience is. Marriage, for example. What is marriage? The myth tells you what it is. It's the reunion of the separated duad. Originally you were one. You are now two in the world, but the recognition of the spiritual identity is what marriage is. It's different from a love affair. It

---

29. Campbell, *The Mythic Dimension*, 5–6; italics in original.
30. Lewis, "Myth Became Fact," in *God in the Dock*, 67.

has nothing to do with that. It's another mythological plane of experience.[31]

At some point each person faces such questions of significance, meaning, and proper ethical behavior. As children mature they ask adults the "How" and "Why" questions of life. Adults find themselves between the twin mysteries of birth and death wondering about the meaning of their existence and the significance of the tragedies and blessings they encounter. And finally the aged, with the wisdom that comes with years, look to the inevitability of their own deaths and wonder what, if anything, is next. As seen earlier, Campbell states that to all of these questions myth provides wisdom and guidance because, "It has always been the prime function of mythology and rite to supply the symbols that carry the human spirit forward, in counteraction to those other constant human fantasies that tend to tie it back."[32]

In an interview with Bill Moyers, Campbell remarked, "The individual has to find an aspect of myth that relates to his own life."[33] Campbell follows this remark by explaining the four aspects of myth that enable each person to tap into myth in a way that meets immediate needs and addresses the eight questions posed earlier by Atwood. Campbell notes that myth, first, has a *mystical* element to it. This aspect addresses questions of origin and makes one aware of the mystery of human existence. Second is the aspect of *cosmology*. This feature identifies the transcendent in the material. "You strike a match, what's fire? You can tell me about oxidation, but that doesn't tell me a thing."[34] This second function reveals the mystery behind all existence.

The third function of myth is *sociological*; it teaches the individual how to live within his or her society. "As a tool, studying each other's myths may aid in developing greater intimacy in both interpersonal and group relationships as understanding between individuals and groups grow."[35] This aspect of myth differs from traditional religion since it will vary from culture to culture: "You can have a whole mythology for polygamy, a whole mythology for monogamy. Either one's okay. It depends on where you are."[36] This aspect addresses questions of right and wrong behavior within any given culture. And the fourth aspect of myth is the *pedagogical* one. This purpose instructs how to act as the ideal man or woman while undergoing any circumstance.

31. Campbell, *The Power of Myth*, 6.
32. Campbell, *The Hero with a Thousand Faces*, 11.
33. Campbell, *The Power of Myth*, 31.
34. Ibid.
35. Jennings, "Communication and Myth," 4.
36. Campbell, *The Power of Myth*, 31.

Even when the reason given for the prosperity of the wicked (or the suffering of the righteous) do not satisfy, myth still provides for the immediate need of how to respond when reason fails and one must live by faith. When taken together, these four functions show that myth gives meaning to life.

Human beings must have a meaning beyond mere survival or existence and myth provides that meaning in a number of ways. First, myth enables individuals to transcend daily life by enabling them to see their activities in a greater scheme of global or even eternal significance.

The anonymous Swedish proverb, "Shared joy is a double joy; shared sorrow is half a sorrow" applies to myth since myths allow individuals to see beyond their solitary and immediate joy by giving it the meaning of a blessing from on high. For someone to receive an unexpected (or better, an undeserved) favor, this turns a simple circumstance of "luck" into something meaningful since now there is a greater power showing approval and favor.

Also, pain and suffering are alleviated by myth. Pain is more bearable if we believe it has some deeper meaning beyond suffering as an end in itself. If a higher power deems me to suffer for a reason I cannot see but I know He (She, It?) knows, then I am better able to endure it since it is no longer random but purposeful. Thus, for Lewis, Christianity's promise of Romans 8:28, that "we know that God causes all things to work together for good to those who love God, to those who are called according to His purpose" is one each person wants to believe concerning his or her own situation.

This ability of myth to help understand experiences such as pain or pleasure was seen by Lewis as one of myth's abiding principles. Because humans have both the capacity to think and to experience but are unable to do both simultaneously, myth provides a way for people to think about experience. He observes:

> Human intellect is incurably abstract. Pure mathematics is the type of successful thought. Yet the only reality we experience is concrete — this pain, this pleasure, this dog, this man. While we are loving the man, bearing the pain, enjoying the pleasure, we are not intellectually apprehending Pleasure, Pain or Personality. When we begin to do so, on the other hand, the concrete realities sink to the level of mere instances or examples: we are no longer dealing with them, but with that which they exemplify . . . You cannot *study* Pleasure in the moment of the nuptial embrace, nor repentance while repenting, nor analyzed the nature of humor while roaring with laughter. But when else can you really know these things?[37]

---

37. Lewis, "Myth Became Fact," in *God in the Dock*, 65–66; italics in original.

As Lewis considered this problem, he realized that myth provided a means whereby one could concretize the abstract thus allowing both the mind and emotions to bear on the experience. He writes,

> Of this tragic dilemma myth is the partial solution. In the enjoyment of a great myth we come nearest to experiencing as a concrete what can otherwise be understood only as an abstraction . . . it is only while receiving the myth as a story that you experience the principle concretely.[38]

So myth's significance to the individual is that it provides a way for a person to understand and articulate an experience.

A second way myth is significant to an individual is by providing a way to explain the unexplainable. Since there will always be realms of the known and unknown, humans will always want to understand what cannot be perceived through the senses.

Myth helps answer such questions as: Do we exist before birth? Are there souls in some celestial realm awaiting bodies? What happens after death? Do we return in another form or as another person? Do we become angelic or spiritual beings or do we simply return to the earth? Are the good deeds in this life rewarded and the bad deeds punished (or vice versa)? What is one to make of coincidences or matters of good (and bad) luck? Is it nothing more than time and chance? What about apparent miracles and the mysteries that lie beyond the realm of natural explanations? And finally, what is one to think about the universe beyond what humans can discover? If there are realms impossible for human exploration, how can anyone say what is there?

Myths are able to answer and explain such dilemmas. By being able to bridge the natural and supernatural, myths provide a way to understand what otherwise would be senseless and maddening. Whether it's the death of one child through an accident, or the loss of a hundred thousand people by a tsunami, myth supplies answers and provides comfort where human logic cannot; myth gives hope to the heart and provides a reason to the mind. Myth serves as a translator of thought; it is able to take a thought or event that by itself is abstract and present it in a way that humans can relate to. As Lewis observes:

> When we translate we get abstraction—or rather, dozens of abstractions. What flows into you from the myth is not truth but reality (truth is always *about* something, but reality is that *about which* truth is), and, therefore every myth becomes the

38. Ibid., 66.

father of innumerable truths on the abstract level. Myth is the mountain whence all the different streams arise which become truths down here in the valley; *in hac valle abstractionis*. Or, if you prefer, myth is the isthmus which connects the peninsula world of thought with the vast continent we really belong to. It is not, like truth, abstract; nor is it, like direct experience, bound to the particular.[39]

So myth can help make sense and bring reason to an otherwise senseless experience. Disasters and tragedies are typically senseless and defy reason and explanations; myth provides a backdrop story that puts the event in a context with cause and result.

A third way myth is significant on the individual level is in its ability to provide understanding to the operations of the natural world. Myths can help make sense out of the randomness of natural disasters. A drought or flood can mean the end of a person's living or life; so the role of human and divine responsibility is important. Is a drought the response of an angry deity and, if so, is there a way to remedy the situation? Campbell refers to the "magical" aspect of myth, "where the symbols are employed to achieve magically-caused effects; e.g. Navaho rain rites; the Mass."[40]

Within Christianity, the narrative account of the life of the apostle Paul and an encounter on the isle of Malta illustrates such a belief. As the apostle was collecting sticks for a fire, he was bitten in the hand by what was known to be a poisonous viper. The response of the natives was "Undoubtedly this man is a murderer, and though he has been saved from the sea, justice has not allowed him to live." But later, when no harm came to Paul, "they changed their minds and began to say that he was a god."[41] While the specific details of their belief system is not discussed, there is enough evidence to conclude that to the native mind a supernatural power was operating in the realm of nature, first to punish and then to prove Paul's deity.

While controversial, some individuals might contend that science itself ventures into the realm of myth when it postulates theories to explain origins it cannot verify by experiment. For instance, evolution and the Big Bang are both considered theories since they are conclusions based on the available evidence. One theory explains the origin of humanity, the other the origin of matter. But all myths of origin are based on the evidence available at the time with new evidence becoming available at any moment. As Lewis observes,

39. Ibid.; italics in original.
40. Campbell, *Sake and Satori*, 257.
41. Acts 28:1–6.

> To the biologist Evolution is a hypothesis. It covers more of the facts than any other hypothesis at present on the market and is therefore to be accepted unless, or until, some new supposal can be shown to cover still more facts with even few assumptions.[42]

And even if one disagrees with referring to scientific theories as "myth," it remains true that the discoveries made by science raise more questions of origins and thus deepen the mystery and awe of human existence. As Lewis said of creation, "It is a very *long* story, with a complicated plot; and we are not, perhaps, very attentive readers."[43]

A fourth way myth is significant to the individual concerns the role models it offers and the examples it provides of individuals responding to the exigencies of life. All children look up to someone whether it is parent, older sibling, or relative, and as they get older their heroes are often strangers whether real (actors and sports figures) or imaginary (comic book or video game figures). Even as adults, role models are discovered in real life, movies, the news, and literature.

Myth is uniquely fitted to provide role models since, unlike the God of religions such as Judaism or Christianity, mythological deities typically are not omnipresent, omnipotent, or omniscient. The gods of myth are slightly better than humans except in power and knowledge. Like humans, the gods are driven by reason and emotion and have to respond to unanticipated events and consequences. But since they are close to human and yet are divine, they can provide mere mortals an example of how a nobler (or at least a greater) being behaves.

And as individuals grow and mature, myth provides what Campbell refers to as a "pedagogical" function by offering examples of how an individual is to behave in each stage of life; he says myth carries

> a person through the inevitable stages of a lifetime. And these are the same today as they were in the paleolithic caves: as a youngster you're dependent on parents to teach you what life is, and what your relationship to other people has to be, and so forth; then you give up that dependence to become a self-responsible authority; and, finally, comes the stage of yielding: you realize that the world is in other hands. And the myth tells you what the values are in those stages in terms of the possibilities of your particular society.[44]

42. Lewis, "The Funeral of a Great Myth," in *Christian Reflections*, 85.
43. Lewis, *Miracles*, 99; italics in original.
44. Maher and Briggs, *An Open Life,* 32.

So myth can provide an ideal role model that the individual can relate to and emulate on a practical level. The goal is not to be perfect, but to be mature.

While not a major focus in the writings of C. S. Lewis,[45] the role model or "hero" is a popular theme in mythology and one Joseph Campbell discussed in depth. In his classic work, *The Hero with a Thousand Faces*, he argues that a single hero, or archetype, appears within myths throughout the world despite variety in culture, language, time, and location. "A hero ventures forth from the world of common day into a region of supernatural wonder: fabulous forces are there encountered and a decisive victory is won: the hero comes back from this mysterious adventure with the power to bestow boons on his fellow man."[46] The hero is the good within each individual; he "symbolizes our ability to control the irrational savage within us."[47]

The hero, according to Campbell, goes through three stages: Departure, Initiation, and Return. In myth these stages are dramatic and often involve supernatural beings but on a common, experiential, level each individual passes through the same stages.

The first stage, departure, sometimes referred to the "call to adventure,"[48] is the moment an individual is beckoned to go outside of his society to an unknown region that consists of both danger and treasure. This region can be a forest, desert, mountaintop, or unknown island, but it is always unfamiliar and threatening. Here the hero will meet and engage danger in the form of unimaginable and supernatural creatures. This first stage, as all three stages, is complex with subplots such as an initial refusal of the hero to venture out into danger or the involvement of others who support him. But the key of the first stage is the initial movement away from the safety of one's home and people.

The second stage is initiation. "This is a favorite phase of the myth-adventure."[49] This stage takes place once the hero has arrived at his destination and must confront danger and trials. Usually the hero has one objective in mind, but to accomplish it he must undergo a series of trials and meet numerous dangers. As with the first stage, initiation can involve subplots involving temptation of the opposite sex or an authority role such as a fa-

---

45. "I am describing and not accounting for myths. To inquire how they arise . . . is quite outside my purpose. I am concerned with the effect of myths as they act on the conscious imagination of minds more or less like my own . . ." (Lewis, *An Experiment in Criticism*, 44–45).

46. Campbell, *The Hero with a Thousand Faces*, 30.

47. Campbell, *The Power of Myth*, xiv.

48. Campbell, *The Hero with a Thousand Faces*, 58.

49. Ibid., 97.

ther, but the primary focus is the engagement of the hero with danger or an enemy.

The third and final stage of a hero consists of the return. Campbell explains,

> When the hero-quest has been accomplished, through penetration to the source, or through the grace of some male or female, human or animal, personification, the adventurer still must return with his life-transmuting trophy. The full round, the norm of the monomyth, requires that the hero shall now begin the labor of bringing the runes of wisdom, the Golden Fleece, or his sleeping princess, back into the kingdom of humanity, where the boon may redound to the renewing of the community, the nation, the planet, or the ten thousand worlds.[50]

So he has accomplished his appointed task and returns to bestow on others a hard-won prize.

This hero motif is important because it is universal and timeless; it is in its essence, fundamental to being human. One of Campbell's greatest contributions to mythology was to identify this theme throughout the world. When asked why his book was entitled *The Hero with a Thousand Faces* he responds,

> Because there is a certain typical hero sequence of actions which can be detected in stories from all over the world and from many periods of history. Essentially, it might even be said there is but one archetypal mythic hero whose life has been replicated in many lands by many, many people. A legendary hero is usually the founder of something—the founder of a new age, the founder of a new religion, the founder of a new city, the founder of a new way of life. In order to found something new, one has to leave the old and go in quest of the seed idea, a germinal idea that will have the potentiality of bringing forth that new thing.[51]

So, unlike religion that grows out of a specific culture and the beliefs of a segment of people, the hero of myth is possessed by each individual. Though Campbell understands religion as culture-specific, he says the typical myth is also culturally-specific. There is a specific mono-myth that emerges from the many different variations on the theme of heroes that speaks to people regardless of context because all people, in passing from childhood to

50. Ibid., 193.
51. Ibid., 136.

adolescence to adulthood, undergo trials and tribulations, as well as joys and successes.

This is why myth and the role of hero is significant to the individual, because everyone is a hero. As opposed to the traditional definition of the word as someone, usually a man, who distinguishes himself from everyone else by an act of courage or ability and is regarded as a role model, Campbell's idea of a hero is universal. For instance, the common act of birth makes both the mother and child heroes. Agreeing with Freud's colleague, Austrian psychoanalyst Otto Rank (1884–1939), Campbell states:

> [E]veryone is a hero in birth, where he undergoes a tremendous psychological as well as physical transformation, from the condition of a little water creature living in a realm of amniotic fluid into an air-breathing mammal which ultimately will be standing. That's an enormous transformation, and had it been consciously undertaken, it would have been, indeed, a heroic act. And there was a heroic act on the mother's part, as well, who had brought all this about.[52]

While some individuals may perform acts recognized by their culture as heroic, each individual must be understood as a hero since everyone starts out a hero and continues a heroic journey as he or she grows to adulthood.

The acts of heroism, in Campbell's thinking, are the stages of growth each individual undergoes. From birth to puberty to adulthood,

> This is the fundamental psychological transformation that everyone has to undergo . . . That's the basic motif of the universal hero's journey—leaving one condition and finding the source of life to bring you forth into a richer or mature condition.[53]

Each human being is a living myth and grows through various stages of myth.

For both Campbell and Lewis, myth's significance to the individual does not disappear in the face of science and technology. Myth has the capability to morph and fit comfortably into any culture and to use the cultural tools to its own advantage. "Despite our very scientific modern culture, mythology still connects with our human hearts because it appeals to transcendence, that is, a reality outside of the world that gives meaning and purpose to our existence within the world."[54]

52. Campbell, *The Power of Myth*, 124–25.

53. Ibid., 124.

54. Godawa, "Avatar," 16.

Myth is essential to the individual. Each person has his or her own myth; we create our own mythology. People and things that are important to us, the things we value, become objects around which we build myths. In a normal lifetime each person passes through various stages looking ahead with eager expectation to adulthood or sentimentally back on childhood, mythologizing each stage. And even though we accept the culturally dictated myths of ethical behavior and origins, we nevertheless value even more the myths that arise from our own dreams and ambitions. As Campbell observes,

> You see, myths do not come from a *concept* system; they come from a *life* system; they come out of a deeper center . . . Myths come from where the heart is, and where the experience is even as the mind may wonder why people believe those things. The myth does not point to a fact; the myth points beyond facts to something that informs the fact.[55]

To Campbell and Lewis, myth is comprised of what goes on around us as interpreted by what goes on inside us. What Lewis says about faith could be applied to myth:

> Faith, as we know it, does not flow from philosophical argument alone; nor from experience of the Numinous alone; nor from moral experience alone; nor from history alone; but from historical events which at once fulfil and transcend the moral category, which link themselves with the most numinous elements in Paganism, and which (as it seems to us) demand as their pre-supposition the existence of a Being who is more, but not less, than the God who many reputable philosophers think they can establish.[56]

Like faith, myth arises out of a combination of philosophy, experience, morality, and history. Myth is significant to the individual since it provides guidance on questions of value that are beyond the reach of science and by offering a worldview that provides the holistic orientation one needs to make sense of the human experience.

55. Maher and Briggs, *An Open Life*, 21; italics in original.
56. Lewis, "Is Theism Important," in *God in the Dock*, 175.

MYTH AND THE SIGNIFICANCE OF SOCIETY AND CULTURE

Because culture is comprised of individuals, myth has a societal as well as individual significance. "The myths of a culture are those stories it takes seriously—the ones that are thought to be key to its identity."[57]

The role of myth in culture is cyclical; myths are passed down from previous generations and then are adopted by a more educated and technologically advanced people who pass them on to a more technologically advanced culture which finds ways to embrace the myth even if it thinks itself too educated to believe such stories. As Atwood observes:

> Myths are stories that are central to their cultures and that are taken seriously enough that people organize their ritual and emotional lives around them, and can even start wars over them. Such stories go underground, as it were, when the core statements about truth and reality repeated in the stories cease to be entirely, factually believed. But they then emerge in other guises, such as Art, or political ideologies.[58]

Not only is the essence of myth human, but the essence of culture is mythical. When asked if appreciation of myth is relevant to the present time, Campbell responds '[T]he great realization of mythology is the immanence of the divine—here and now—you don't have to go anywhere else for it"[59] and Lewis says that he "defines myths by their effect on us."[60] Both men agreed in the timeless relevance of myth.

People in highly technological cultures are often quick to dismiss the influence of myth, but as noted earlier Campbell points out that science and myth:

> don't conflict. Science is breaking through now into the mystery dimensions. It's pushed itself into the sphere the myth is talking about. It's come to the edge.[61]

Myth cannot be removed from culture since culture is comprised of myth as much as it is of individuals. Even in a culture as technologically advanced as the modern West, myth has a place because of its role in helping us to participate in certain mysteries of life. As Campbell points out,

57. Atwood, *In Other Worlds*, 49.
58. Ibid., 51–55.
59. Maher and Briggs, *An Open Life*, 32.
60. Lewis, *An Experiment in Criticism*, 56.
61. Campbell, *The Power of Myth*, 132.

But the role of myth will be what it has always been: to render in contemporary terms the mysteries of our own inner life, and the relationship of these mysteries to the cosmic life—because we are all parts of the cosmos. So myth has got to deal with the human system in relation to the mystery of the universe.[62]

Since myth is able to provide a means of bringing timeless principles to apply to the individual experience of any age, it is hard to imagine a culture thriving, or even surviving, without myth. Speaking of the constant relevance of myth, Peretti observes,

Myths, though old, are part of the present. To retell them is not to join them in the past, but to affirm their existence in the present, to recognize their continuing vitality while representing the messages they bear in new creative acts.[63]

In his criticism of the modern attempts to "demythologize" the New Testament, Lewis quips, "I am sure 'demythologising' the N.T. always really means remythologising it: i.e., clothing it in the popular scientific and historical theories of your own period which are in fact transitory and will soon seem as mythological as those of the first century."[64]

Instead of myth being threatened by science, it is only the traditional religious elements of myth, what Atwood calls "the old religious furniture," that is threatened by knowledge and technology. She writes:

Why this migration of the West's more recent founding mythologies—our once-essential core stories of the Judeo-Christian era—from Earth to Planet X? Possibly because—as a society—we no longer believe in the old religious furniture, or not enough to make it part of our walking "realistic" life. If you have a conversation with the Devil and admit to it, you're liable to end up in a psychiatric ward, not sizzling at the stake. Supernatural creatures with wings and burning bushes that speak are unlikely to be encountered in a novel about stockbrokers unless the stockbrokers have been taking mind-altering substances. But such creatures are thoroughly at home on Planet X.[65]

Atwood points out the worlds of science fiction and myth are not hindered by the limitations of space and time and so the issue of the miraculous taking place in the present world, as claimed by religions such as Judaism and

---

62. Maher and Briggs, *An Open Life*, 117.
63. Peretti, "The Modern Prometheus," 214.
64. Hooper, *The Collected Letters of C. S. Lewis*, 3:1012.
65. Atwood, *In Other Worlds*, 64–65.

Christianity, do not exist in science fiction and myth. Creatures and events that cannot exist on earth can live on another planet, a planet similar to earth in many ways but with enough room given to imagination to allow even the unbelievable to be believable.

Atwood's explanation would seem reasonable to Campbell. For him "the Miracles in the Christ legend"[66] are psychological or metaphorical. An example of the former would be the physical healings, while the feeding of the five thousand is "told in metaphorical, mythological terms."[67] But Lewis does not have difficulty accepting the idea that a Creator can perform miracles.[68] By remaining open to the miraculous, Lewis has no need for an alternate universe. Nevertheless, he says "I like the whole interplanetary idea as a *mythology*" while lamenting, "The more astronomy we know the less likely it seems that other planets are inhabited: even Mars has practically no oxygen."[69]

Both Joseph Campbell and C. S. Lewis saw a timelessness to myth with its themes and figures spanning every culture and age. This is because, as Campbell observes, "One of the main functions of myth . . . [is] to carry a person through the inevitable stages of a lifetime. And these are the same today as they were in the Paleolithic caves."[70] On the individual level, nothing in humanity has changed; so myth remains culturally present and relevant. And as Lewis points out, "I believe that in the huge mass of mythology which has come down to us a good many different sources are mixed—true history, allegory, ritual, the human delight in story telling, etc.,"[71] further confirming that where culture exists myth and mythology will be present. And though both men expressed concern about the negative influence science and technology could have on myth,[72] if either man were alive today he would be able to point to an almost limitless number of examples of myth in modern Western culture.

66. Campbell, *Thou Art That*, 73.

67. Ibid.

68. "The experience of a miracle in fact requires two conditions. First we must believe in a normal stability of nature, which means we must recognize that the data offered by our senses recur in regular patterns. Secondly, we must believe in some reality beyond Nature. When both beliefs are held, and not till then, we can approach with an open mind the various reports which claim that this super- or extra-natural reality has sometimes invaded and disturbed the sensuous content of space and time which make our 'natural' world" (Lewis, "Miracles," in *God in the Dock*, 27).

69. Hooper, *The Collected Letters of C. S. Lewis*, 2:236–37; italics in original.

70. Maher and Briggs, *An Open Life*, 32.

71. Lewis, "Religion Without Dogma?," in *God in the Dock*, 132.

72. Lewis, "Religion and Science," in *God in the Dock*, 72–75; Campbell, *The Power of Myth*, 9.

Allusions to ancient myth are everywhere in contemporary society. Expressions such as the difficulty of a *Herculean* task, deception of a *Trojan horse* or the weakness of an *Achilles heel*, or the tragedy of opening *Pandora's box* reflects ancient myth. Possessing the *Midas touch* signifies an element of good luck while being rich as *Croesus* implies incredible wealth. Many people are unaware that a word used almost everyday, breakfast cereal, derives from *Ceres*, the name of the Roman goddess of harvest and agriculture. Figures of speech traced to myth include "caught between a rock and a hard place" and "between the Devil and deep blue sea," both refer to sailors caught between the monsters Scylla and Charybdis of Greek mythology.

In the field of psychology, a term made famous by Sigmund Freud, the *Oedipus complex*,[73] derives from the mythical king of Thebes, while *narcissism* derives from Narcissus, the mythical young man who fell in love with his own image reflected in a pool of water and wasted away from desire only to be transformed into a flower.

Common medical terms also come from myth. *Hygiene* comes from Hygieia, the Greek goddess of health, while *morphine* derives from Morpheus, a son of Hypnos and the god of dreams.

Other everyday terms have a mythical history. *Chronology* comes from Kronos, in Greek mythology the youngest of the first generations of Titans who became the father of Zeus and was later imprisoned in Tartarus. *Discipline* is from Disciplina, a Roman deity who personified self-control. The opposite of discipline, *Discord*, comes from Discordia, the Greek goddess of chaos while *eros* is handed down from Eros,[74] Greek god of love. *Fauna* finds its origin in Faunus, the Roman god of forest, plain, and field; *fidelity* from Fides, Roman goddess of trust; *flora* from Flora, goddess of plants, flowers, and fertility; and *fortune* from Fortuna, the Roman goddess of fortune and luck. Each of these common terms show the abiding nature of myth.

Some of the most famous works of art show the impact of myth in western culture.[75] Botticelli's *The Birth of Venus* is one of the world's most recognized paintings, and opera selections such as Offenbach's *Orpheus in the Underworld* are heavily influenced by myth.

The world of industry and commerce is not devoid of the influence of mythical characters. The cleanser *Ajax* and running shoes *Nike* find their logos in Greek mythological heroes, *Ajax* the grandson of Zeus, and *Nike* the personification of victory. The insurance company, the Aegis Group, harks

---

73. Campbell, *Pathways to Bliss*, 49–51.

74. Lewis, "The Four Loves," in *The Beloved Works of C. S. Lewis*, 262–75.

75. Campbell, *The Power of Myth*, 162.

back to the *Aegis*, the shield used by both Zeus and his daughter Athena in the *Iliad*.

Myth is also evident in the world of entertainment and movies. The influence of Joseph Campbell's work on myth upon moviemaker George Lucas is significant.[76] When asked if movies create myths and if a movie, like *Star Wars*, fills the modern need for mythical heroes, Campbell said,

> Well, you see, that movie communicates. It is in a language that talks to young people, and that's what counts. It asks, Are you going to be a person of heart and humanity—because that's where the life is, from the heart—or are you going to do whatever seems to be required of you by what might be called "intentional power"? When Ben Kenobi says, "May the Force be with you," he's speaking of the power and energy and life, not of programmed political intentions.[77]

Movies are one of the best modern venues to portray the clash between good and evil and the idealism inherent in myths.

Moviegoers familiar with the 2010 film *Icarus* (or *The Killing Machine*), are reminded of the Greek mythical figure of the same name. In the myth Icarus, the son of Daedalus, attempts to escape from Crete by means of wings his father constructed from feathers and wax but he flew too close to the sun, melting the wax and causing him to fall into the water.

The 2009 movie, *Avatar* (number one in worldwide box office and breaking $2.5 billion dollars) owes much of its success to its appeal to myth and transcendence, a reality outside of this world that can give meaning to life. As movie screenwriter Brian Godawa concludes,

> I believe that the reason for *Avatar's* success lies in [director] James Cameron's skill as a mythmaker. *Avatar* is essentially a postmodern pagan myth on the level of the Babylonian Enuma Elish or the Ugaritic Baal Cycle of ancient Mesopotamia. Like *Avatar*, these epic myths were tales of warring deities of nature embodying the claims of religious and political supremacy.[78]

So an ancient tale first recorded on clay tablets is comfortable being retold in the special effects world of modern Hollywood.

The May 2012 release of the comic book science fiction film, *The Avengers,* features among other super heroes, Thor, the Norse god usually associated with thunder, lightening, and strength, defending the earth

76. Larsen and Larsen, *Joseph Campbell,* 541–45.

77. Campbell, *The Power of Myth,* 143–44.

78. Godawa, "Avatar," 16.

against the arch villain, Loki, another Norse god often associated with trickery and deception.

Names most moderns take for granted, forgetting they are mythical, include the months of the year. The first month, *January*, is named after Janus, the two-faced Roman god looking at the past and future while *March* comes from the Mars (or Ares), the Greek god of war. And the planets too are named after mythical characters. *Jupiter* is the principle god of Roman mythology, *Venus* the Roman god of love and beauty, and *Neptune* is the Roman god of the sea. Constellations named after Greek mythical characters include Cassiopeia, Andromeda, Hercules, and Gemini.

While scholars disagree on the endurance of myth or if modern society can sustain myths, myth's influence is obvious and "Mythology need not be taken seriously in order to have a powerful influence."[79] The mythical idea of hero (or goddess) is not far from how society envisions the compassion of a Mother Teresa, the brilliance of Albert Einstein, or the inventive or commercial power of a Bill Gates or Steve Jobs. Entertainment "goddesses" such as Marilyn Munroe, Madonna, and Lady Gaga bring to mind Aphrodite, the goddess of love, beauty, and pleasure.

The world of business, one of the few places one might not expect myth to be present, often has myth in its "corporate culture." Because myth is human, it is present wherever people gather and form communities.

> There is a mythology in every group—our social club, our family, our profession, our subculture, our ethnic group, our religion and denomination, our city, our neighborhood, our friendships, etc. Our mythology changes as our culture changes—from one generation to the next, from one presidential administration to the next, from one decade to the next.[80]

Myth's adaptability makes it able to be reinvented in any context and able to appeal to any people irrespective of time, race, or technological advancements. As Daniel Peretti observes in his book on ancient myth,

> A myth exists as nothing more than potential for meaning in a person's mind, likely learned from a book, until it comes into being as the result of the dialect between personality and context. A situation demands its presence and thus gives it the potential for meaning.[81]

79. Hurst, "Western Cultural Mythology."

80. Stout, "What is Mythology?"

81. Peretti, "The Modern Prometheus," 10.

Myth's importance in culture is due in part to the fact that myth grants stability and continuity to a culture. A culture that shares a myth also shares the history, values, and perspectives contained in the myth. Such a connection ties individuals to one another and to previous generations, the greater society, the environment, and to the world of the supernatural. And as mythologists such as Joseph Campbell point out, by studying other myths we find a shared connection with people very different from ourselves, and perhaps even with our enemies.

Myths also add weight to the authority of a culture. Events such as warfare, hunting, holidays, laws, social structures, arts and crafts, religions and rituals, and other recurring cultural events are given further weight when understood as originating from a deity or even when the event or experience can be related to a myth. Thus, for example, Lewis would write of his World War I combat experience as an infantry officer:

> But for the rest, the war—the frights, the cold, the smell of H.E. [high explosives], the horribly smashed men still moving like half-crushed beetles, the sitting or standing corpses, the landscape of sheer earth without a blade of grass, the boots worn day and night till they seemed to grow to your feet—all this shows rarely and faintly in memory. It is too cut off from the rest of my experience and often seems to have happened to someone else. It is even in a way unimportant. One imaginative moment seems now to matter more than the realities that followed. It was the first bullet I heard—so far from me that it "whined" like a journalist's or a peacetime poet's bullet. At that moment there was something not exactly like fear, much less like indifference: a little quavering signal that said, "This is War. This is what Homer wrote about."[82]

He found meaning for and correlation between his experience and the mythological warfare writings of Homer. In a moment of crisis, there was meaning in mythology.

Myth has often been understood as pertaining to wild tales that can be proven false. But it has more to do with assumptions one makes about reality and often involves maters of morality. At other times the term is used to imply the significance of something, not its validity. No one calls into question the veracity of a topic of "mythical proportions"; such matters are so grave as to require the full attention.

Joseph Campbell certainly believed in the lasting power of myth, but he understood myth as originating from the human imagination with the

82. Lewis, *Surprised by Joy*, 196.

purpose of providing answers to the great questions of human existence as well as offering meaning and purpose to life. When asked if life has a purpose, Campbell answered "I don't believe life has a purpose. Life is a lot of protoplasm with an urge to reproduce and continue in being." When pressed to explain he said:

> Just sheer life cannot be said to have a purpose, because look at all the different purposes it has all over the place. But each incarnation, you might say, has a potentiality, and the mission of life is to live that potentiality. How do you do it? My answer is, "Follow your bliss." There's something inside you that knows when you're in the center, that knows when you're on the beam or off the beam. And if you get off the beam to earn money, you've lost your life. And if you stay in the center and don't get any money, you still have your bliss.[83]

For Joseph Campbell, myth reflects human potentiality and translates this potentiality into stories, signs, symbols, and rituals that allow individuals and cultures to find hope and meaning. And as the earth's population grows, its need of myth remains, but its scope broadens. Campbell declares:

> Myths and dreams come from the same place. They come from realizations of some kind that have then to find expression in symbolic form. And the only myth that is going to be worth thinking about in the immediate future is one that is talking about the planet, not the city, not these people, but the planet, and everybody on it. That's my main thought for what the future myth is going to be.[84]

Campbell observed that myth is as ancient and universal as the human race. People have always had myths because they need myths; myths are what it means to be human. And by studying myth Campbell was able to identify common themes throughout the world, themes that religion separated and compartmentalized by emphasizing one theme to the exclusion of others. He found a better way in rising above the distinctives of religion and looking for the commonalities of each belief system. He wrote:

> The comparative study of the mythologies of the world compels us to view the cultural history of mankind as a unit; for we find that such themes as the fire-theft, deluge, land of the dead, virgin birth, and resurrected hero have a worldwide

---

83. Campbell, *The Power of Myth*, 229.
84. Ibid., 32.

distribution—appearing everywhere in new combinations while remaining, like the elements of a kaleidoscope, only a few and always the same.

Thus it was in an ancient commonality of human visionary experience that Campbell sought for the roots of mythology. The entire superstructure of world mythology and religious thought, he asserted, might be better understood by starting with these humble foundations.[85]

So, like the person who stands back far enough until all the items in the distance resemble each other, Campbell stood back and looked at religion and myth and was able to identify the elements that resembled the others and it was these elements that he believed should make up one's faith. Instead of a world of religions at odds with one another, humanity could instead focus on what all people held in common. He states:

Once we have broken free of the prejudices of our own provincially limited ecclesiastical, tribal, or national rendition of the world archetypes, it becomes possible to understand that the supreme initiation is not that of the local motherly fathers, who then project aggression onto the neighbors for their own defense. The good news, which the World Redeemer brings and which so many have been glad to hear, zealous to preach, but reluctant, apparently, to demonstrate, is that God is love, that He can be, and is to be, loved, and that all without exception are his children.[86]

Campbell perceived myth as a way to demonstrate the oneness of humanity and to break down the walls of division caused by people believing their religion is the only true one.

C. S. Lewis approached the understanding and importance of myth with a different presupposition, especially with respect to Christianity. Instead of understanding myth as the source of Christianity and as a way to weave it seamlessly into all beliefs, Lewis believed the triune God of Christianity used myth as a means of communicating truth that would later be revealed in Jesus Christ and the Bible. The difference for Lewis concerned whether one included the supernatural in one's presupposition:

If you start from a naturalistic philosophy, then something like the view of Euhemerus [Greek mythographer, late fourth century BC] or the view of [James George] Frazer is likely to result. But I am not a naturalist. I believe that in the huge mass

85. Larsen and Larsen, Joseph Campbell, 442–43.

86. Campbell, The Hero of a Thousand Faces, 157–58.

of mythology which has come down to us a good many different sources are mixed—true history, allegory, ritual, the human
delight and storytelling, etc. but among these sources I include
the supernatural, both diabolical and divine.[87]

Lewis did not think myths were only stories that involved the gods. Rather,
he believed that there was one true God, the God of Christianity, who was
originally behind and using myth as a means of communication with the
human race. Lewis conceded that if the claims of Jesus and Christianity as
revealed in the Bible were wrong, then one would still expect the similarities
found in myth since myths address questions common to all humanity. But
if the God of the Bible exists, and if He created humanity and seeks ways to
communicate with this creation, then myths are an ideal mode because of
that same commonality among all myths. For Lewis, the life of Jesus Christ
was not the *result* of mythical tales of a hero dying and rising, but rather
myths *foretold* the coming of Jesus Christ as God prepared the human race
for his coming:

> If my religion is erroneous then occurrences of similar motives
> and pagan stories are, of course, instances of the same, or similar
> error. But if my religion is true, and the stories may well be a
> *preparatio evangelica*, a divine hinting in poetic and ritual for at
> the same central truth which was later focused and (so to speak)
> is historicised in the Incarnation.[88]

Joseph Campbell and C. S. Lewis approach myth and Christianity from opposite ends. Campbell believed that religion, in this case Christianity, starts
in myth. As humans struggle to find meaning in life, they turn to the imagination and from the imagination comes myth and a spiritual existence.
"Like dreams, myths are products of the human imagination"[89] As a result
of this process, myths ultimately end up at a final destination be it a person
(god), or a place (paradise), or a constant recycling (reincarnation). But
myth must lead somewhere and in the Christian faith it arrives at the triune
God revealed in the life, death, and physical resurrection of Jesus Christ.

But as Campbell points out, the idea of a savior is not unique to Christianity. As he says, "The interesting thing is that when you read the life of
the saviors—Jain saviors, Buddhist saviors, Hindu saviors, the Christ—the
same motifs are there, time and time and time again."[90] What Christianity

---

87. Lewis, "Religion Without Dogma," 132.

88. Ibid.

89. Campbell, *The Inner Reaches of Outer Space*, 55.

90. Maher and Briggs, *An Open Life*, 60.

did is take the universal mythical motif of savior and apply it to its own savior, Jesus Christ. So Christianity grows out of elements of myth because myth has always been in the mind of humanity.

But Lewis argues the opposite. He contends that the human imagination is able to devise myth because God has implanted within the human psyche a realization of His existence and involvement in creation. It was Lewis's love and respect of myth that actually triggered his belief in the incarnation, once he made this myth—Christian connection. Lewis writes:

> To me, who first approached Christianity from a delighted interest in, and reverence for, the best pagan imagination, who loved Balder before Christ and Plato before St. Augustine, the anthropological argument against Christianity has never been formidable. On the contrary, I could not believe Christianity if I were forced to say that there were a thousand religions in the world of which 999 were pure nonsense and the thousandth (fortunately) true. My conversion, very largely, dependent on recognizing Christianity as the completion, the actualization, the entelechy, of something that had never been wholly absent from the mind of man. And I still think that the agnostic argument from similarities between Christianity and paganism works only if you know the answer. If you start by knowing on other grounds that Christianity is false, then the pagan stories may be another nail in its coffin: just as if you started by knowing that there were no such things as crocodiles then the various stories about dragons might help to confirm your disbelief. But if the truth or falsehood of Christianity is the very question you are discussing, and the argument from anthropology is surely a *petitio*.[91]

Lewis argues along lines similar to the apostle Paul in Romans 1:19–20 that "For what can be known about God is plain to them, because God has shown it to them. For his invisible attributes, namely, his eternal power and divine nature, have been clearly perceived, ever since the creation of the world, in the things that have been made. So they are without excuse." Lewis concludes that in any given culture humanity creates myth that reveal something of the divine nature.

Both men understood myth as a social force that reinforces cultural values. But Lewis would not put long-term value on myth. As he said in *The Four Loves,* "All that is not eternal is eternally out of date."[92] Because he was supernaturalist and believed the triune God would bring time and creation

---

91. Lewis, "Religion Without Dogma," in *God in the Dock,* 132.

92. Lewis, *The Four Loves,* in *The Beloved Works of C. S. Lewis,* 287.

to a conclusion, that "When all things are subjected to him, then the Son himself will also be subjected to him who put all things in subjection under him, that God may be all in all,"[93] Lewis saw something greater than myth and realized that myth did not have eternal significance. Myth was not an end in itself; instead myth was a shadow, a reflection of something greater, and the purpose of myth was to prepare and point people to that something greater, the gospel of Jesus Christ. But as Robert Segal notes:

> For Campbell, myth is not only necessary for the deepest human fulfillment but also sufficient. One needs nothing else, including therapy. In fact, therapy is only for those without myth . . . Myth for Campbell contains all the wisdom humans need. They need only learn to interpret it. They need never venture beyond it. Moreover, myth is easy to interpret. It has a single meaning, even if "sages" are required to decipher that meaning.[94]

Joseph Campbell understood myth the way C. S. Lewis understood the person of Jesus Christ. While Campbell saw myth as an end in itself and all religions and metaphysical beliefs, even those concerning Christ, through the lens of myth, Lewis's approach was, "I believe in Christianity as I believe that the Sun has risen, not only because I see it, but because by it I see everything else."[95] Lewis looked at myth as a vehicle of communication imparted by God to his creation.

Joseph Campbell and C. S. Lewis devoted much of their lives, teaching, and writing to understanding the role of myth in religion and in a technological society. On the *importance* of myth the men agreed that myth has a place and plays a significant role in culture irrespective of how technologically primitive or advanced the culture might be. But concerning the *specifics* of myth and the relationship myth has to the Christian faith, the men came to very different conclusions.

93. 1 Cor 15:28.
94. Segal, *Joseph Campbell*, 260.
95. Lewis, "Is Theology Poetry?," in *The Weight of Glory*, 92.

7

Conclusion

The purpose of this book has been to answer the question: "What was the meaning and significance of myth as understood by Joseph Campbell and C. S. Lewis and how did each man apply his understanding of myth to the Christian faith?" Secondarily, attention was given to the place of myth in a highly technological society.

Beyond meeting immediate physical needs, two of the most basic characteristics of humanity are knowing and worshiping — the pursuit of intellectual and spiritual endeavors. No individual or culture can exist in a state of meaninglessness. Being human, even in an age of highly advanced technology, consists not only of physical, sensory experiences, but also involves the process of thought, imagination, and emotion; concepts commonly referred to as matters of the "heart." As far back as can be determined humanity has sought answers for the origins of the universe and the meaning of human existence as well as for the existence of a deity (or deities) and the possibility of life after death.

One means through which such answers are found and expressed that has universal appeal on both the individual and cultural levels is myth. Even in a highly scientific and technological age, myth provides a way of making sense of the human condition and offers answers to the many "why" questions that inevitably arise in times of tragedy or while considering the many enigmas and dilemmas of life. Like religion, myth can help define humanity to such a degree that many people see myth as synonymous with religion; myth satisfies where discursive statements fail. The capacity to imagine allows humans to create myths that serve as a bridge to span the chasm between humanity and eternity; myth is a means of explaining the

supernatural as well as other questions of human origins and the ﹍
ties of life.

We humans have an innate desire to know and to understand, ﹍
fore we analyze, consider, intellectualize, and seek a rational explan﹍ ﹍
But intellectualization alone is inadequate. Because some matters lie beyond
the intellect, they frequently elude being understood in familiar terms and
concepts. In order to address such matters, humanity turns to the imagination by which it can transcend statements and systems. In ways not easily
understood, imagination is able to turn the mind away from thinking in
categories and systems and, instead, enables one to conceptualize. Imagination allows one to think in terms of metaphors, images, pictures, and myths.
Myth is a means by which one can make sense of experiences that seem void
of meaning or purpose.

But as this book has shown in the study of the genre of myth, myth is
difficult, if not impossible, to define. Although one may contemplate or see
evidence of myth a number of times in an average day, myth is nevertheless
ageless and filled with universal meaning as it reveals the human condition.
Irrespective of how one approaches it, myth is universally understood as a
way of understanding life and of one's place in it. Myth is a term that signifies far more than a discredited popular belief; it is part of comprehending
what it is to be human.

Two men who devoted much of their life and learning to the subject
of myth were Joseph Campbell and C. S. Lewis. Both men grew up in religious homes (Campbell in the Roman Catholic Church, Lewis first in the
Church of Ireland then the Church of England), and were exposed to the
doctrines of the Christian faith from infancy. From a young age each man
had an understanding of the Christian faith in which myth was a significant
component and served as a means of explaining historical and doctrinal
issues such as miracles, the virgin birth, and the physical resurrection and
ascension of Jesus Christ.

Few authors were able to articulate Christian mythology as clearly or
argue it more forcefully than C. S. Lewis. For Lewis, as for all Christian
mythologists (such as J. R. R. Tolkien and George MacDonald), wisdom
consists of not focusing on the self, but on God. To such authors, it was not
surprising that concepts such as rebirth and renewal, of dying and rising
again, were found in cultures since the one true God used it as a means of
communication. When encountering the dynamic of myth people do not
simply tap into the deeper recesses of the human mind. They get a fleeting
glimpse of some other remote world.

Experiencing the loss of his mother to cancer while a young boy caused
Lewis to doubt the existence of a loving and sovereign God. At a similar

age Campbell, deeply impressed by the beliefs and culture of Native Americans, wondered how such people outside of his own Roman Catholicism answered the existential questions of origins and meaning. And as both men matured and thought through their questions they arrived at very different conclusions. Throughout his life, Campbell consistently maintained that much of Christianity was based on myths that developed around the historical person of Jesus of Nazareth; Christianity was one myth among many equally valid religious myths throughout the world. But Lewis came to understand Christianity as the belief that Jesus Christ was the Son of God, born of a virgin, who lived, taught, performed miracles, was crucified, and physically resurrected and ascended to heaven as recorded in the four Gospel accounts.

Campbell's knowledge of myth was extensive and his insights instructive. As he compared and contrasted the myths of many cultures and religions he was able to identify four purposes of myth: to make one aware of the universe and of one's place in it; to offer structure to an otherwise chaotic existence; to validate the ethical code of the culture in which the myth arose; and finally, to provide guidance as one passes through the stages of life such as youth, middle age, and death. In other words, myth provides a worldview that is both universal and enduring.

Lewis admitted to having little interest in religion as a young boy, referring to his mother's death when he was almost ten as his first real religious experience. This clash of idea against experience, of his being told of a loving and caring God who was evidently oblivious to the prayers of a young boy for his dying mother, resulted in Lewis finding little comfort in religion. He instead withdrew into a childhood world of make-believe, fantasy, and myth, especially the Norse myths.

As both men matured they shared a love for learning. Campbell studied at Dartmouth College and Columbia University, traveled extensively throughout Europe and the United States, and learned to speak French, German, Latin, and Japanese. His understanding of myth was influenced by the works of Sigmund Freud and Carl Jung, and by his exposure to Native Americans, Asian philosophy, and Hindu practices. The more Campbell traveled and read, the more similarities he identified between people of different religious beliefs and those of no religion. In time, he came to see organized religion as a divider and myth as a unifier of humanity. He noticed that people everywhere have the same basic needs and questions: Who am I? Where did I come from? Why am I here? And what, if anything, happens to me when I die? And, as Campbell observed, certain themes keep reoccurring in every answer irrespective of the culture, geography, time, or religious belief. This led him to believe that if people could learn to see beyond their sectarian religious beliefs, to set aside their doctrinal distinctives, and realize what their beliefs had in common with other beliefs, much of the warring and factions that plague humanity could be relieved if not resolved.

C. S. Lewis also had a passion for learning. As an undergraduate student at Oxford, he won a triple first, the highest honors in three areas of study, and for close to thirty years he taught at Magdalen College, Oxford, later becoming the first Professor of Medieval and Renaissance English at Cambridge University and a fellow of Magdalene College. As Campbell learned French, German, Latin, and Japanese, Lewis became fluent in Greek, Latin, and French. As Freud and Jung influenced Campbell's thinking on myth, so the writings of Plato, Samuel Taylor Coleridge, G. K. Chesterton, George MacDonald, influenced Lewis. Lewis's close personal and professional relationships with authors J. R. R. Tolkien, Charles Williams, and Dorothy Sayers additionally shaped his understanding of myth.

Students of these two authors may be surprised by the paradoxes of comparison and contrast. Critics of Campbell are quick to point to his dismissive attitude toward the Christian faith and his approach of categorizing many aspects of the faith as mythical. But, as this book has shown, Campbell believed in a historical Jesus, a man who lived, taught, healed, and went about doing good. Campbell believed Jesus lived an exemplary life and that the Bible is not only a collection of sacred writings, but that it also provides the wisdom needed to live a fruitful and satisfying life. And as this book points out, although he abandoned the Roman Catholic faith as a young adult, even on his deathbed, certain rituals of the Roman Catholic Church (crossing himself in prayer) remained.

Supporters of C. S. Lewis who make much of his orthodoxy in Christian theology, his belief and defense of a triune God, virgin birth, physical resurrection and ascension of Jesus are surprised by his reservations of the inspiration and inerrancy of all Scripture and of his mythical reading of books such as Job and Jonah.

Each of these authors surprise supporters and critics alike and both have been unfairly represented by each side. As demonstrated in this book, what each man said and how each man has been portrayed is not always consistent.

Another similarity between the two men is that, even though they acknowledged the influence of others to their own understanding of myth, each man went beyond what he learned from others to become a well-known figure in his own right. While C. S. Lewis credits J. R. R. Tolkien with helping him understand Christian doctrine by seeing it through the lens of myth, Lewis and Tolkien disagreed about the role theology should have in myth. Tolkien preferred to bury Christian themes deeply so the reader would not feel bullied by doctrine or the theme would not distract from the story. Lewis, on the other hand, preferred to make Christian teachings and symbols prominent in his writings, often giving them a major role, as in the case of the lion, Aslan, in *The Lion, the Witch and the Wardrobe*. Tolkien also had reservations about Lewis's use of many different elements in his stories such as witches, children, and talking animals, thinking they clashed and confused the children for whom Lewis wrote. Tolkien would have preferred an equally deep but less complicated story.

Joseph Campbell often refers to the considerable influence of Sigmund Freud upon his early views of myth by praising Freud's clear discursive style of writing and crediting Freud with helping him see how psychology could better help one understand myth. But Campbell also came to identify major differences between myths and dreams and, unlike Freud, he chose to focus on the cultural and not just the individual. To Campbell, myths are not neurotic projections, they are metaphors by which people live. Myths permeate whole societies and shape cultural patterns.

Most authors addressing C. S. Lewis, Joseph Campbell, myth, and Christianity do so as separate disciplines. There are some, though surprisingly few, books exclusively on Lewis's thinking on myth or Campbell's understanding of Christianity outside of Roman Catholicism and none that engage the thinking of both men on these topics simultaneously. Much of the work on these men focuses on Lewis's writings on Christianity and Campbell's approach to myth. Though this is understandable, more interdisciplinary studies of their thinking is needed. Although it was beyond the scope of this present study, there are several themes relating to Lewis, Campbell, myth, and Christianity that could be pursued in future studies.

First, understanding Campbell's and Lewis's hermeneutics would be helpful. Both men often quote the Bible and they both respect its authority as a source of spiritual and religious truth, but they also speak of its mythical nature. Campbell and Lewis believed that the man Jesus lived in Israel and was a great teacher and healer. But while Lewis believed he was the Son of God and ascended to Heaven following his physical resurrection, Campbell did not. What rationale did Campbell use to read half a verse as literal and the next half as mythical, and how would such an approach apply to other literature, such as his writings?

On the other hand, Lewis, as well as Campbell, did not understand the Old Testament story of Jonah to be historical even though Jesus used it as an example of his own resurrection, "For just as Jonah was three days and three nights in the belly of the great fish, so will the Son of Man be three days and three nights in the heart of the earth" (Matt. 12:40, English Standard Version). Further research into how each man interpreted the biblical text and identified its genre would be a helpful step in better understanding their application of myth to Christianity. What were the hermeneutical presuppositions of each author? Such a study would look not only at how each man understood the biblical text, but also at how each approached the nature and interpretation of literature. For Lewis, whose academic specialty was English literature, such a study would be an especially rich endeavor.

A second helpful investigation would be the question of whether myth helps or hinders religious belief. For some religions this question may be moot, but for others it is vitally important. A large number of Jews, Christians, and Muslims would be greatly offended to be told that Moses's experience at the burning bush, Jesus's virgin birth, bodily resurrection and ascension, or the revelations Mohammed received that are recorded in the Quran were not historical events, but simply tales that arose around each individual. For many believers such an approach undermines the very foundation of their belief system and further divides the very believers that adherents of myth seek to bring together. More interdisciplinary study of myth, religion, and history is needed.

A third area of study concerns the influence of culture upon myth and myth upon culture. As demonstrated in this study, myth has an enduring quality that enables it to be adapted to changes in culture. Myth is not limited to the religion of indigenous peoples, but is found in all cultures, including the highly technological West. Does myth progress in the same sense that peoples and societies are said to progress or is such an understanding faulty? Do myths, or the meaning of myth, change as civilization changes? Just as some scholars argue that to translate a text from one language to another can change the meaning, can it also be argued that as myths are handed down from one generation to another their purpose and meaning also change? If so, do such changes matter or is myth pliable enough that, so long as the genre remains, the lessons learned are free to change?

A final investigation relevant to this book would involve further clarification on Joseph Campbell's personal beliefs regarding the theology of Christianity in general and Roman Catholicism specifically. Throughout his many books and lectures, C. S. Lewis is clear about his position regarding the basic tenets of the Christian faith such as human sin, the virgin birth, the deity, miracles, and the physical resurrection and ascension of Jesus Christ. Indeed, to many readers and Lewis scholars his clarity on such issues is his greatest contribution. But what did Campbell believe about such doctrines?

To understand Campbell's criticism of Christianity it is important to recognize his lack of clarity on the subject. In his many and varied references to "Church" and "Christianity," one has to be aware of the context. Sometimes Campbell's reference is specifically to his own experience in a

Roman Catholic church while at other times his comments pertain to Roman Catholicism in general. But there are also instances where he addresses Christianity in so broad a context that he includes Protestant faiths as well. While speaking of Christianity in monolithic terms is convenient, it has the unfortunate result of making generalizations where a better sense of nuance and distinction would present a clearer and fairer representation. To some degree Campbell's background, disappointment, and disagreements with Roman Catholicism blinded him to broader Christian ideas and thought resulting in his mistaking the part for the whole.

Joseph Campbell was a well-travelled reader and scholar familiar with the history, themes, and lessons of myths the world over. His books, lectures, interviews, and television series show a person comfortable with talking about the harm caused by religion and the advantages that come as a result of a greater understanding and appreciation of myth. But on a personal level great teachers believe something, so what did Joseph Campbell believe about God? Did he believe in a personal God? If so, did he believe individuals are alienated from God by sin (or something else)? Did he believe in an existence after death, and if so, what distinguishes one's eternal destiny? Campbell is without doubt one of the leading authorities on the world's belief systems and he is transparent on his disagreements with Roman Catholicism, but many questions and apparent contradictions remain as to what he personally believed concerning the very questions myth is supposed to answer. More is known about what he did not believe than what he did believe.

After answering the questions of the meaning and significance of myth and its place in the Christian faith as understood by Campbell and Lewis, there remains the corresponding question of myth's place in culture and its significance in the Christian faith today, decades after the passing of Campbell and Lewis. As seen in this book, both men contributed greatly to the study in their day, but the influence of technology in the 1960s of C. S. Lewis and the 1980s of Joseph Campbell does not seem as significant as its influence today. Does myth still have a place in contemporary society and do Lewis and Campbell, though dead, still speak?

As shown in this book, myth appears evident at the dawn of human history and will evidently be present at its close. Myth helps people find meaning in life, it assists in building a coherent worldview, a hermeneutic of experience, and it provides a way to communicate life experience to others. Myths are a construct of reality and belief and a means to express what one believes, individually and culturally. Creating, thinking, and sharing myth are activities that provide self-identity and inform a person's view of reality.

In spite of advances in technology, science, medicine, and education, humanity has changed very little. Wars and rumors of war still abound and understanding others, whether on the other side of the world or just across the street, shows little sign of improvement. Irrespective of their differences on the meaning of myth, Joseph Campbell and C. S. Lewis both acknowledged the commonality of myth, that myth is a part of the human condition, and both men see in myth a way forward for humanity.

Joseph Campbell reminds us of our humanity and the fact that there is only one race, the human race, and that most human tragedies are self-inflicted. Though we enjoy the reading of the science fiction invasion from another planet, we realize most of our calamities and catastrophes are of our own making. Campbell's familiarity with myth and his research into myths ancient and modern, combined with his insights into psychology and sociology, resulted in his being uniquely able to remind us how much we all have in common. No one wants to, or can, live a meaningless existence. As we age and pass through various stages of life, each of us must face new challenges. And as we grow older, and often even long before old age, the prospect of death haunts our thinking.

Joseph Campbell believed myth provided direction for such human dilemmas. For him, by better understanding our own myths and the myths of others, we are better able to understand ourselves, to appreciate the differences in cultures, and to work to establish a more prosperous and peaceful global community. Since myth originates in the human imagination, no one myth is superior. Campbell reminds us that our asking the same questions is more important than our arriving at different answers.

C. S. Lewis also believed myth provides direction for the human condition and, if he were alive today, Lewis, like Campbell, would encourage a greater understanding and appreciation of myth on a personal and cultural level. But where Campbell and Lewis disagree is in their conclusions. Campbell sees myth as an end in itself. Myth, correctly understood and appreciated, will result in a better understanding and appreciation of self and of others. But Lewis says that myth's universality points humanity in another direction, to something greater, to a personal, loving, and eternal "other." Myths serve as hints, as clues, they are a suspicion that something more is going on than life under the sun. And while Lewis agrees with Campbell that myth helps us to understand ourselves and one another, Lewis adds that myth also helps people better understand the love of the triune God as well.

The study of the Humanities bridges a number of disciplines and explores the human condition through the question, "What does it mean to be human in an age of advanced technology?" This book has addressed this question by exploring the thinking of Joseph Campbell and C. S. Lewis regarding both myth and religion and by investigating the influence and presence of myth in today's philosophy, media, ethics, history, literature, art, music, and religion. This comparison and critique of these men and their approaches to myth will enable students and scholars working in these disciplines to integrate the thoughts of Joseph Campbell and C. S. Lewis with respect to myth and Christianity in further reflections upon the relationship between humans and technology.

Bibliography

Adams, Jay E. *A Call to Discernment: Distinguishing Truth from Error in Today's Church*. Eugene, OR: Harvest, 1987.

Adler, Mortimer J. *Truth in Religion: The Plurality of Religions and the Unity of Truth*. New York: Macmillan, 1990.

Aeschliman, Michael D. *The Restitution of Man: C. S. Lewis and the Case Against Scientism*. Grand Rapids: Eerdmans, 1983.

Andriolo, Karin R. "Myth and History: A General Model and Its Application to the Bible." *American Anthropologist* New Series 83/2 (1981) 261–84. Online: http://o-www.jstor.org.helin.uri.edu/stable/pdfplus/676670.pdf.

Armstrong, Karen. *A Short History of Myth*. New York: Canongate, 2005.

Arndt, William F., and F. Wilbur Gingrich. *A Greek-English Lexicon of the New Testament and Other Early Christian Literature* by Walter Bauer. Chicago: University of Chicago Press, 1957.

"Art and Irrationality." Albert Ellis and REBT: A Rational Oasis blog. April 8, 2008. Online: http://albert-ellis.blogspot.com/2008/04/art-and-irrationality.html.

Asimov, Isaac. *Words from the Myths*. Boston: New American Library, 1969.

Atwood, Margaret. *In Other Worlds: SF and the Human Imagination*. New York: Doubleday, 2011.

Bachofen, J. J. *Myth, Religion, and Mother Right*. Princeton: Princeton University Press, 1967.

Barbour, Ian. *Ethics in an Age of Technology*. San Francisco: Harper, 1993.

———. *Religion and Science: Historical and Contemporary Issues*. San Francisco: HarperCollins, 1997.

Barenbaum, Nichol B. "Jung, Carl Gustav." *World Book Advanced*. World Book, 2011. Online: http://www.worldbookonline.com/advanced/printarticle?id=ar292580.

Barfield, Owen. *Owen Barfield on C. S. Lewis*. Oxford: Barfield, 2011.

———. *Poetic Diction: A Study in Meaning*. Oxford: Barfield, 2010.

Barkman, Adam. "It's NOT 'All in Plato': C. S. Lewis' Theory of Myth." *CSL: The Bulletin of the New York C. S. Lewis Society* 40/5 (2009) 1–8.

Barthes, Roland. *Mythologies*. Edited and translated by Annette Lavers. New York: Hill and Wang, 1972.

Batto, Bernard F. *Slaying the Dragon: Mythmaking in the Biblical Tradition*. Louisville: Westminster John Knox, 1992.

Bell, James Stuart, and Anthony Palmer Dawson, eds. *From the Library of C. S. Lewis: Selections from Writers Who Influenced his Spiritual Journey.* Colorado Springs: WaterBrook, 2004.

Bettelheim, Bruno. *The Uses of Enchantment: The Meaning and Importance of Fairy Tales.* New York: Vintage, 1977.

Beversluis, John. *C. S. Lewis and the Search for Rational Religion.* Grand Rapids: Eerdmans, 1985.

Birenbaum, Harvey. *Myth and Mind.* Lanham, MD: University Press of America, 1988.

Birzer, Bradley J. *J. R. R. Tolkien's Sanctifying Myth: Understanding Middle-Earth.* Wilmington, DE: ISI, 2003.

Bloom, Allen. *The Closing of the American Mind.* New York: Simon and Schuster, 1987.

Bloom, Harold, ed. *Modern Critical Interpretations: J. R. R. Tolkien's* Lord of the Rings. Philadelphia: Chelsea, 2000.

Bock, Darrell L. *Jesus according to Scripture: Restoring the Portrait from the Gospels.* Grand Rapids: Baker Academic, 1990.

———. *Studying the Historical Jesus: A Guide to Sources and Methods.* Grand Rapids: Baker Academic, 2002.

Boynton, Richard W. *Beyond Mythology.* New York: Doubleday, 1952.

Brockway, Robert W. *Myth from the Ice Age to Mickey Mouse.* Albany: State University of New York Press, 1993.

Bromiley, Geoffrey W. *Theological Dictionary of the New Testament: Abridged in One Volume.* Edited by Gerhard Kittel and Gerhard Friedrich. Grand Rapids: Eerdmans, 1985.

Brown, Dave. "Real Joy and True Myth." Online: http://www.geocities.com/athens/forum/3505/LewisJoy.html.

Bulfinch, Thomas. *Bulfinch's Mythology.* Middlesex: Hamlyn, 1968.

Burnson, Scott R., and Jerry L. Walls. *C. S. Lewis and Francis Schaeffer: Lessons for a New Century from the Most Influential Apologists of Our Time.* Downers Grove, IL: InterVarsity, 1998.

Bush, Randall. "The Suffering of God as an Aspect of the Divine Omniscience." *Journal of the Evangelical Theological Society* 51/4 (2008) 769–84.

Buttrick, Arthur. *The Interpreter's Bible.* Vol. 11, *Philippians–Hebrews.* Nashville: Abingdon, 1978.

Caird, G. B. *The Language and Imagery of the Bible.* Philadelphia: Westminster, 1980.

Campbell, Joseph. *The Flight of the Wild Gander: Explorations in the Mythological Dimensions of Fairy Tales, Legends, and Symbols.* New York: HarperCollins, 1969.

———. *The Hero with a Thousand Faces.* Princeton: Princeton University Press, 1949.

———. *The Hero's Journey: a Biographical Portrait.* DVD. The Joseph Campbell Foundation, 2003.

———. *The Inner Reaches of Outer Space: Metaphor as Myth and as Religion.* New York: Harper & Row, 1986.

———. *The Masks of God.* New York: Viking, 1968.

———. *The Masks of God: Primitive Mythology.* New York: Viking, 1959.

———. *The Mythic Dimension: Selected Essays, 1959–1987.* Edited by Antony Van Couvering. New York: HarperCollins, 1997.

———. *Mythic Worlds, Modern Words: On the Art of James Joyce.* Novato, CA: New World Library, 2003.

———. *Myths to Live By.* New York: Penguin, 1972.

———. *Occidental Mythology: The Masks of God*. New York: Penguin, 1964.

———. *Pathways to Bliss: Mythology and Personal Transformation*. Novato, CA: New World Library, 2004.

———. *The Power of Myth with Bill Moyers*. New York: Doubleday, 1988.

———. *Thou Art That: Transforming Religious Metaphor*. Novato, CA: New World Library, 2001.

———. *Sake and Satori: Asian Journals—Japan*. Novato, CA: New World Library, 2002.

Carnell, Corbin Scott. "Imagination." In *The C. S. Lewis Readers' Encyclopedia*, edited by Jeffrey D. Schultz and John G. West Jr., 214. Grand Rapids: Zondervan, 1998.

Carpenter, Humphrey, ed. *The Letters of J. R. R. Tolkien*. New York: Houghton Mifflin, 2000.

———. *Tolkien: A Biography*. Boston: Houghton Mifflin, 1977.

Carson, D. A. *The Gagging of God: Christianity Confronts Pluralism*. Grand Rapids: Zondervan, 1996.

———. *The Intolerance of Tolerance*. Grand Rapids: Eerdmans, 2012.

Catechism of the Catholic Church. Mahwah, NJ: Paulist, 1994.

Cavanaugh, William T. *The Myth of Religious Violence: Secular Ideology and the Roots of Modern Conflict*. New York: Oxford University Press, 2009.

Chance, Jane. *Tolkien and the Invention of Myth: A Reader*. Lexington: The University of Kentucky Press, 2004.

Chesterton, G. K. *The Everlasting Man*. London: Hodder and Stoughton, 1925.

Childs, Brevard S. *Myth and Reality in the Old Testament*. Eugene, OR: Wipf & Stock, 2009.

Christians, Clifford G., and Jay M. Hook. *Jacques Ellul: Interpretive Essays*. Champaign: University of Illinois Press, 1981.

Christopher, Joe R. "Archetypal Patterns in *Till We Have Faces*." In *The Longing for a Form: Essays on the Fiction of C. S. Lewis*, edited by Peter J. Schaakel, 193–212. Kent, OH: Kent State University Press, 1977.

Cline, Austin. "C. S. Lewis and J. R. R. Tolkien: Friendship and Disagreements Over Christian Theology." Online: Http://atheism.about.com/od/cslewisnarnia/a/jrrtolkein.htm.

Cobble, William J. "C. S. Lewis' Understanding of God's Work in Paganism." *Journal of Theta Alpha Kappa* 25/2 (2001) 16–29.

Collins, Tom. "Mythic Reflections: Thoughts on Myth, Spirit, and Our Times." *In Context: A Quarterly of Humane Sustainable Culture* (Winter 1985–86) 52. Online: http://www.context.org/ICLIB/IC12/Campbell.htm.

Como, James. "Mere Lewis." *Wilson Quarterly (1976–)* 18/2 (1994) 109–17. Online: http://www.jstor.org/stable/40258859.

Connolly, Sean. *Inklings of Heaven: C. S. Lewis and Eschatology*. Herefordshire, UK: Gracewing, 2007.

Coogan, Michael David, trans. *Stories from Ancient Canaan*. Louisville: Westminister, 1978.

Corduan, Winfried. *A Tapestry of Faiths: The Common Threads Between Christianity and World Religions*. Downers Grove, IL: InterVarsity, 2003.

Degh, Linda. *Legend and Belief*. Bloomington: Indiana University Press, 2001.

De Haan, Mart. *C. S. Lewis: The Story of A Converted Mind*. Grand Rapids: RBC Ministries, 2010.

De Lange, Simon Blaxland. *Owen Barfield: Romanticism Come of Age—a Biography.* Sussex: Temple Lodge, 2006.

Demy, Timothy J. "Faith and Force: Religious Values and the Tragedy of War." Paper presented as part of the "War and Faith Conference" at Goodenough College, London, June 18, 2010.

———. "In the Pillory—C. S. Lewis and The Two Cultures." Paper presented as part of the "Oxford Roundtable" at Harris Manchester College, Oxford, London, March 2010.

———. "Technology, Progress, and the Human Condition in the Life and Thought of C. S. Lewis." PhD diss., Salve Regina University, 2005.

Dickerson, Matthew. *The Mind and the Machine.* Grand Rapids: Brazos, 2011.

Dickerson, Matthew, and David O'Hara. *From Homer to Harry Potter: A Handbook on Myth and Fantasy.* Grand Rapids: Brazos, 2006.

———. *Narnia and the Fields of Arbol: The Environmental Vision of C. S. Lewis.* Lexington: University of Kentucky Press, 2009.

Dinkler, E. *The Interpreter's Dictionary of the Bible.* Vol. 3, *K-Q.* Edited by George Arthur Buttrick. Nashville: Abingdon, 1962.

Donaldson, Mara E. *Holy Places Are Dark Places: C. S. Lewis and Paul Ricoeur on Narrative Transformation.* Lanham, MD: University Press of America, 1988.

Dorman, S. "Fictionalizing Lewis." *Mythprint: The Monthly Bulletin of the Mythopoeic Society* 47/12 (2010) n.p.

Dorsett, Lyle W. *The Essential C. S. Lewis.* New York: Macmillan, 1988.

Downing, Christine. "Sigmund Freud and the Greek Mythological Tradition." *Journal of the American Academy of Religion* 43/1 (1975) 3–14. Online: http://0-www.jstor.org.helin.uri.edu/stable/pdfplus/1460730.pdf?acceptTC=true.

Downing, David C. "The Discarded Mage: Lewis the Scholar-Novelist on Merlin's Moral Taint." *Christian Scholars' Review* 27/4 (1998) 406–15.

———. *Into the Region of Awe: Mysticism in C. S. Lewis.* Downers Grove, IL: InterVarsity, 2005.

———. *The Most Reluctant Convert.* Downers Grove, IL: InterVarsity, 2002.

———. *Planets in Peril: A Critical Study of C. S. Lewis's Ransom Trilogy.* Amherst: University of Massachusetts Press, 1992.

Dundes, Alan. *Sacred Narrative: Readings in the Theory of Myth.* Berkeley: University of California Press, 1984.

Duriez, Colin. *The C. S. Lewis Encyclopedia: A Complete Guide to His Life, Thought, and Writings.* Wheaton, IL: Crossway, 2000.

———. *J. R. R. Tolkien and C. S. Lewis: The Story of their Friendship.* Sparkford, UK: J. H. Haynes, 2003.

Eco, Umberto. *Travels in Hyper Reality.* New York: Harcourt Brace, 1986.

Edwards, Bruce L. *C. S. Lewis: Life, Works, and Legacy.* Vol. 1, *An Examined Life.* Westport, CT: Prager, 2007.

———. *C. S. Lewis: Life, Works, and Legacy.* Vol. 2, *Fantasist, Mythmaker, and Poet.* Westport, CT: Prager, 2007.

———. *C. S. Lewis: Life, Works, and Legacy.* Vol. 3, *Apologist, Philosopher, and Theologian.* Westport, CT: Prager, 2007.

———. *C. S. Lewis: Life, Works, and Legacy.* Vol. 4, *Scholar, Teacher, and Public Intellectual.* Westport, CT: Prager, 2007.

Elgin, Don D. "True and False Myth in C. S. Lewis' 'Till We Have Faces.'" *The South Central Bulletin* 41/4 (1981) 98–101.

Eliade, Mircea. *Myth and Reality*. New York: Harper & Row, 1963.

———. *The Myth of the Eternal Return*. Translated by Willard R. Trask. New York: Pantheon, 1954.

———. *Myths, Dreams and Mysteries: The Encounter between Contemporary Faiths and Archaic Realities*. London: Harvill, 1961.

———. *Patterns in Comparative Religion*. London: Sheed and Ward, 1958.

———. *The Sacred and the Profane: The Nature of Religion*. London: Harcourt, Brace, Jovanovich, 1959.

English Standard Version Study Bible. Wheaton, IL: Crossway, 2008.

Evslin, Bernard. *Heros, Gods and Monsters of the Greek Myths*. New York: Random House, 1966.

Felser, Joseph M. "Was Joseph Campbell a Postmodernist?" *Journal of the American Academy of Religion* 64/2 (1996) 395–417.

Fisher, Dennis. *C. S. Lewis: The Story of a Converted Mind*. Grand Rapids: RBC Ministries, 2010.

Fisher, Matt. "*The Weirdstone of Brisingamen*: 50 Years Young." *Mythprint: The Monthly Bulletin of the Mythopoeic Society* 47/10 (2010) n.p.

Flieger, Verlyn. *Splintered Light: Logos and Language in Tolkien's World*. Rev. ed. Kent, OH: The Kent State University Press, 2002.

Frazer, James George. *The Illustrated Golden Bough: A Study in Magic and Religion*. New York: Simon & Schuster, 1996.

Freud, Sigmund. *Civilization and Its Discontents*. New York: Norton, 2005.

———. *The Future of an Illusion*. Translated by James Strachey et al. London: Hogarth, 1961.

———. *Moses and Monotheism*. Charlestown, SC: Nabu, 2011.

———. *Totem and Taboo*. Madison, NC: Empire, 2012.

Frye, Northrop. *Anatomy of Criticism: Four Essays*. Princeton: Princeton University Press, 1957.

———. *The Educated Imagination*. Bloomington: Indiana University Press, 1964.

———. *Fables of Identity: Studies in Poetic Mythology*. New York: Harcourt, Brace & World, 1963.

Fuller, Edmund. *Myth, Allegory, and Gospel: An Interpretation of J. R. R. Tolkien, C. S. Lewis, G. K. Chesterton, and Charles Williams*. Minneapolis: Bethany Fellowship, 1974.

Garvey, John. "A Storied Faith: Myths, Fables and Parables." *Commonweal*, December 3, 2010, 6.

Gaskell, G. A. *Dictionary of All Scriptures and Myths*. New York: Avenel, 1960.

Gaster, T. H. *The Interpreter's Dictionary of the Bible*. Vol. 3, *K–Q*. Edited by George Arthur Buttrick. Nashville: Abingdon, 1962.

Gibson, Evan K. *C. S. Lewis, Spinner of Tales: A Guide to His Fiction*. Washington, DC: Christian University Press, 1980.

Girard, Rene. *Things Hidden Since the Foundation of the World*. Stanford: Stanford University Press, 1987.

———. "Violence and the Sacred." Translated by Patrick Gregory. Baltimore: Johns Hopkins University Press, 1977.

Global Oneness. "Joseph Campbell Encyclopedia." Online: http://www. experiencefestival.com/ a/Joseph_Campbell/id/1895674.

Glover, Donald E. *C. S. Lewis and the Art of Enchantment*. Athens: Ohio University Press, 1981.

Godawa, Brian. "Avatar: A Postmodern Pagan Myth." *Christian Research Journal* 33/2 (2010) 16.

Goffar, Janine. *The C. S. Lewis Index*. Wheaton, IL: Crossway, 1995.

Grant, Michael. *Myths of the Greeks and Romans*. New York: The New American Library, 1962.

Graves, Robert. *The Greek Myths*. Vol. 1. New York: Penguin, 1960.

Gray, William. *Fantasy, Myth and the Measure of Truth: Tales of Pullman, Lewis, Tolkien, MacDonald and Hoffman*. New York: Palgrave Macmillan, 2009.

Gregory, Brad S. Review of *The Myth of Religious Violence: Secular Ideology and the Roots of Modern Conflict* by William T. Cavanaugh. *First Things* 203 (2010) 57.

Griffin, William. *Clive Staples Lewis: A Dramatic Life*. New York: Harper & Row, 1986.

Groothuis, Douglas. *Christian Apologetics: A Comprehensive Case for Biblical Faith*. Downers Grove, IL: InterVarsity Academic, 2011.

———. "The Power of Myth: Summary Critique." Online: http://www.equip.org/ articles/the-power-of-myth.

Grossman, Walter. "Gruber on the Discernment of True and False Inspiration." *The Harvard Theological Review* 81/4 (1988) 363–87. Online: http://0-www.jstor.org. helin.uri.edu/stable/pdfplus/1509712.pdf?acceptTC=true..

Hall, T. William, ed. *Introduction to the Study of Religion*. San Francisco: Harper & Row, 1978.

Hamilton, Edith. *Mythology*. Boston: Little, Brown, 1942.

Hammond, Barbi. "Differences Between Myth, Fairy Tales, Literary Fantasies and Postmodern Fantasy." Integral Life website. April 17, 2009. Online: https://www. integrallife.com/member/barbi-hammond/blog/differences-between-myth-fairy-tales-literary-fantasies-and-postmodern-fan.

Hannay, Margaret Patterson. "Arthurian and Cosmic Myth in *That Hideous Strength*." *Mythlore* 2/2 (1970) 7–9.

———. *C. S. Lewis*. New York: Frederick Ungar, 1981.

———. "The Mythology of *Out of the Silent Planet*." *Mythlore* 1/4 (1969) 11–14.

———. "The Mythology of *Perelandra*." *Mythlore* 2 (1970) 14–16.

Hannon, James. *The Genesis of Science: How the Christian Middle Ages Launched the Scientific Revolution*. Washington, DC: Regnery, 2011.

Hansen, William F. *Handbook of Classical Mythology*. Oxford: ABC-Clio, 2004.

Harris, R. Laird, Gleason K. Archer, and Bruce K. Waltke. *Theological Wordbook of the Old Testament*. Chicago: Moody, 1980.

Heidel, Alexander. *The Babylonian Genesis: The Story of Creation*. Chicago: University of Chicago, 1963.

Hein, Rolland. *Christian Mythmakers: C. S. Lewis, Madeleine L'Engle, J. R. R. Tolkien, George MacDonald, G. K. Chesterton and Others*. Chicago: Cornerstone, 2002.

———. *George MacDonald: Victorian Mythmaker*. Nashville: Star Song, 1993.

Henry, Carl F. H. *God, Revelation and Authority*. Vol. 1, *God Who Speaks and Shows: Preliminary Considerations*. Waco, TX: Word, 1976.

Herrick, James A. "Sci-Fi's Brave New World: How the Genre Draws Us to Its Own Views of Redemption." *Christianity Today* (February 2009) 20–25.

Hess, Richard S. *Israelite Religions: An Archeological and Biblical Survey.* Grand Rapids: Baker, 2007.

Hexham, Irving. *Understanding World Religions: An Interdisciplinary Approach.* Grand Rapids: Zondervan, 2011.

Holyer, Robert. "The Epistemology of C. S. Lewis's *Till We Have Faces.*" *Anglican Theological Review* 70 (1988) 233–55.

Hooper, Teresa. "Playing by the Rules: Kipling's 'Great Game' vs. 'the Great Dance' in C. S. Lewis's Space Trilogy." *Mythlore* (September 2006) n.p. Online : http://www. thefreelibrary.com/Playing+by+the+rules%3a+Kipling's+%22Great+Game%22+ vs.+%22the+Great+Dance%22+in. . .-a0154698402.

Hooper, Walter. *C. S. Lewis: Companion and Guide.* New York: HarperCollins, 1996.

———. *C. S. Lewis: Reading for Meditation and Reflection.* New York: HarperCollins, 1992.

———, ed. *The Collected Letters of C. S. Lewis.* Vol. 1, *Family Letters, 1905–1931.* New York: HarperCollins, 2004.

———, ed. *The Collected Letters of C. S. Lewis.* Vol. 2, *Books, Broadcasts, and the War, 1931–1949.* New York: HarperCollins, 2004.

———, ed. *The Collected Letters of C. S. Lewis.* Vol. 3, *Narnia, Cambridge, and Joy, 1950–1963.* New York: HarperCollins, 2007.

———. *Of Other Worlds: C. S. Lewis, Essays and Stories.* New York: Harcourt, Brace & World. 1966.

———. *On Stories and Other Essays on Literature.* New York: Harcourt Brace Jovanovich, 1982.

———, ed. *They Stand Together: The Letters of C. S. Lewis to Arthur Greeves (1914–1963).* London: Collins, 1979.

Howard, Thomas. *The Achievement of C. S. Lewis: A Reading of His Fiction.* Wheaton, IL: Harold Shaw, 1980.

———. "The 'Moral Mythology' of C. S. Lewis." *Modern Age* 22 (Fall 1978) 384–92.

———. *Narnia and Beyond: A Guide to the Fiction of C. S. Lewis.* San Francisco: Ignatius, 2006.

Houston, James M. "C. S. Lewis's Concern for the Future of Humanity." *Knowing and Doing: A Teaching Quarterly for Discipleship of Heart and Mind* (Spring 2006) n.p.

Hurst, Ed. "Western Cultural Mythology." Online: http://soulkiln.org/bible/cultmyth. html.

Huttar, Charles. "*Till We Have Faces*: A Myth Retold." In *The C. S. Lewis Readers' Encyclopedia*, edited by Jeffrey D. Schultz and John G. West Jr., 403–4. Grand Rapids: Zondervan, 1998.

Hyde, Lewis. *Trickster Makes this World: Mischief, Myth, and Art.* New York: North Point, 1998.

Ingham, Tanya. "George MacDonald: An Original Thinker." *Knowing and Doing, C. S. Lewis Institute* (Spring 2009) 1–6. Online: http://www.cslewisinstitute.org/ webfm_send/614.

Jennings, Katherine Lynn. "Communication and Myth: Joseph Campbell's Concepts of Myth Exemplified in C. S. Lewis's *The Lion, The Witch and the Wardrobe.*" Master's thesis, Central Missouri State University, 1993.

Kattsoff, L. O. "The Discernment of Moral Attributes." *Philosophy and Phenomenological Research* 29/1 (1968) 68–83.

Keefe, Carolyn. *C. S. Lewis: Speaker and Teacher.* Grand Rapids: Zondervan, 1971.

Kilby, Clyde S. "*Till We Have Faces*: An Interpretation." In *The Longing for a Form: Essays on the Fiction of C. S. Lewis*, edited by Peter J. Schakel, 171–81. Kent, OH: Kent State University Press, 1977.

Kirk, G. S. *Myth: Its Meaning and Functions in Ancient and Other Cultures*. Cambridge: Cambridge University Press, 1970.

Kitchen, Kenneth A. *On the Reliability of the Old Testament*. Grand Rapids: Eerdmans, 2003.

Krohn, Kaarle. *Folklore Methodology*. Translated by Roger L. Welsch. Austin: University of Texas Press, 1971.

Kushner, Harold. *When Bad Things Happen to Good People*. New York: Anchor, 2004.

Lamberth, David. "Discernment and Practice: Questions for a Logic of Revelation— Response to William Abraham." *The Harvard Theological Review* 95/3 (2002) 273–76.

Larsen, Stephen, and Robin Larsen. *Joseph Campbell: A Fire in the Mind: The Authorized Biography*. Rochester, VT: Inner Traditions, 2002.

Leeming, David A. "Myth and Therapy." *Journal of Religion and Health* 40/1 (2001) 115–19.

———. *The World of Myth*. New York: Oxford University Press, 1990.

Leonard, Daniel. "Myth and Symbol According to Joseph Campbell: An Evaluation." PhD diss., Pontificia Universita Gregoriana, 1997.

Levi-Strauss, Claude. *Myth and Meaning: Cracking the Code of Culture*. New York: Schocken, 1979.

———. *Totemism*. Translated by Rodney Needham. Boston: Beacon, 1962.

Lewis, Clive Staples. *The Abolition of Man*. New York: Macmillan, 1955.

———. *All My Road Before Me: The Diary of C. S. Lewis, 1922–1927*. Edited by Walter Hooper. Orlando: Harcourt Brace Jovanovich, 1991.

———. *The Allegory of Love*. New York: Oxford University Press, 1968.

———. *The Beloved Works of C. S. Lewis: Surprised by Joy, Reflections on the Psalms, The Four Loves, The Business of Heaven*. New York: Inspirational, n.d.

———. *Beyond Personality: The Christian Idea of God*. New York: Macmillan, 1945.

———. *The Business of Heaven: Daily Readings from C. S. Lewis*. Edited by Walter Hooper. San Diego: Harcourt Brace Jovanovich, 1984.

———. *The C. S. Lewis Bible*. New York: HarperCollins, 2010.

———. *Christian Reflections*. Grand Rapids: Eerdmans, 1995.

———. *The Complete C. S. Lewis Signature Classics*. New York: HarperCollins, 2005.

———. *The Essential C. S. Lewis*. Edited with an introduction by Lyle W. Dorsett. New York: Macmillan, 1988.

———. *An Experiment in Criticism*. Cambridge: Cambridge University Press, 1961.

———. *The Four Loves and C. S. Lewis Speaks His Mind*. Recorded lectures by the author. Compact disc. Alliance for Christian Media, 2007.

———, ed. *George MacDonald: An Anthology*. New York: Macmillan, 1947.

———. *God in the Dock: Essays on Theology and Ethics*. Edited by Walter Hooper. Grand Rapids: Eerdmans, 1970.

———. *The Great Divorce*. New York: HarperCollins, 1946.

———. *A Grief Observed*. Greenwich, CT: Seabury, 1963.

———. *That Hideous Strength*. New York: Macmillan, 1965.

———. *The Joyful Christian*. New York: Macmillan, 1977.

————. *Lost Aeneid: Arms and the Exile.* Edited by A. T. Reyes. New Haven, CT: Yale University Press, 2011.

————. *Mere Christianity.* New York: Macmillan, 1952.

————. *Miracles.* New York: Macmillan, 1969.

————. *Of Other Worlds: Essays and Stories.* New York: Harcourt, Brace & World, 1966.

————. *Out of the Silent Planet.* New York: Macmillan, 1965.

————. *Perelandra.* New York: Macmillan, 1965.

————. *The Pilgrim's Regress.* Grand Rapids: Eerdmans, 1986.

————. *A Preface to* Paradise Lost. London: Oxford University Press, 1956.

————. *Present Concerns.* Edited by Walter Hooper. San Diego: Harcourt Brace Jovanovich, 1986.

————. *The Problem of Pain.* New York: HarperCollins, 1940.

————. *Reflections on the Psalms.* New York: Harcourt, Brace, 1958.

————. *Selected Literary Essays.* Edited by Walter Hooper. Cambridge: Cambridge University Press, 1979.

————. *Surprised by Joy.* New York: Harcourt, Brace & World, 1955.

————. *That Hideous Strength: A Modern Fairy-Tale for Grown-Ups.* New York: Macmillan, 1946.

————. *They Asked for a Paper: Papers and Addresses.* London: Geoffrey Bless, 1962.

————. *Till We Have Faces; A Myth Retold.* New York: Harcourt, Brace, 1956.

————. "The Weight of Glory." Sermon preached in Church of St Mary the Virgin, Oxford, on June 8, 1942. Online: http://www.verber.com/mark/xian/weight-of-glory.pdf.

————. *The Weight of Glory.* New York: HarperCollins, 1980.

————. *What Christians Believe.* New York: HarperCollins, 2005.

————. *A Year with C. S. Lewis.* Edited by Patricia S. Klein. New York: HarperCollins, 2003.

Lincoln, Bruce. *Theorizing Myth: Narrative, Ideology, and Scholarship.* Chicago: University of Chicago Press, 1999.

Lindsley, Art. *C. S. Lewis's Case for Christ: Insights from Reason, Imagination and Faith.* Downers Grove, IL: InterVarsity, 2005.

Lindvall, Terry. "Joy and Sehnsucht." *Mars Hill Review* 8 (Summer 1997) 25-38. Online: http://www.leaderu.com/marshill/mhr08/hall1.html.

Livingston, G. Herbert. *The Pentateuch in Its Cultural Environment.* Grand Rapids: Baker, 1974.

Lovelock, James. *Gaia: A New Look at Life on Earth.* Oxford: Oxford University Press, 2000.

Keller, Timothy J. *The Reason for God: Belief in an Age of Skepticism.* New York: Dutton, 2008.

MacSwain, Robert, and Michael Ward. *The Cambridge Companion to C. S. Lewis.* Cambridge: Cambridge University Press, 2010.

Maher, John M., and Dennis Briggs, eds. *An Open Life: Joseph Campbell in Conversation with Michael Toms.* New York: Harper & Row, 1989.

Malinowski, Bronsilaw. *Myth in Primitive Psychology.* Westport, CT: Negro Universities Press, 1971.

Manlove, C. N. *C. S. Lewis: His Literary Achievement.* New York: St. Martin's, 1987.

Markos, Louis. "Culture, Religion, Philosophy, and Myth: What Christianity Is Not." *Christian Research Journal* 29/2 (2006) n.p. Online: http://www.equip.org/articles/culture-religion-philosophy-and-myth/.

———. "From Homer to Christ: Why Christians Should Read the Pagan Classics." Email attachment to author, June 10, 2009.

———. "Lewis Agonistes: Wrestling with the Modern and Postmodern World." Email attachment to author, June 9, 2009.

———. *The Life and Writings of C. S. Lewis.* Compact disc. Chantilly, VA: The Teaching Company, 2000.

———. "The Myth Made Fact." Email attachment to author, June 9, 2009.

———. "Pressing Forward: Alfred Lord Tennyson and the Victorian Age." Email attachment to author, June 9, 2009.

———. "What Christianity is *Not*." Email attachment to author, June 8, 2009.

Marlantes, Karl. *What It Is Like to Go to War.* New York: Atlantic Monthly, 2011.

Martin, Thomas L. *Reading the Classics with C. S. Lewis.* Grand Rapids: Baker, 2000.

Martindale, Wayne, and Jerry Root. *The Quotable Lewis.* Wheaton, IL: Tyndale, 1990.

Martindale, Wayne, Jerry Root, and Linda Washington. *The Soul of C. S. Lewis: A Meditative Journey through Twenty-Six of His Best Loved Writings.* Carol Stream, IL: Tyndale, 2010.

Matthews, Kenneth Ernest. "C. S. Lewis and the Modern World." PhD diss., University of California, Los Angeles, 1983.

McClintock, John, and James Strong. *Cyclopedia of Biblical, Theological, and Ecclesiastical Literature.* 12 vols. Grand Rapids: Baker, 1981.

McGrath, Alistar E. *C. S. Lewis: A Life. Eccentric Genius. Reluctant Prophet.* Carol Stream, IL: Tyndale, 2013.

———. *The Intellectual World of C. S. Lewis.* Malden, MA: Wiley, 2013.

———, ed. *The J. I. Packer Collection.* Downers Grove, IL: InterVarsity, 1999.

Miller, Eric. "So What Is the Historian's Vocation?" *Books and Culture* (January–February 2012) 22.

Milton, John. *Milton's Comus.* Minneapolis: Fili-Quarian Classics, 2010.

Moorman, Charles. "Space Ship and Grail: The Myths of C. S. Lewis." *College English* 18/8 (1957) 401–5.

Morgan, Lewis Henry. *League of the Iroquois (A Classic Study of the American Indian Tribe with Original Illustrations).* New York: Citadel, 1993.

Morgan-Browne, H. P. "Critics and the Spirit of Discernment." *Music and Letters* 11/4 (1930) 397–400.

Morris, William. *The Earthly Paradise.* London: Routledge, 2001.

Munzinger, Andre. *Discerning the Spirits: Theological and Ethical Hermeneutics in Paul.* Cambridge: Cambridge University Press, 2007.

Murray, A. S. *Manual of Mythology: Greek and Roman, Norse, and Old German, Hindoo and Egyptian Mythology.* Lexington, KY: Forgotten Books, n.d.

Murrell, Beatrix. "The Imaginal Within The Cosmos: Projection and the Numinosum." Online: http://www.bizcharts.com/stoa_del_sol/imaginal/imaginal2.html.

Nicholi, Armand, Jr. *The Question of God: C. S. Lewis and Sigmund Freud Debate God, Love, Sex, and the Meaning of Life.* New York: Free Press, 2002.

Orr, James. *The Problem of the Old Testament.* London: Nisbett, 1907.

Orwell, George. "The Scientists Take Over: George Orwell's review of C. S. Lewis, *That Hideous Strength* (1945)." *Manchester Evening News*, August 16, 1945. Online: http://www.lewisiana.nl/orwell/.

Osborn, Diane K. *A Joseph Campbell Companion: Reflections on the Art of Living.* New York: HarperCollins, 1991.

Oswalt, John N. *The Bible Among the Myths.* Grand Rapids: Zondervan, 2009.

Packer, J. I. *Knowing God.* Downers Grove, IL: InterVarsity, 1973.

Pals, Daniel L. *Eight Theories of Religion.* Oxford: Oxford University Press, 2006.

Panofsky, Dora, and Erwin Panofsky. *Pandora's Box: The Changing Aspects of Mythical Symbol.* Princeton: Princeton University Press, 1956.

Parini, Jay. *John Steinbeck: A Biography.* New York: Henry Holt, 1995.

Patterson, Nancy-Lou. "Thesis, Antithesis, and Synthesis: The Interplanetary Trilogy of C. S. Lewis." *CLS: The Bulletin of the New York C. S. Lewis Society* 16/8 (1985).

Payne, Leanne. *Real Presence: The Christian Worldview of C. S. Lewis as Incarnational Reality.* Wheaton, IL: Crossways, 1988.

———. *Real Presence: The Holy Spirit in the Works of C. S. Lewis.* Westchester, IL: Cornerstone, 1979.

Peabody, Josephine Preston. *Old Greek Stories Told Anew.* Whitefish, MT: Kissinger, 2010.

Pearce, Joseph. *Literary Giants: Literary Catholics.* San Francisco: Ignatius, 2005.

———. *Tolkien: Man and Myth.* San Francisco: Ignatius, 1998.

Peretti, Daniel. "The Modern Prometheus: The Persistence of an Ancient Myth in the Modern World, 1950 to 2007." PhD diss., Indiana University, 2009.

Phemister, Mary Anne, and Andrew Lazo. *Mere Christians: Inspiring Stories of Encounters with C. S. Lewis.* Grand Rapids: Baker, 2009.

Phillips, Justin. *C. S. Lewis in a Time of War.* New York: HarperCollins, 2002.

Pinnock, Clark H. "Theology and Myth: An Evangelical Response to Demythologizing." *Bibliotheca Sacra* (July 1971) 215–26.

Purtill, Richard. *J. R. R. Tolkien: Myth, Morality and Religion.* San Francisco: Ignatius, 1984.

Reddy, Albert F. "*Till We Have Faces*: 'An Epistle to the Greeks.'" *Mosaic* 13 (1980) 153–64.

Reilly, R. J. *Romantic Religion: A Study of Owen Barfield, C. S. Lewis, Charles Williams, J. R. R. Tolkien.* Great Barrington, MA: Lindisfarne, 2006.

Reppert, Victor. *C. S. Lewis's Dangerous Idea: In Defense of the Argument from Reason.* Downers Grove, IL: InterVarsity, 2003.

Rose, H. J. *Handbook of Greek Mythology.* New York: Dutton, 1929.

———. *Gods and Heroes of the Greeks.* New York: Meridan, 1958.

Rosenberg, Donna, and Sorelle Baker. *Mythology and You.* Columbus, OH: McGraw Hill, 2006.

Rosenbladt, Rod. "Middle Earth Invades History." *His Magazine* (April 1972) 4–7.

Ryken, Leland, James C. Wilhoit, and Tremper Longman III. *Dictionary of Biblical Imagery.* Downers Grove, IL: InterVarsity Academic, 1998.

Samet, Elizabeth D. "Warrior Code: A Vietnam Veteran Offers a Deeply Personal Look at the Ordeal of Combat." *The New York Times Book Review*, September 18, 2011, 15.

Sammons, Martha C. *"A Far Off Country": A Guide to C. S. Lewis's Fantasy Fiction.* New York: University Press of America, 2000.

———. *War of the Fantasy Worlds: C. S. Lewis and J. R. R. Tolkien on Art and Imagination.* Santa Barbara: ABC-CLIO, 2010.

Sayer, George. *Jack: A Life of C. S. Lewis.* Wheaton, IL: Crossway, 1994.

Schakel, Peter J. *Reason and Imagination in C. S. Lewis: A Study of Till We Have Faces.* Grand Rapids: Eerdmans, 1984.

Schultz, Jeffrey D., and John G. West Jr. *The C. S. Lewis Readers' Encyclopedia.* Grand Rapids: Zondervan, 1998.

Schwartz, Sanford. *C. S. Lewis on the Final Frontier.* New York: Oxford University Press, 2009.

Scorgie, Glen G. *Dictionary of Christian Spirituality.* Grand Rapids: Zondervan, 2011.

Seaward, Christine M. "The Theodicy of C. S. Lewis: A Christian Defense of a Good God in a World of Evil and Suffering." Master's thesis., California State University, Dominguez Hills, 2000.

Segal, Robert A. *Joseph Campbell: An Introduction.* New York: Penguin, 1990.

———. *Myth: A Very Short Introduction.* Oxford: Oxford University Press, 2004.

———. "The Romantic Appeal of Joseph Campbell." *Christian Century* (April 4, 1990) 332–35. Online: http://www.religion-online.org/showarticle.asp?title=766.

———. *Theorizing About Myth.* Amherst: University of Massachusetts Press, 1999.

Seton, Ernest Thompson. *Woodcraft and Indian Lore: A Classic Guide from a Founding Father of the Boy Scouts of America.* New York: Skyhorse, 2007.

Sibley, Brian. *C. S. Lewis through the Shadowlands: The Story of His Life with Joy Davidman.* New York: Revell, 1985.

Simkins, Ronald. *Creator and Creation: Nature in the Worldview of Ancient Israel.* Peabody, MA: Hendrickson, 1994.

Simonson, Martin. *The Lord of the Rings and the Western Narrative Tradition.* Zurich: Walking Tree, 2008.

Slater, Mason. "Mythology and Meaning: How We Read the Scriptures." *Koinonia* blog, Novermber 2010. Online: http://www.koinoniablog.net/2010/11/mythfology-and-meaning.html.

Smith, Huston. *The World's Religions.* New York: HarperCollins, 1991.

Smith, Mark. *The Early History of God: Yahweh and the Other Deities in Ancient Israel.* New York: Harper and Row, 1990.

———. *The Origins of Biblical Monotheism.* Oxford: Oxford University Press, 2001.

Snyder, Thomas Lee. *Myth Conceptions: Joseph Campbell and the New Age.* Grand Rapids: Baker, 1995.

Soulen, Richard N. *Handbook of Biblical Criticism.* 2nd ed. Atlanta: John Knox, 1981.

Sparks, Kenton L. *Ancient Texts for the Study of the Hebrew Bible.* Peabody, MA: Hendrickson, 2005.

Spence, Lewis. *Myths and Legends of Babylonia and Assyria.* Norwalk, CT: Easton, 1997.

Sprague, Duncan. "The Unfundamental C. S. Lewis: Key Components of Lewis's View of Scripture." Mars Hill Review 2 (May 1995) 53–63. Online: http://www.leaderu.com/marshill/mhr02/lewis1.html.

Stahl, John H. "The Nature and Function of Myth in the Christian Thought of C. S. Lewis." *Christian Scholar's Review* 7 (1978) 330–36.

Starr, Charlie. "The Triple Enigma: Fact, Truth, and Myth as the Key to C. S. Lewis's Epistemological Thinking." DA thesis, Middle Tennessee State University, 2001.

Starr, Nathan Comfort. *C. S. Lewis's "Till We Have Faces": Introduction and Commentary.* New York: Seabury, 1968.

Stevenson, W. T. *History as Myth: The Import for Contemporary Theology.* New York: Seabury, 1969.

Storey, John. *Cultural Theory and Popular Culture: An Introduction.* 4th ed. Athens: The University of Georgia Press, 2006.

Stout, James Harvey. "What Is Mythology?" Myths-Dreams-Symbols: The Unconscious World of Dreams website. N.d. Online: http://www.mythsdreamssymbols.com/importanceofmyth.html.

Svehla, Catherine. "Blisters on the Way to Bliss." 2010. Online: http://www.catherinesvehla.com/Blisters-Bliss-Hero%20FINAL.pdf.

Sykes, Egerton. *Who's Who in Non-Classical Mythology.* New York: Oxford University Press, 1952.

Talbott, Thomas. "C. S. Lewis and the Problem of Evil." *Christian Scholars' Review* 7 (1987) 36–51.

Tennyson, G. B. *A Barfield Reader: Selections from the Writings of Owen Barfield.* Hanover, NH: University Press of New England, 1999.

Tennyson, G. B., and Jane Hipolito. *Owen Barfield on C. S. Lewis.* Oxford: Barfield, 2011.

Tighe, Mary. *Psyche, with Other Poems.* 3rd ed. London: Paternoster-Row, 1811. Online: http://web.nmsu.edu/~hlinkin/.

Tillyard, E. M. W. *Myth and the English Mind: From Piers Plowman to Edward Gibbon.* New York: Collier, 1962.

Toelken, Barre. *The Dynamics of Folklore.* Logan: Utah State University Press, 1996.

Tolkien, Christopher. *The Monsters and The Critics and Other Essays.* London: Allen & Unwin, 1983.

Tolkien, J. R. R. *The Legend of Sigurd and Gudrun.* Edited by Christopher Tolkien. New York: Houghton Mifflin Harcourt, 2009.

———. *The Lord of the Rings.* Boston: Houghton Mifflin, 1954.

———. *The Tolkien Reader.* New York: Ballantine, 1966.

Totaro, Rebecca. "Regaining Perfection: The Ransom Trilogy as a Re-embodiment of the Neoplatonic Model." *CSL: The Bulletin of the C. S. Lewis Society* 22/10 (1991).

Travers, Michael. *C. S. Lewis: Views from Wake Forest: Collected Essays on C. S. Lewis.* Wayne, PA: Zossima, 2008.

Trexler, Robert. "George MacDonald: Merging Myth and Method." *CSL: The Bulletin of the C. S. Lewis Society* 34/4 (2003).

Ulrech, John C. "Prophets, Priests, and Poets: Toward a Definition of Religious Fiction." *Cithara* 22/2 (May 1983) 3–31.

Urang, Gunnar. *Shadows of Heaven: Religion and Fantasy in the Writing of C. S. Lewis. Charles Williams, and J. R. R. Tolkien.* Philadelphia: Pilgrim, 1971.

Van Der Weele, Steve J. "From Mt. Olympus to Glome: C. S. Lewis's Dislocation of Apuleius's 'Cupid and Psyche' in *Till We Have Faces.*" In *The Longing for a Form: Essays on the Fiction of C. S. Lewis,* edited by Peter J. Schakel, 182–92. Kent OH: Kent State University Press, 1977.

Vanhoozer, Kevin J. *Is There a Meaning in This Text?* Grand Rapids: Zondervan, 1998.

Vaus, Will. *Mere Theology: A Guide to the Thought of C. S. Lewis.* Downers Grove, IL: InterVarsity, 2004.

Veyne, Paul. *Did the Greeks Believe in Their Myths? An Essay on the Constitutive Imagination.* Translated by Paula Wissing. Chicago: University of Chicago Press, 1983.

Walsh, Chad. *C. S. Lewis: Apostle to the Skeptics*. New York: Macmillian, 1949.

————. "C. S. Lewis: Critic, Creator, and Cult Figure." *Seven: An Anglo-American Literary Review* 2 (1981) 66–80.

————. *The Literary Legacy of C. S. Lewis*. New York: Harcourt Brace Jovanovich, 1979.

Walton, John H. *Ancient Near Eastern Thought and the Old Testament: Introducing the Conceptual World of the Hebrew Bible*. Grand Rapids: Baker Academic, 2006.

Ward, Michael. *Planet Narnia: The Seven Heavens in the Imagination of C. S. Lewis*. New York: Oxford University Press, 2008.

Weatherby, H. L. "Two Medievalists: Lewis and Eliot on Christianity and Literature." *Sewanee Review* 78 (Spring 1970) 330–47.

Weaver, Richard. *Ideas Have Consequences*. Chicago: University of Chicago Press, 1948.

White, Luther William. *The Image of Man in C. S. Lewis*. Nashville: Abingdon, 1969.

White, Michael. *C. S. Lewis: A Life*. New York: Carroll & Graf, 2004.

Wiener, Richard L., and Thomas J. Kramer. "Ministerial Discernment: An Application of the Lens Model to the Study of Decision Making." *Review of Religious Research* 29/1 (1987) 57–68.

Willis, John Randolph. *Pleasures Forever: The Theology of C. S. Lewis*. Chicago: Loyola University Press, 1983.

Witherington, Ben, III. *Is There A Doctor in the House? An Insider's Story and Advice on Becoming a Bible Scholar*. Grand Rapids: Zondervan, 2011.

Wright, G. Ernest. *The Old Testament against Its Environment*. London: SCM, 1950.

Wright, Marjorie Evelyn. "The Vision of the Cosmic Order in the Oxford Mythmakers." In *Imagination and the Spirit: Essays in Literature and the Christian Faith Presented to Clyde S. Kilby*, edited by Charles Huttar, 259–76. Grand Rapids: Eerdmans, 1971.

Wriglesworth, Cha. "Myth Maker, Unicorn Maker: C. S. Lewis and the Reshaping of Medieval Thought." *Mythlore* (September 22, 2006) n.p. Online: http://www.thefreelibrary.com/Myth+maker,+unicorn+maker%3A+C.S.+Lewis+and+the+reshaping+of+medieval. . .-a0154698397.

Young, Jonathan. "Joseph Campbell's Mythic Journey." *New Perspectives Magazine* (July 1994). Online: http://www.folkstory.com/campbell/campbell.html.

Made in United States
North Haven, CT
22 January 2023

31461838R00153